Y THE LAST MAN — Ring of Truth

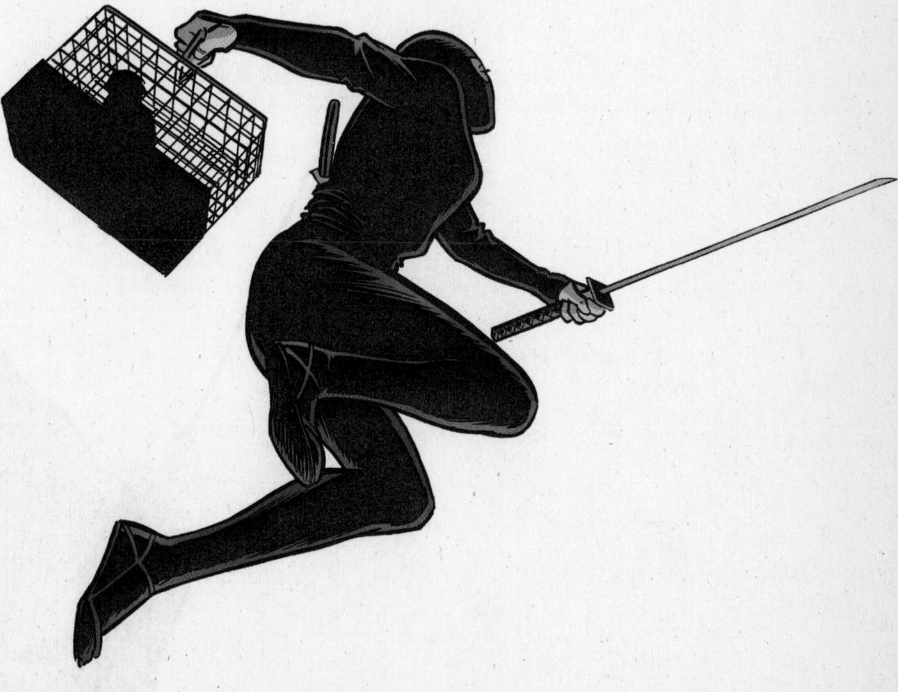

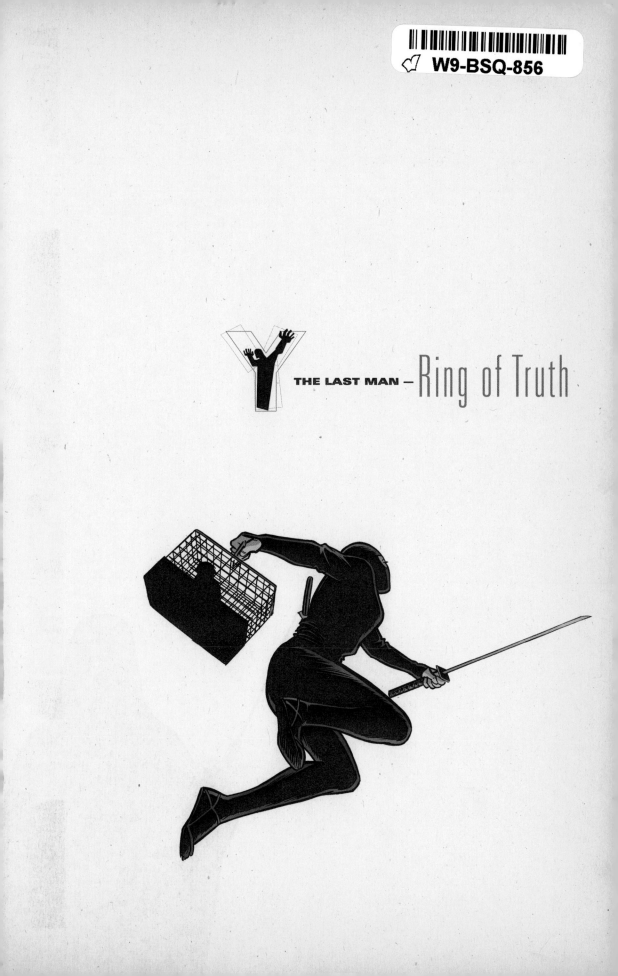

Y: THE LAST MAN – Ring of Truth

Brian K. Vaughan
Writer

Pia Guerra
Penciller

José Marzán, Jr.
Inker

Zylonol
Colorist

Clem Robins
Letterer

Massimo Carnevale
Original series covers

Y: THE LAST MAN created by Brian K. Vaughan and Pia Guerra

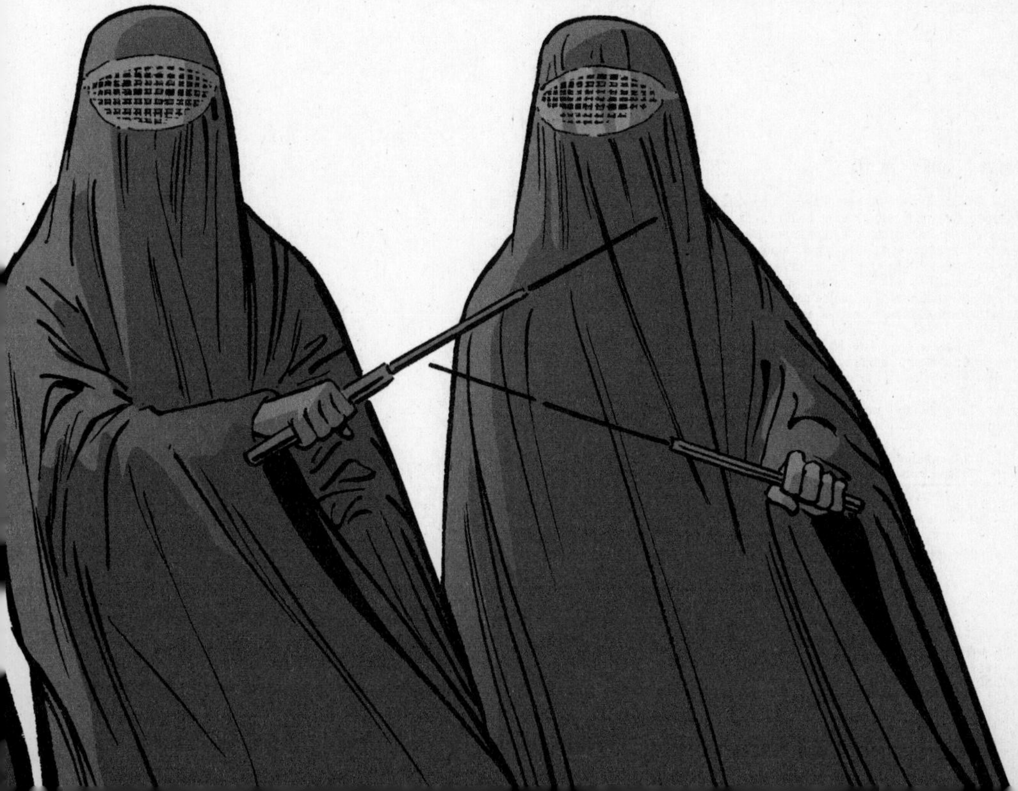

Will Dennis
Editor – Original Series

Casey Seijas
Assistant Editor – Original Series

Scott Nybakken
Editor

Robbin Brosterman
Design Director – Books

Louis Prandi
Publication Design

Karen Berger
Senior VP – Executive Editor, Vertigo

Bob Harras
VP – Editor-in-Chief

Diane Nelson
President

Dan DiDio and **Jim Lee**
Co-Publishers

Geoff Johns
Chief Creative Officer

John Rood
Executive VP – Sales, Marketing and Business Development

Amy Genkins
Senior VP – Business and Legal Affairs

Nairi Gardiner
Senior VP – Finance

Jeff Boison
VP – Publishing Operations

Mark Chiarello
VP – Art Direction and Design

John Cunningham
VP – Marketing

Terri Cunningham
VP – Talent Relations and Services

Alison Gill
Senior VP – Manufacturing and Operations

Hank Kanalz
Senior VP – Digital

Jay Kogan
VP – Business and Legal Affairs, Publishing

Jack Mahan
VP – Business Affairs, Talent

Nick Napolitano
VP – Manufacturing Administration

Sue Pohja
VP – Book Sales

Courtney Simmons
Senior VP – Publicity

Bob Wayne
Senior VP – Sales

Y: THE LAST MAN — RING OF TRUTH

DC Comics, 1700 Broadway, New York, NY 10019
A Warner Bros. Entertainment Company.
Printed in the USA. Fifth Printing.
ISBN: 978-1-4012-0487-7
Cover illustrations by Massimo Carnevale.
Logo design by Terry Marks.

SUSTAINABLE FORESTRY INITIATIVE

Certified Chain of Custody
Promoting Sustainable Forestry
www.sfiprogram.org
SFI-01042
APPLIES TO TEXT STOCK ONLY

Library of Congress Cataloging-in-Publication Data

Vaughan, Brian K.
  Y, the last man. Vol. 5, Ring of truth / Brian K. Vaughan Pia Guerra, José Marzán, Jr.
    p. cm.
  "Originally published in single magazine form as Y: The Last Man 24-31."
  ISBN 978-1-4012-0487-7
  1. Graphic novels. I. Guerra, Pia. II. Marzán, José. III. Title. IV. Title: Ring of truth.
  PN6728.Y2V386 2012
  741.5'973–dc23
                                    2012039381

THE LAST MAN – Contents

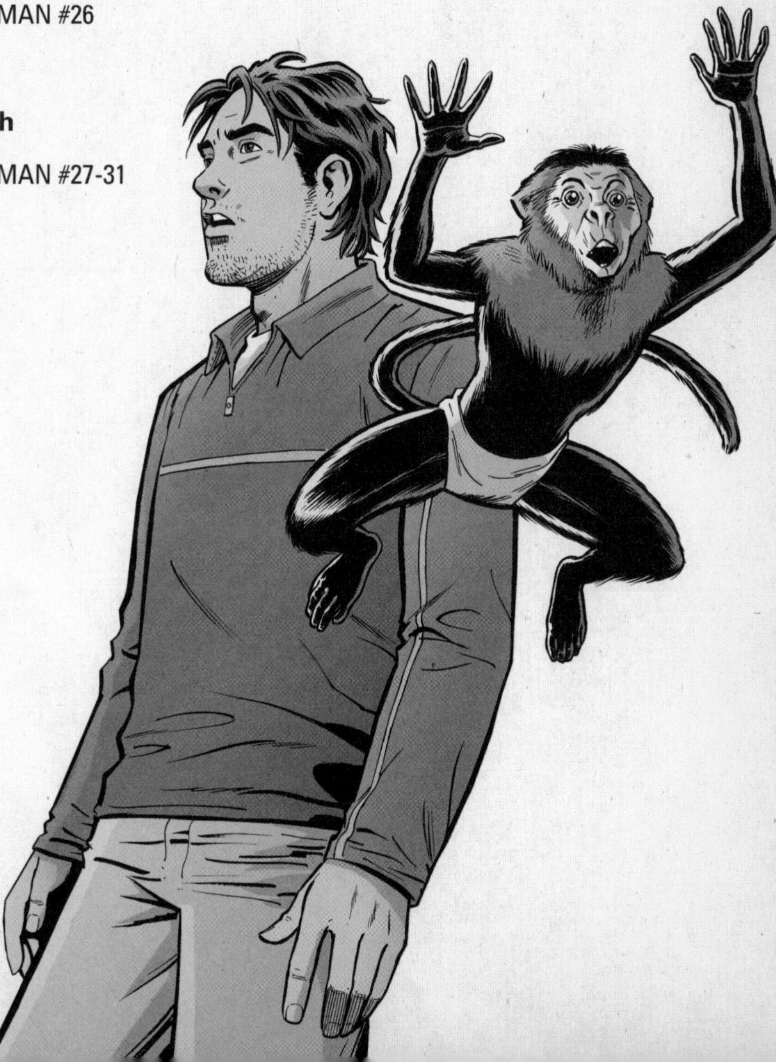

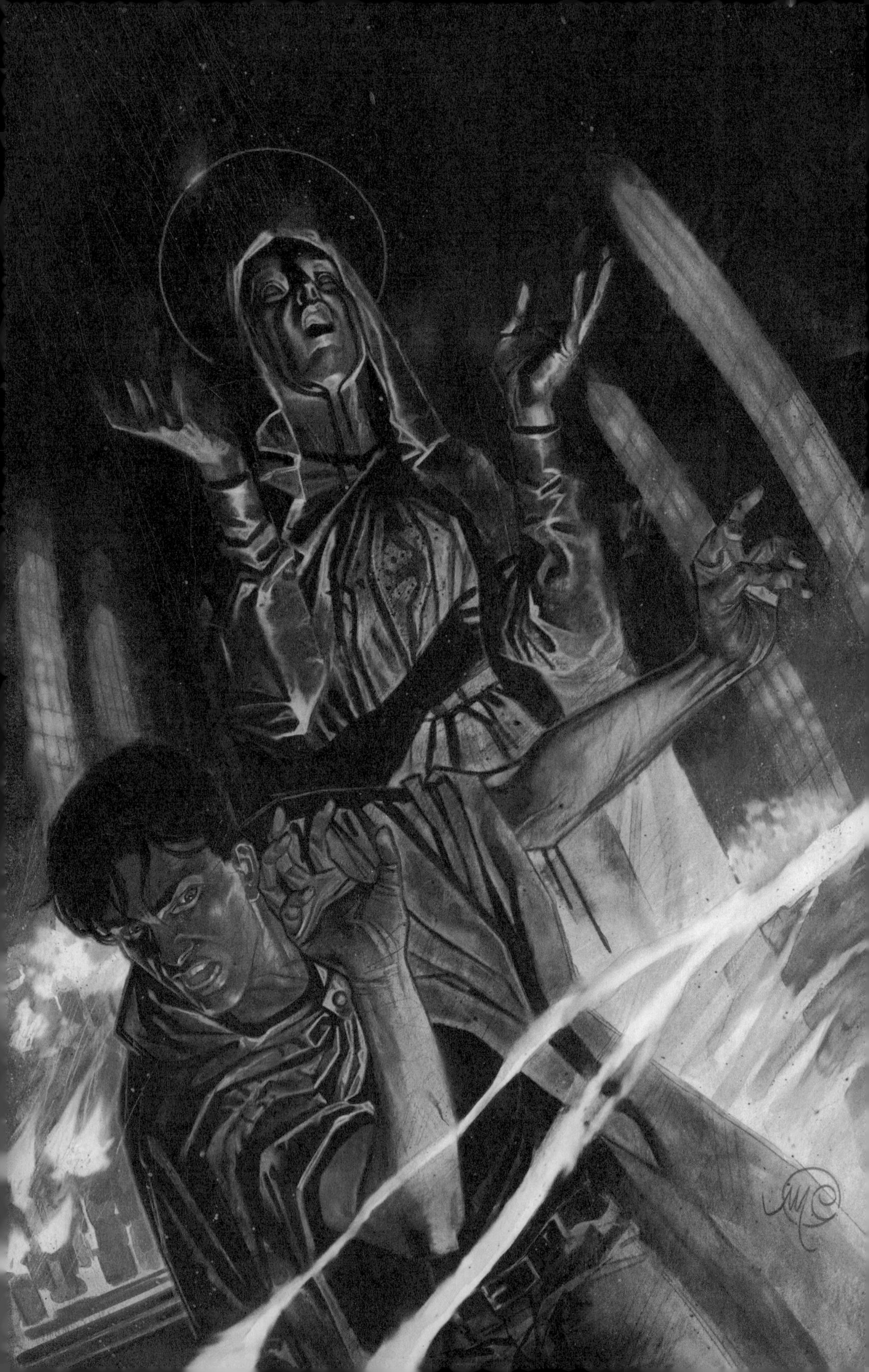

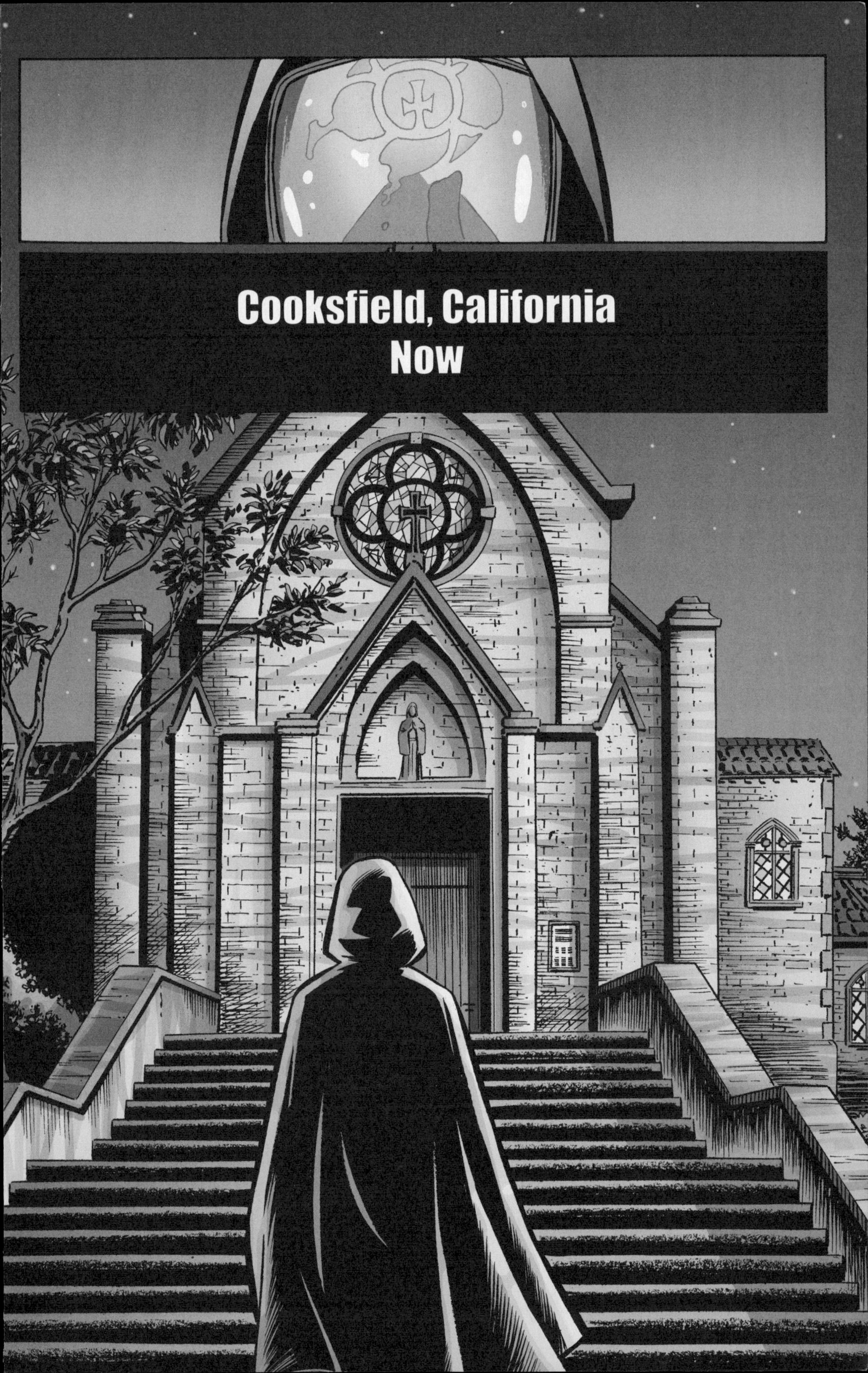
Cooksfield, California
Now

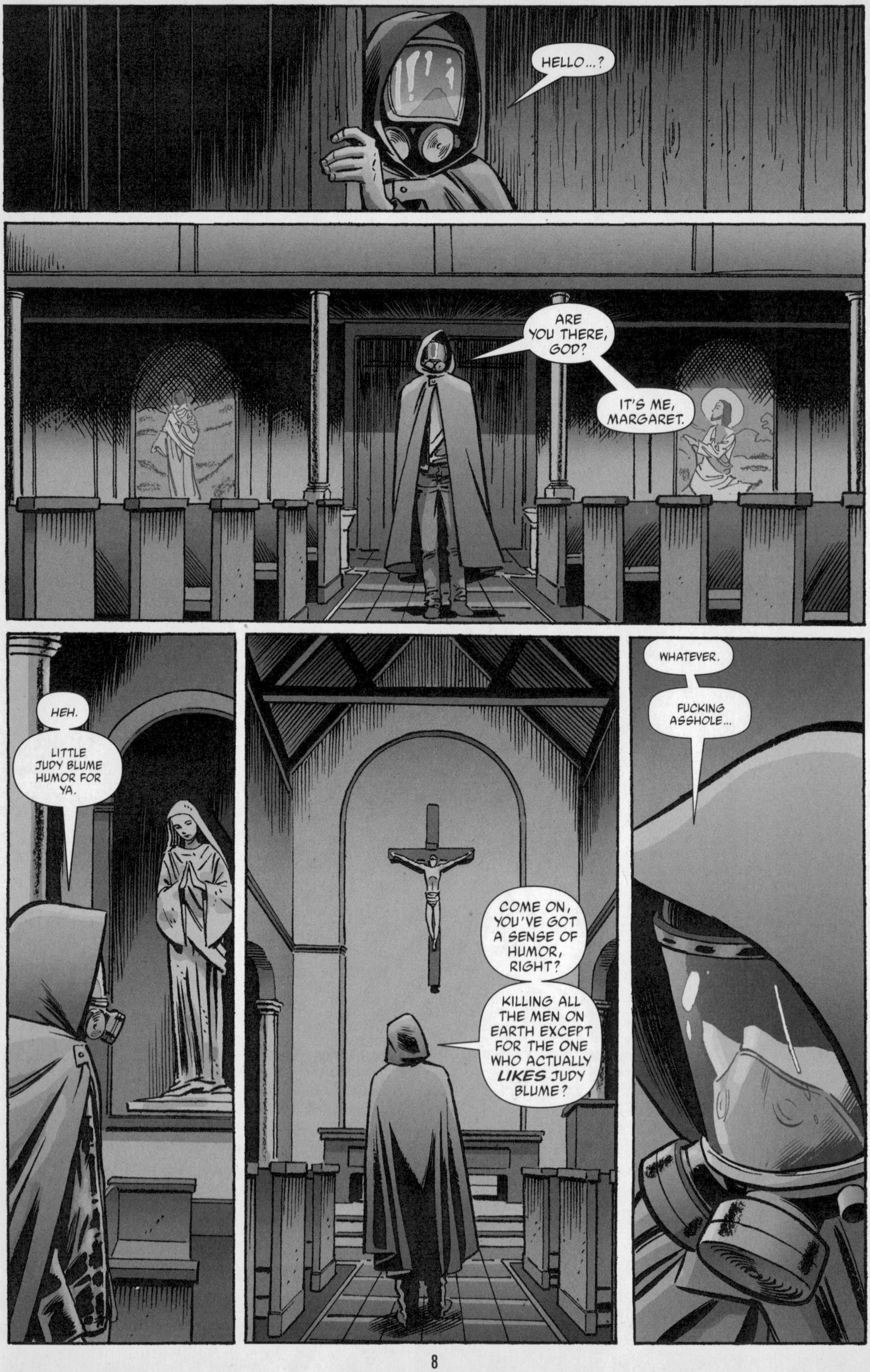
HELLO...?
ARE YOU THERE, GOD?
IT'S ME, MARGARET.
HEH.
LITTLE JUDY BLUME HUMOR FOR YA.
COME ON, YOU'VE GOT A SENSE OF HUMOR, RIGHT?
KILLING ALL THE MEN ON EARTH EXCEPT FOR THE ONE WHO ACTUALLY LIKES JUDY BLUME?
WHATEVER.
FUCKING ASSHOLE...

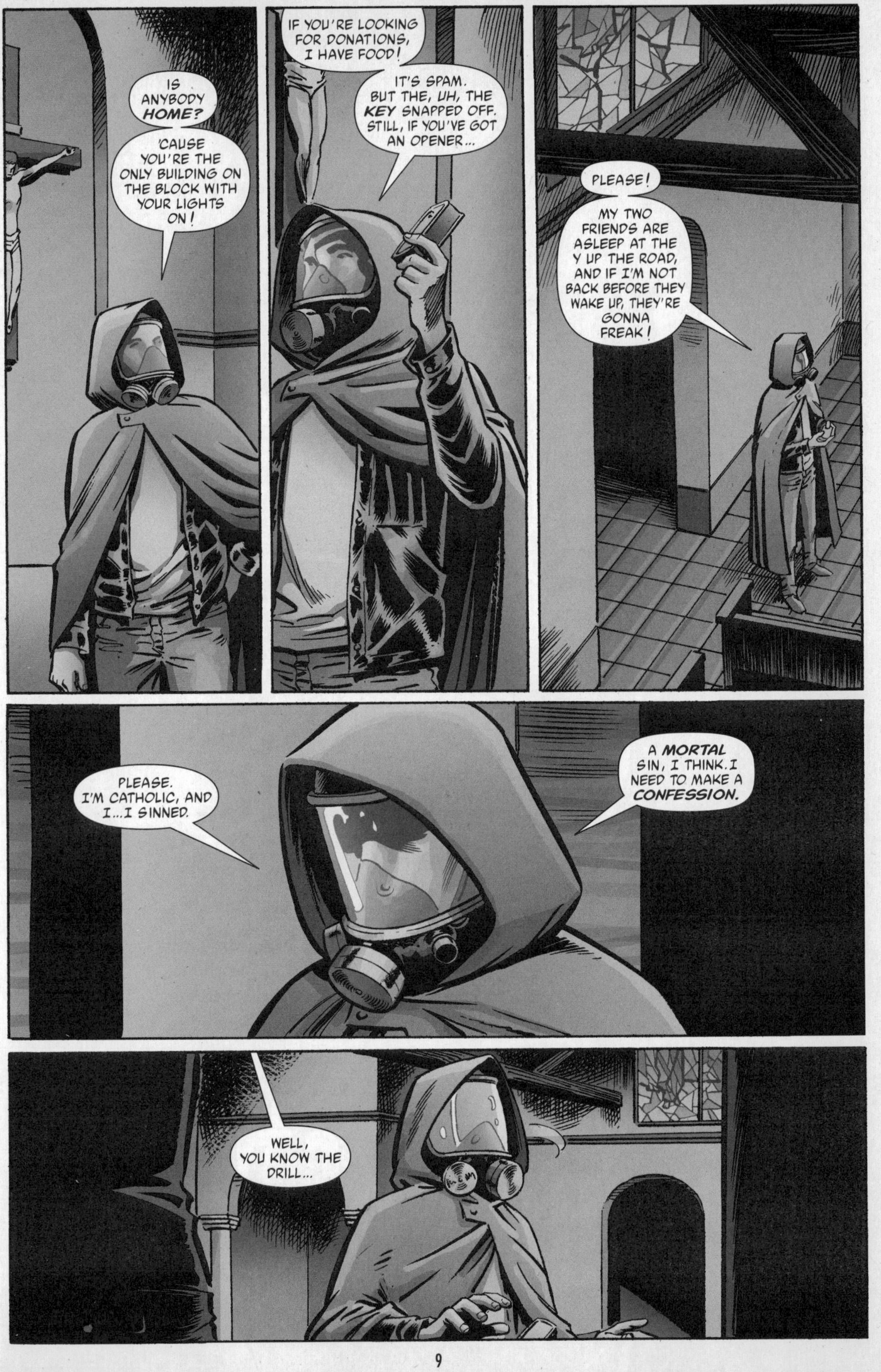
IS ANYBODY HOME?
'CAUSE YOU'RE THE ONLY BUILDING ON THE BLOCK WITH YOUR LIGHTS ON!
IF YOU'RE LOOKING FOR DONATIONS, I HAVE FOOD!
IT'S SPAM. BUT THE, UH, THE KEY SNAPPED OFF. STILL, IF YOU'VE GOT AN OPENER...
PLEASE!
MY TWO FRIENDS ARE ASLEEP AT THE Y UP THE ROAD, AND IF I'M NOT BACK BEFORE THEY WAKE UP, THEY'RE GONNA FREAK!
PLEASE. I'M CATHOLIC, AND I...I SINNED.
A MORTAL SIN, I THINK. I NEED TO MAKE A CONFESSION.
WELL, YOU KNOW THE DRILL...

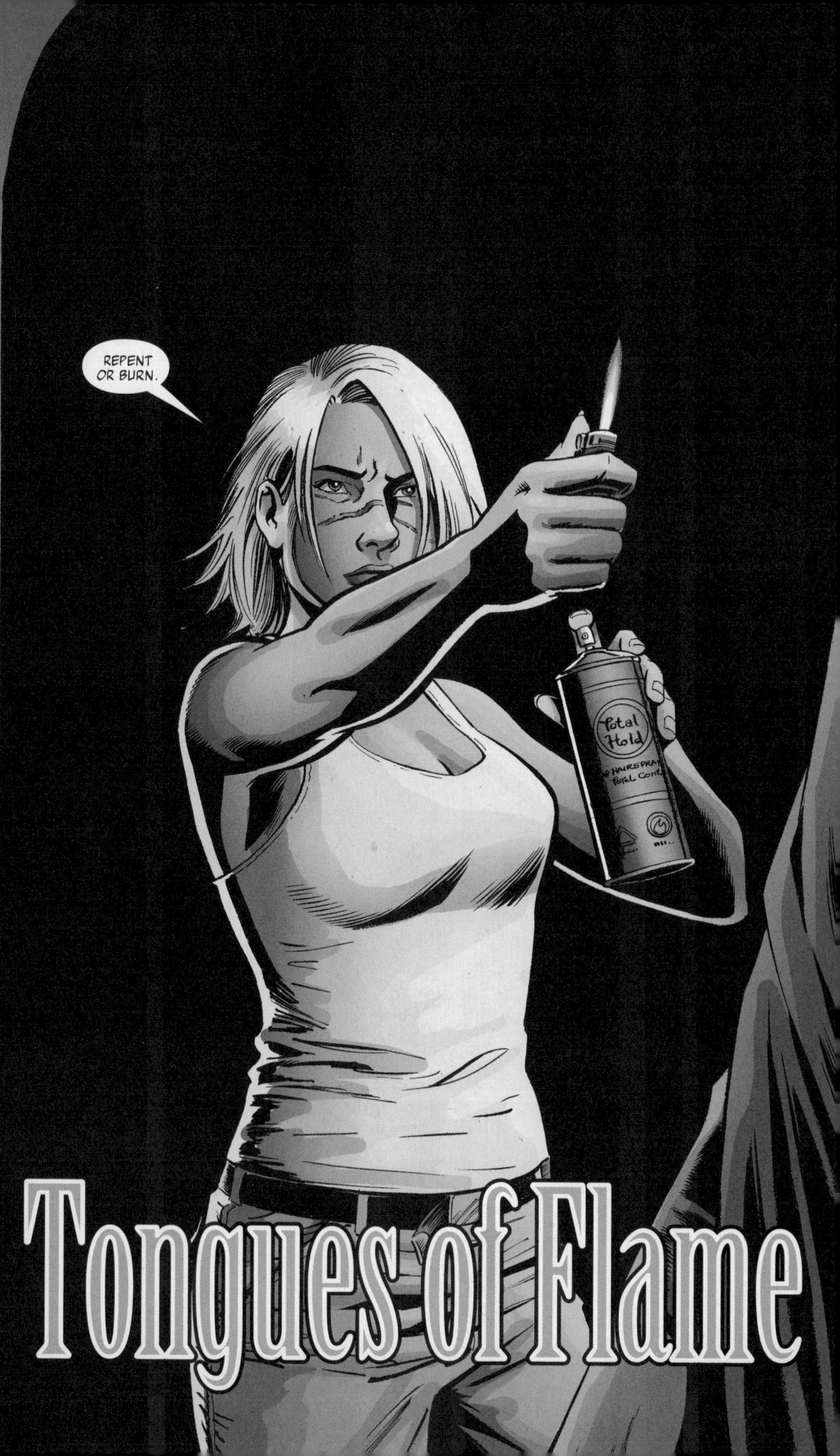
REPENT OR BURN.
Total Hold
Tongues of Flame

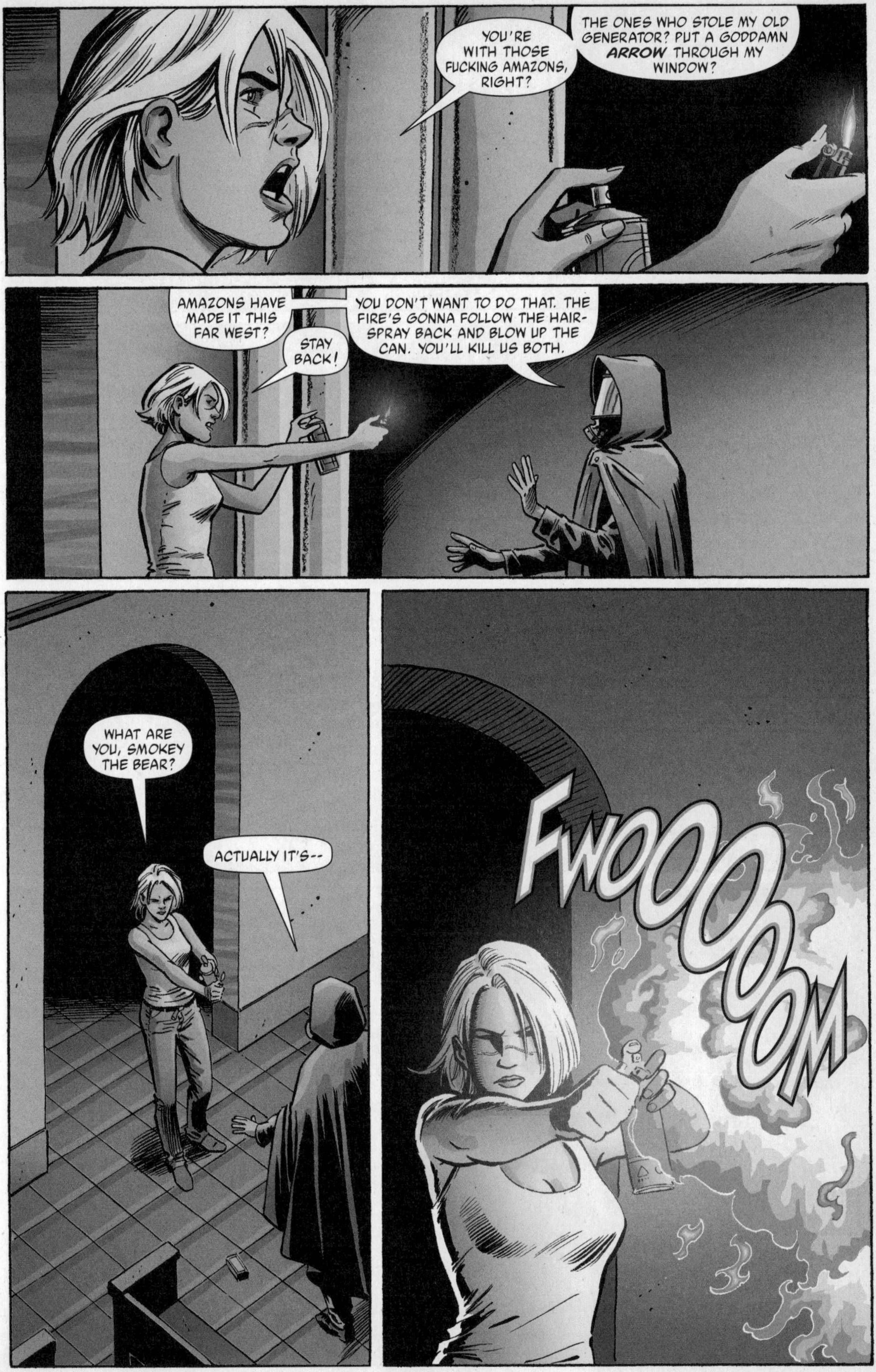
YOU'RE WITH THOSE FUCKING AMAZONS, RIGHT?
THE ONES WHO STOLE MY OLD GENERATOR? PUT A GODDAMN ARROW THROUGH MY WINDOW?
AMAZONS HAVE MADE IT THIS FAR WEST?
STAY BACK!
YOU DON'T WANT TO DO THAT. THE FIRE'S GONNA FOLLOW THE HAIR-SPRAY BACK AND BLOW UP THE CAN. YOU'LL KILL US BOTH.
WHAT ARE YOU, SMOKEY THE BEAR?
ACTUALLY IT'S--
FWOOOOOOM

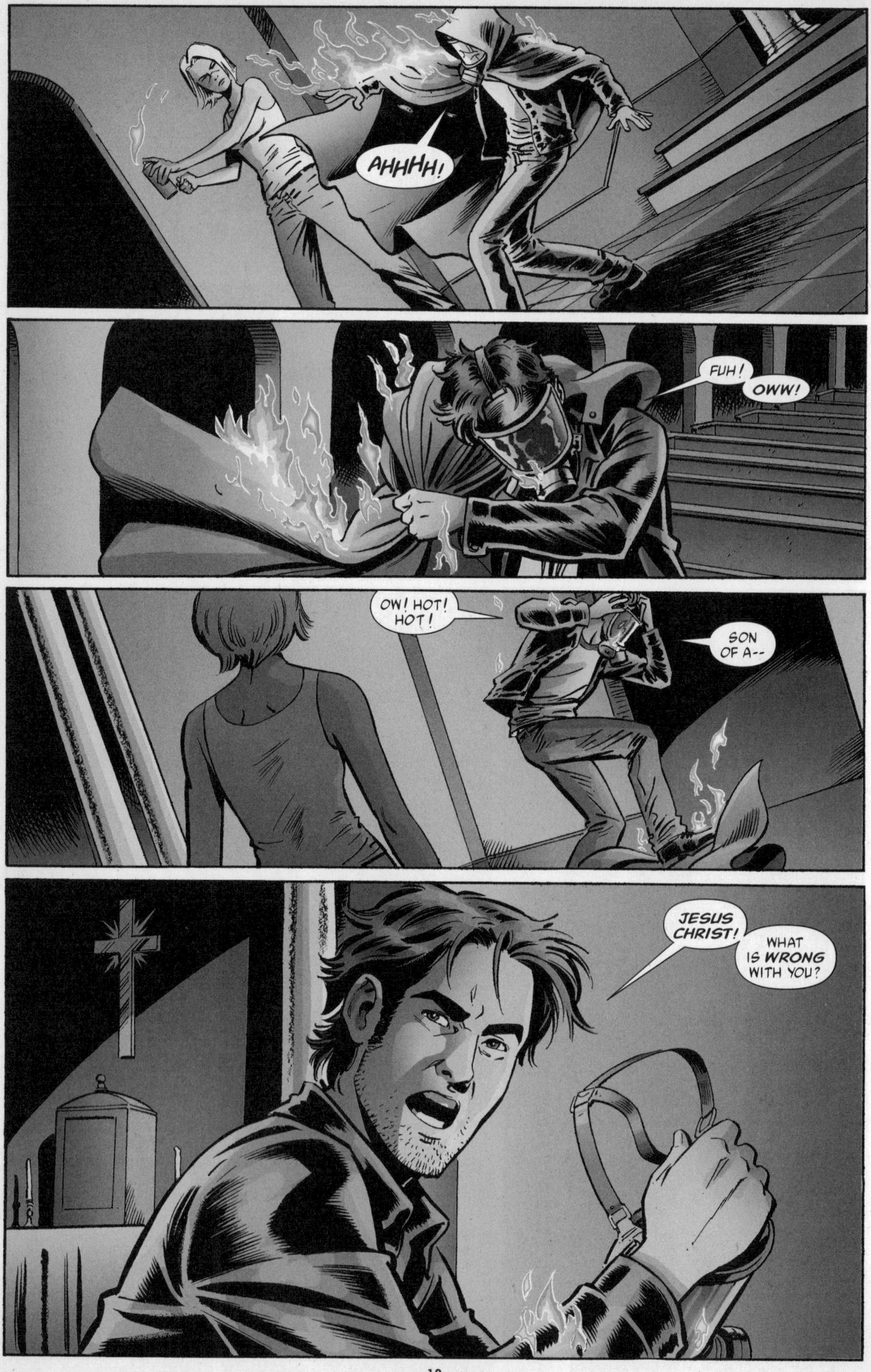
AHHHH!
FUH!
OWW!
OW! HOT! HOT!
SON OF A--
JESUS CHRIST!
WHAT IS WRONG WITH YOU?

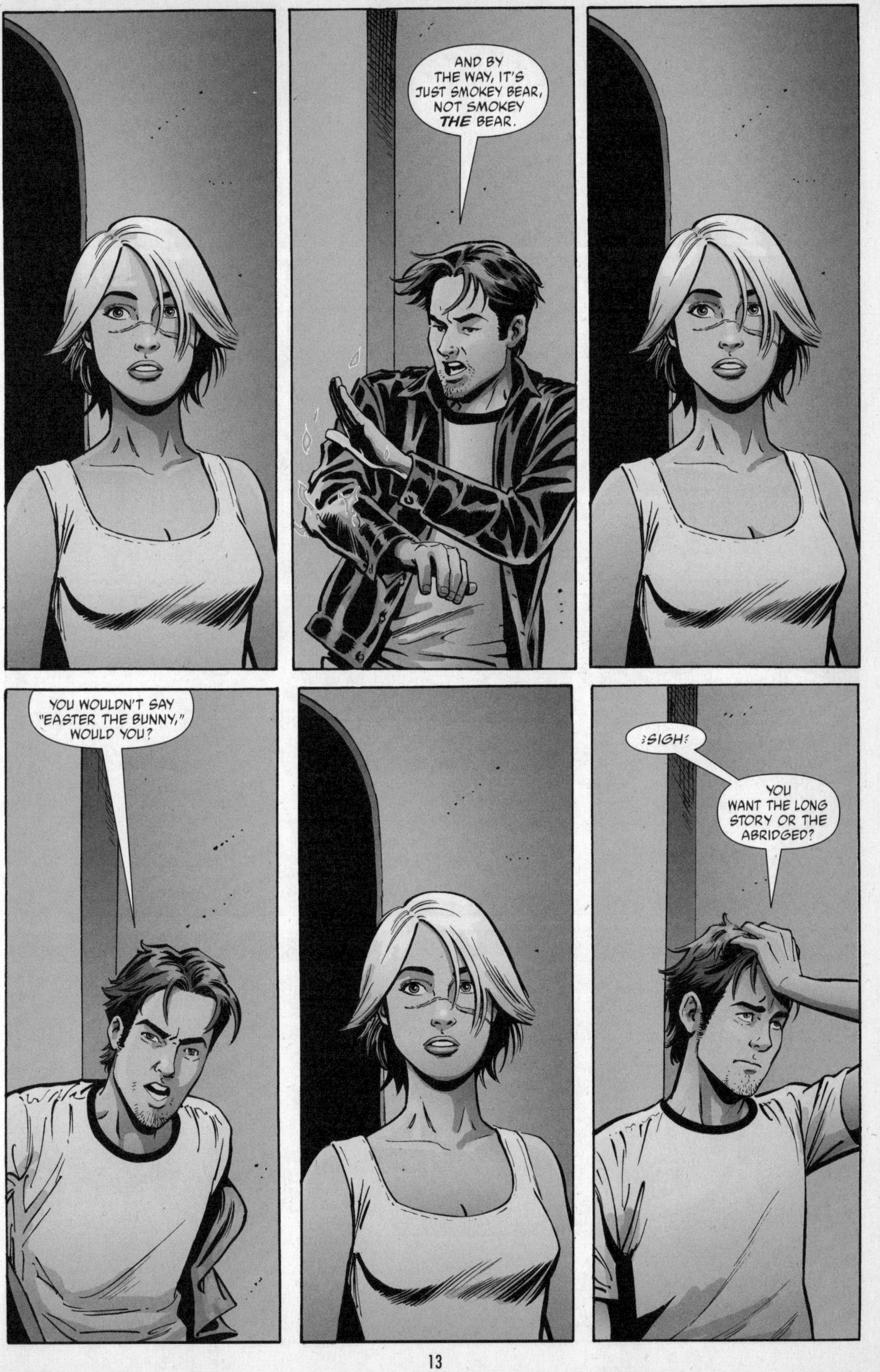
AND BY THE WAY, IT'S JUST SMOKEY BEAR, NOT SMOKEY **THE** BEAR.
YOU WOULDN'T SAY "EASTER THE BUNNY," WOULD YOU?
SIGH
YOU WANT THE LONG STORY OR THE ABRIDGED?

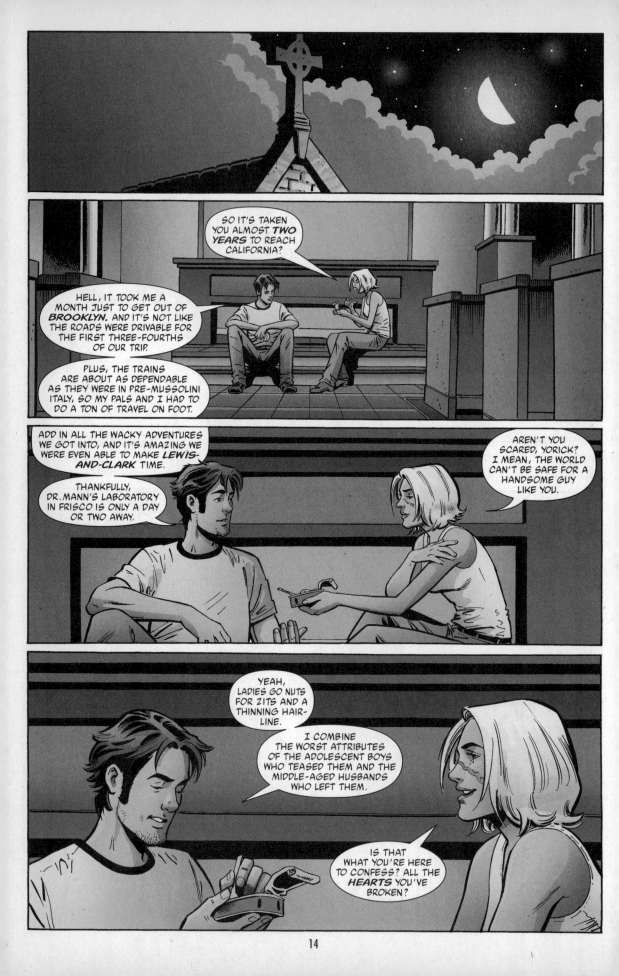

SO IT'S TAKEN YOU ALMOST **TWO YEARS** TO REACH CALIFORNIA?

HELL, IT TOOK ME A MONTH JUST TO GET OUT OF **BROOKLYN.** AND IT'S NOT LIKE THE ROADS WERE DRIVABLE FOR THE FIRST THREE-FOURTHS OF OUR TRIP.

PLUS, THE TRAINS ARE ABOUT AS DEPENDABLE AS THEY WERE IN PRE-MUSSOLINI ITALY, SO MY PALS AND I HAD TO DO A TON OF TRAVEL ON FOOT.

ADD IN ALL THE WACKY ADVENTURES WE GOT INTO, AND IT'S AMAZING WE WERE EVEN ABLE TO MAKE **LEWIS-AND-CLARK** TIME.

THANKFULLY, DR. MANN'S LABORATORY IN FRISCO IS ONLY A DAY OR TWO AWAY.

AREN'T YOU SCARED, YORICK? I MEAN, THE WORLD CAN'T BE SAFE FOR A HANDSOME GUY LIKE YOU.

YEAH, LADIES GO NUTS FOR ZITS AND A THINNING HAIR-LINE.

I COMBINE THE WORST ATTRIBUTES OF THE ADOLESCENT BOYS WHO TEASED THEM AND THE MIDDLE-AGED HUSBANDS WHO LEFT THEM.

IS THAT WHAT YOU'RE HERE TO CONFESS? ALL THE **HEARTS** YOU'VE BROKEN?

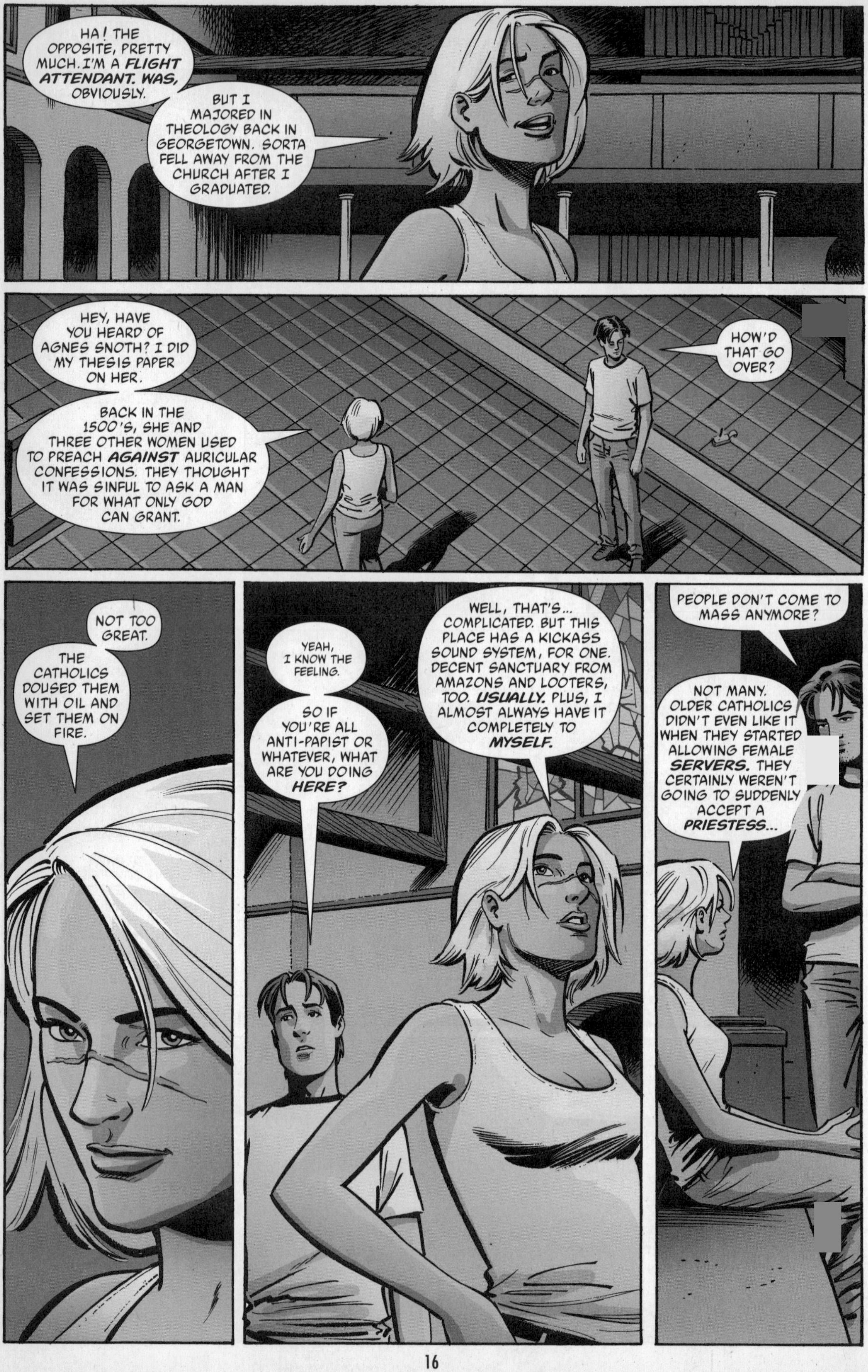
HA! THE OPPOSITE, PRETTY MUCH. I'M A FLIGHT ATTENDANT. WAS, OBVIOUSLY.
BUT I MAJORED IN THEOLOGY BACK IN GEORGETOWN. SORTA FELL AWAY FROM THE CHURCH AFTER I GRADUATED.
HEY, HAVE YOU HEARD OF AGNES SNOTH? I DID MY THESIS PAPER ON HER.
BACK IN THE 1500'S, SHE AND THREE OTHER WOMEN USED TO PREACH AGAINST AURICULAR CONFESSIONS. THEY THOUGHT IT WAS SINFUL TO ASK A MAN FOR WHAT ONLY GOD CAN GRANT.
HOW'D THAT GO OVER?
NOT TOO GREAT.
THE CATHOLICS DOUSED THEM WITH OIL AND SET THEM ON FIRE.
YEAH, I KNOW THE FEELING.
SO IF YOU'RE ALL ANTI-PAPIST OR WHATEVER, WHAT ARE YOU DOING HERE?
WELL, THAT'S... COMPLICATED. BUT THIS PLACE HAS A KICKASS SOUND SYSTEM, FOR ONE. DECENT SANCTUARY FROM AMAZONS AND LOOTERS, TOO. USUALLY. PLUS, I ALMOST ALWAYS HAVE IT COMPLETELY TO MYSELF.
PEOPLE DON'T COME TO MASS ANYMORE?
NOT MANY. OLDER CATHOLICS DIDN'T EVEN LIKE IT WHEN THEY STARTED ALLOWING FEMALE SERVERS. THEY CERTAINLY WEREN'T GOING TO SUDDENLY ACCEPT A PRIESTESS...

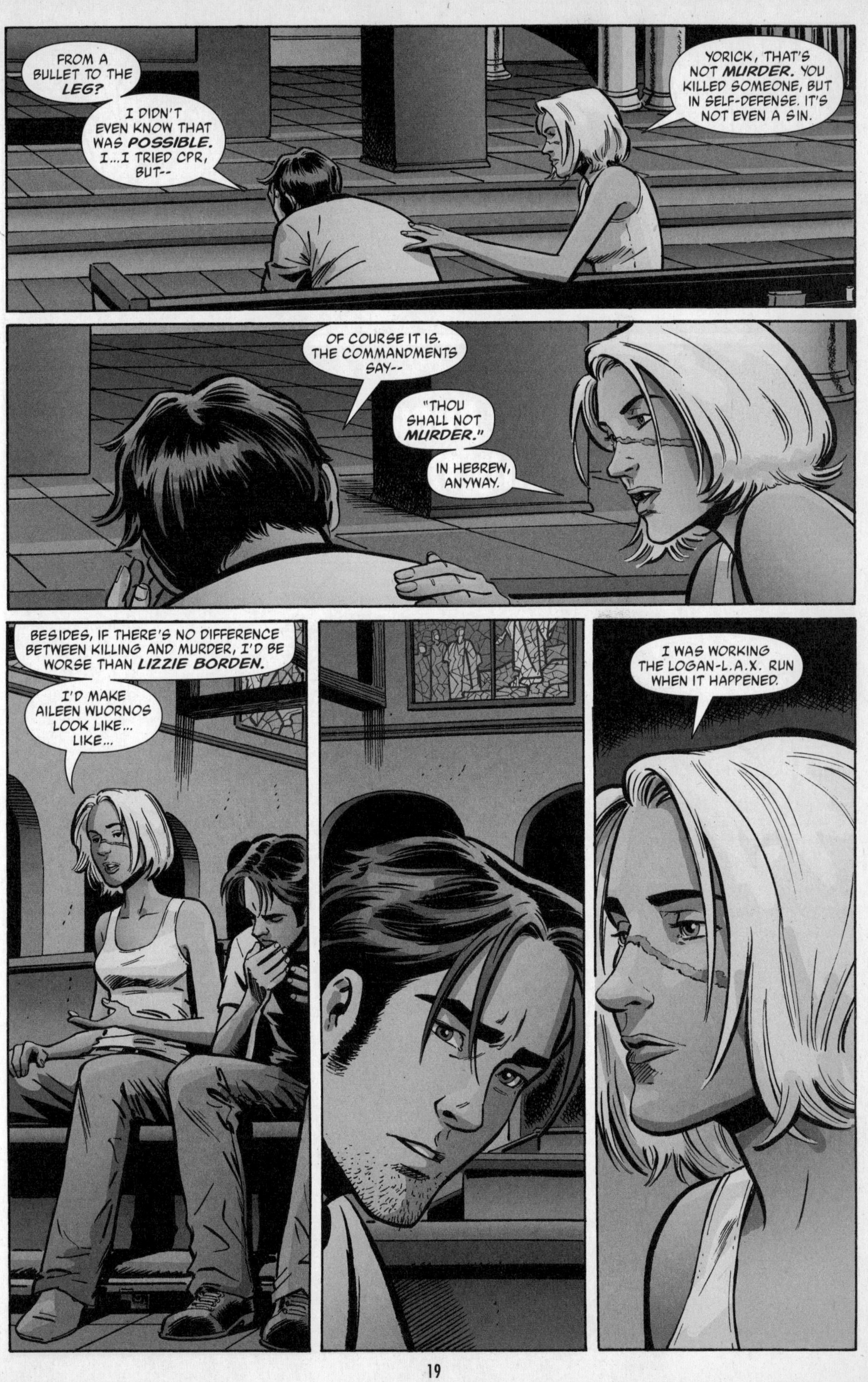
FROM A BULLET TO THE LEG?
I DIDN'T EVEN KNOW THAT WAS POSSIBLE. I...I TRIED CPR, BUT--
YORICK, THAT'S NOT MURDER. YOU KILLED SOMEONE, BUT IN SELF-DEFENSE. IT'S NOT EVEN A SIN.
OF COURSE IT IS. THE COMMANDMENTS SAY--
"THOU SHALL NOT MURDER."
IN HEBREW, ANYWAY.
BESIDES, IF THERE'S NO DIFFERENCE BETWEEN KILLING AND MURDER, I'D BE WORSE THAN LIZZIE BORDEN.
I'D MAKE AILEEN WUORNOS LOOK LIKE... LIKE...
I WAS WORKING THE LOGAN-L.A.X. RUN WHEN IT HAPPENED.

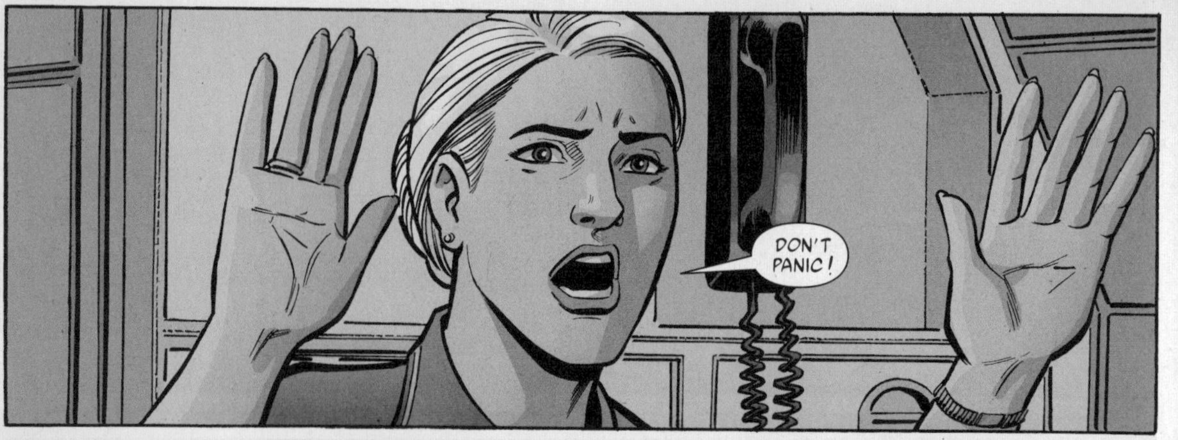
DON'T PANIC!

15,000 Feet Above Cooksfield
July 17, 2002

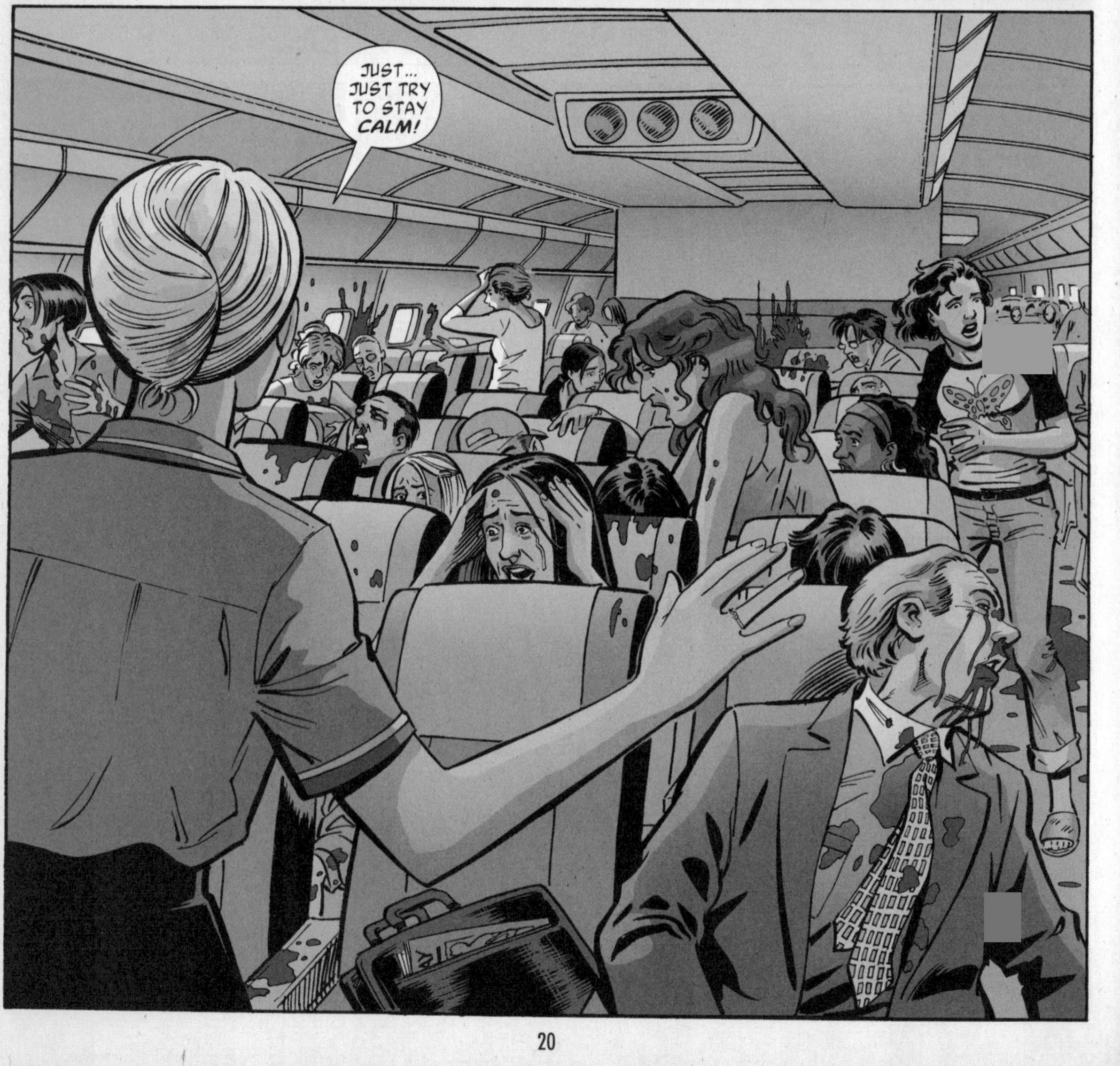
JUST... JUST TRY TO STAY CALM!

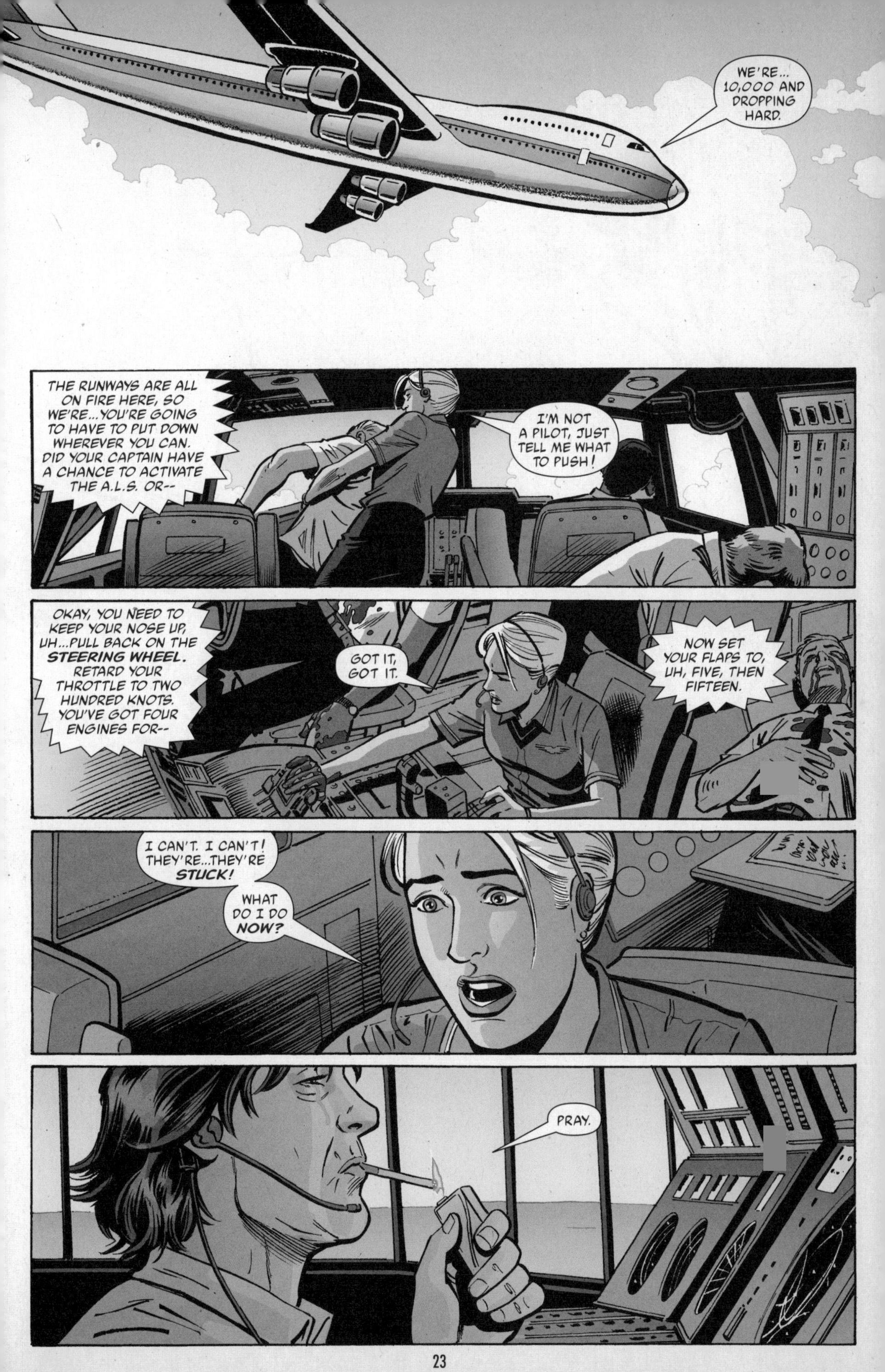
WE'RE... 10,000 AND DROPPING HARD.
THE RUNWAYS ARE ALL ON FIRE HERE, SO WE'RE...YOU'RE GOING TO HAVE TO PUT DOWN WHEREVER YOU CAN. DID YOUR CAPTAIN HAVE A CHANCE TO ACTIVATE THE A.L.S. OR--
I'M NOT A PILOT, JUST TELL ME WHAT TO PUSH!
OKAY, YOU NEED TO KEEP YOUR NOSE UP, UH...PULL BACK ON THE STEERING WHEEL. RETARD YOUR THROTTLE TO TWO HUNDRED KNOTS. YOU'VE GOT FOUR ENGINES FOR--
GOT IT, GOT IT.
NOW SET YOUR FLAPS TO, UH, FIVE, THEN FIFTEEN.
I CAN'T. I CAN'T! THEY'RE...THEY'RE STUCK!
WHAT DO I DO NOW?
PRAY.

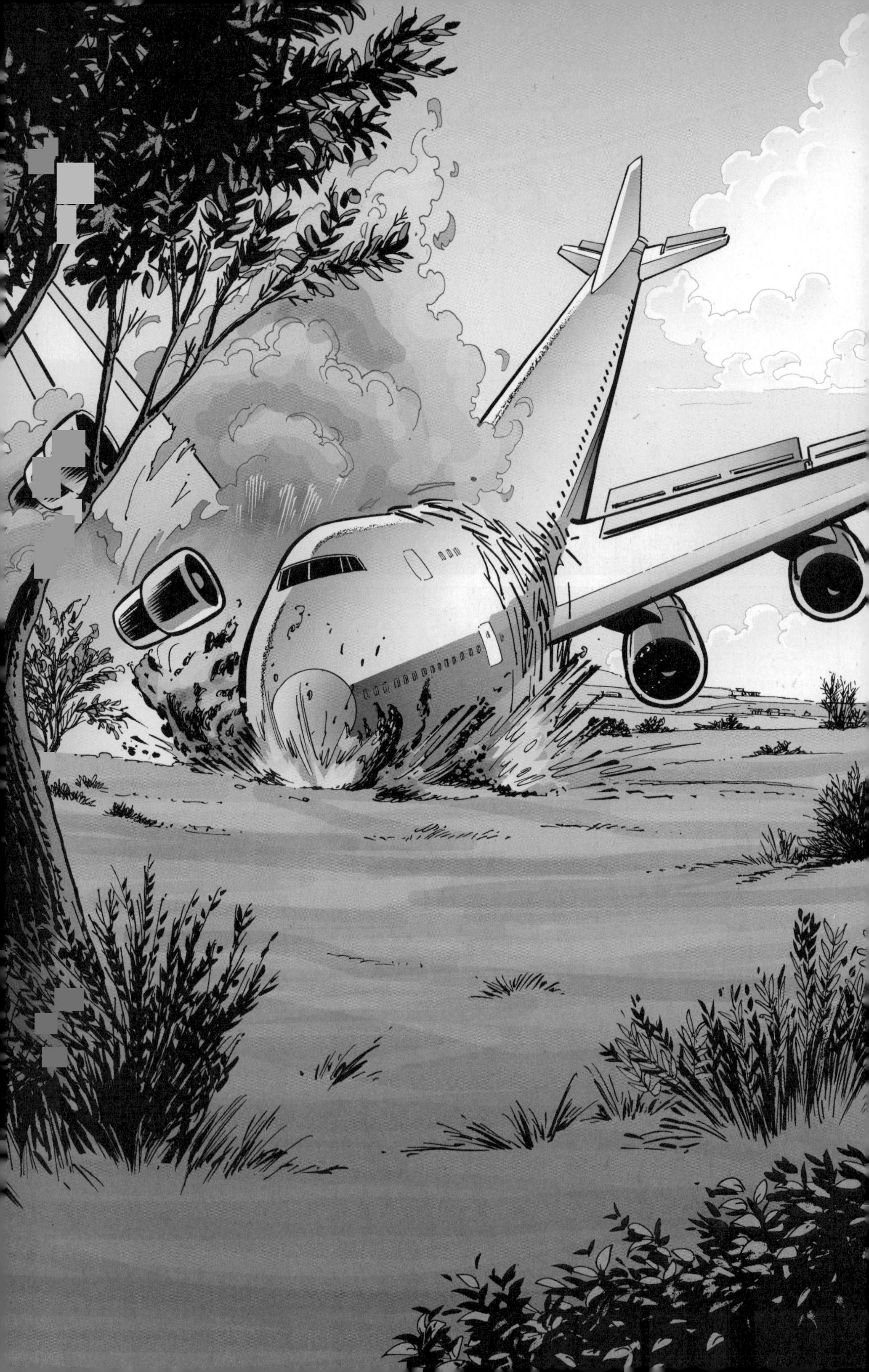

THE CEMETERIES FILLED UP FAST, SO I BROUGHT WHAT REMAINS I COULD FIND AT THE CRASH SITE BACK TO THIS OLD CHURCHYARD.

NEXT THING I KNOW, I'M A *CARETAKER*.

HOW MANY OTHER WOMEN SURVIVED?

BETH, YOU DIDN'T *KILL* ANYONE. THOSE THREE WOMEN WOULDN'T EVEN BE *ALIVE* IF--

I TOOK A FEW FLIGHT MANUALS FROM THE LIBRARY LAST YEAR. FIGURED OUT THAT MY CAPTAIN HAD PROBABLY ACTIVATED THE *AUTOMATIC LANDING SYSTEM* BEFORE HE DIED. THAT'S WHY THE FLAPS WERE LOCKED.

IF I HADN'T TOUCHED ANYTHING... THE ENTIRE *PLANE* MIGHT HAVE MADE IT.

25

26

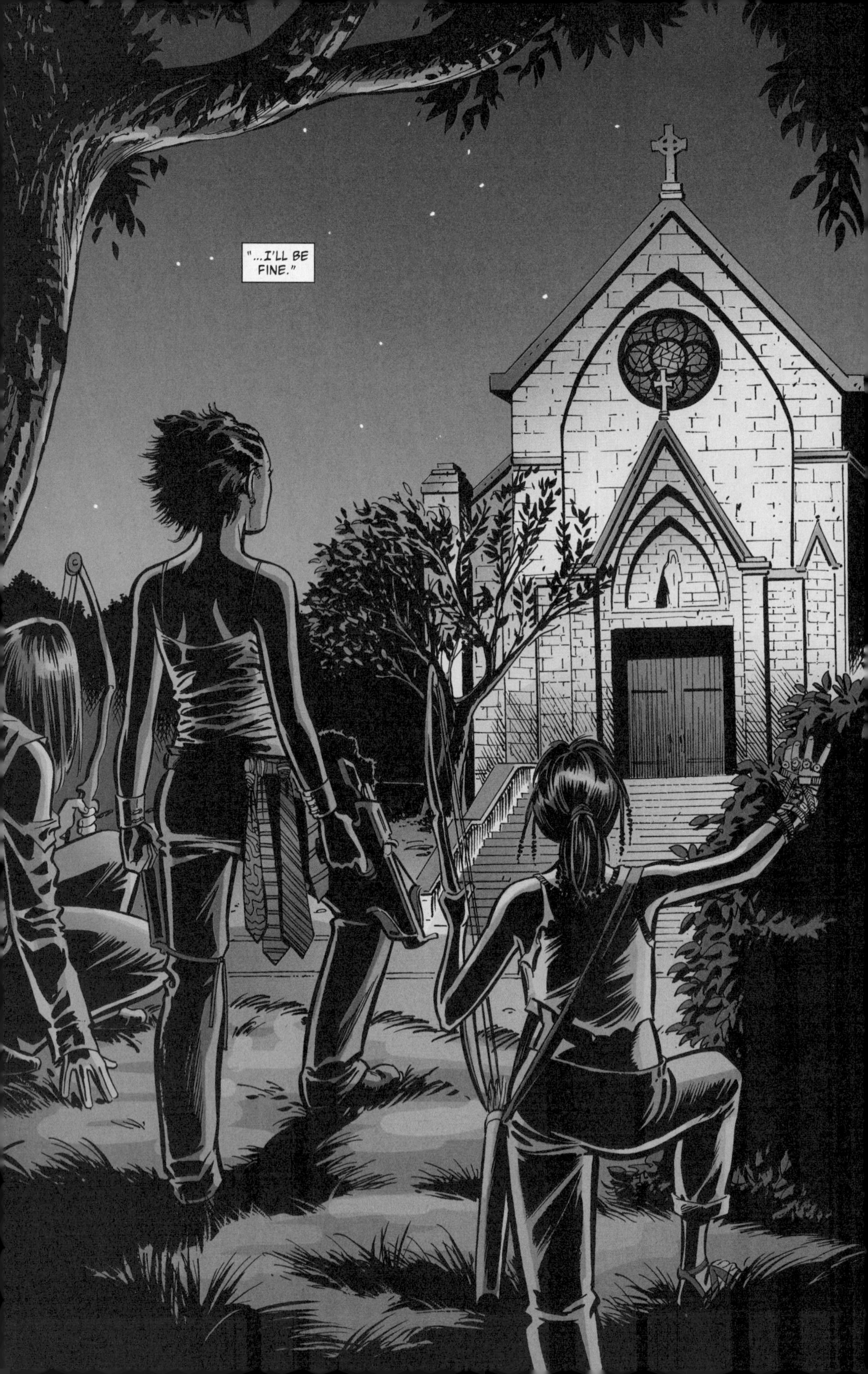
"...I'LL BE FINE."

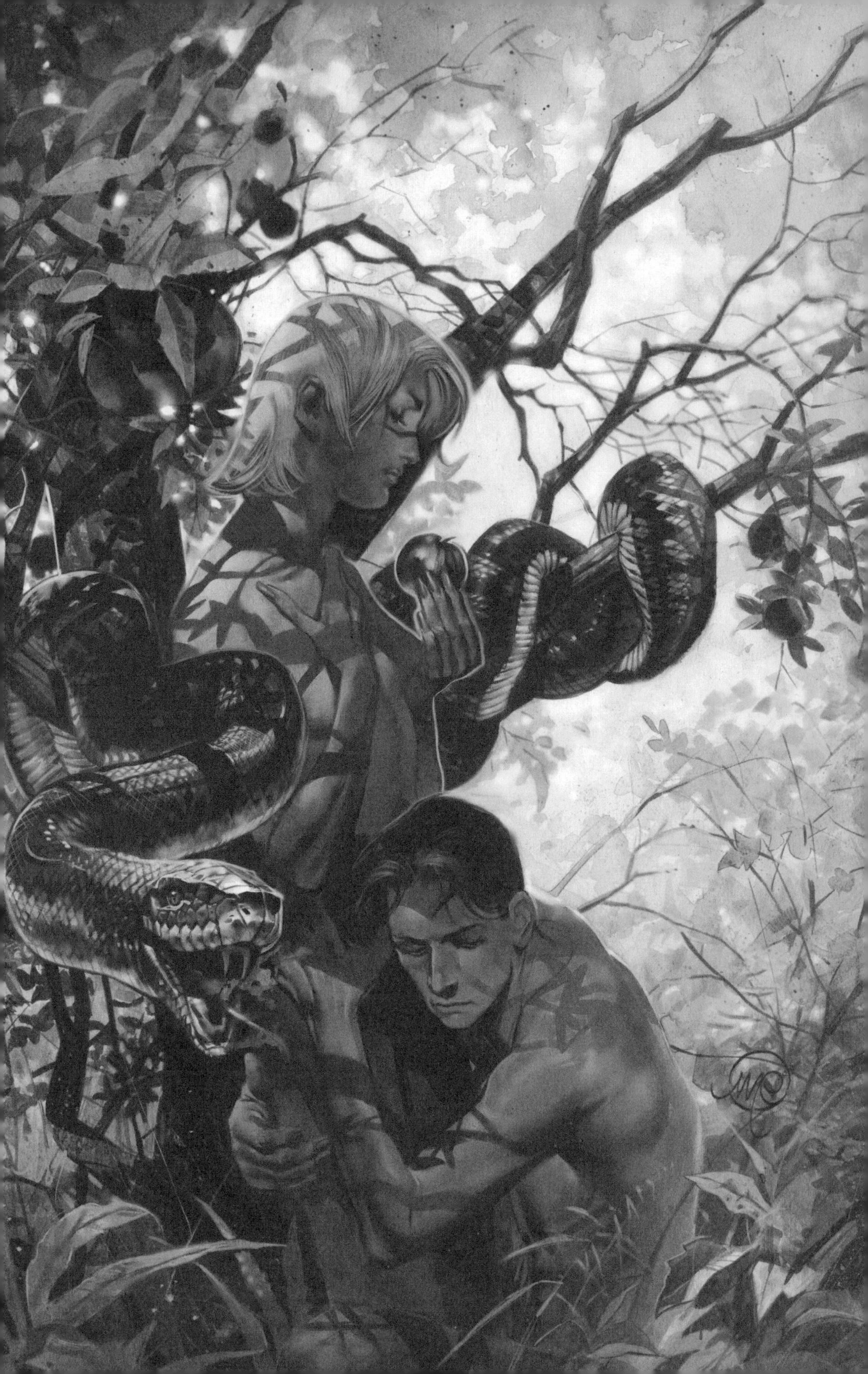

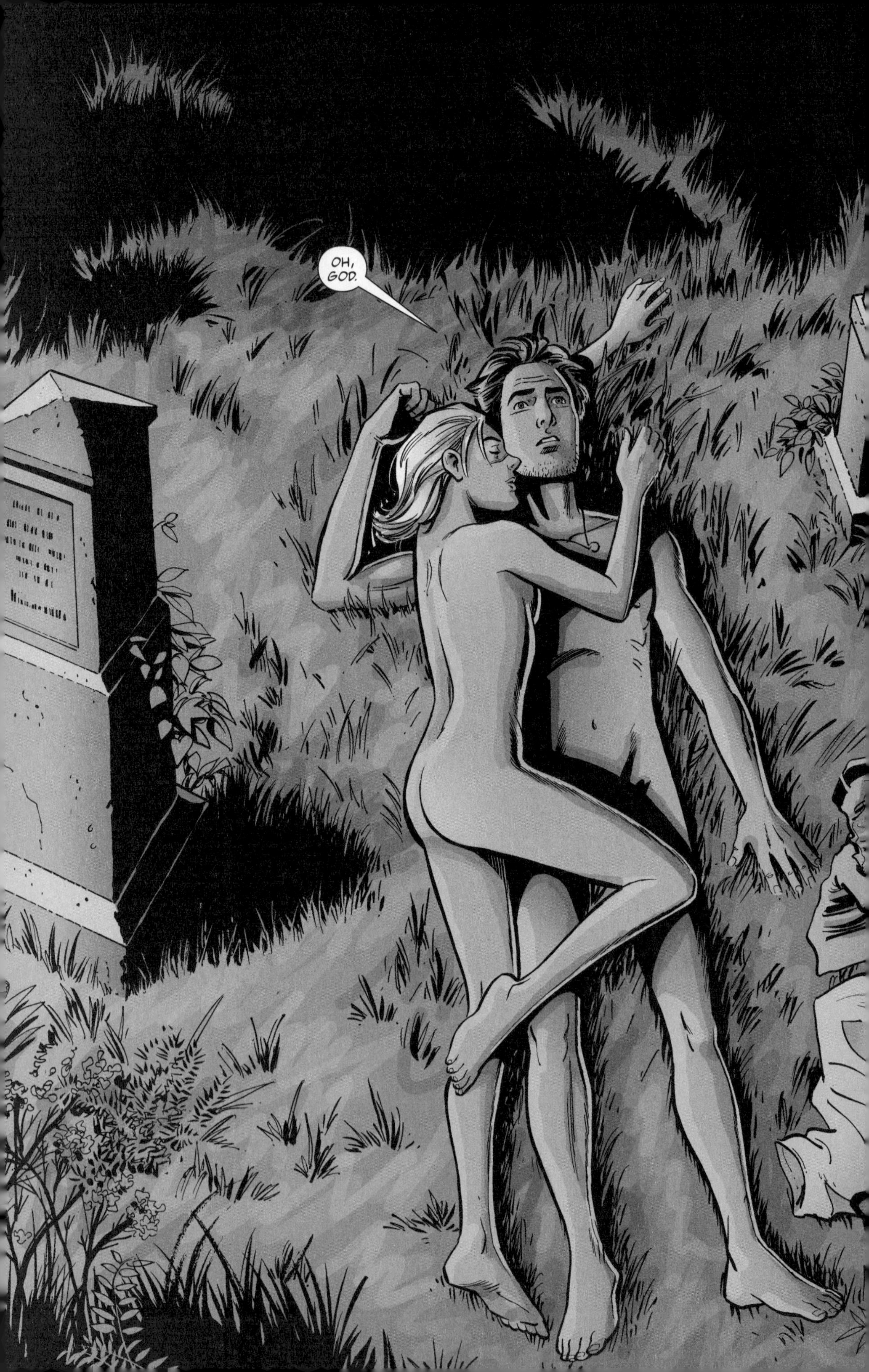
OH, GOD.

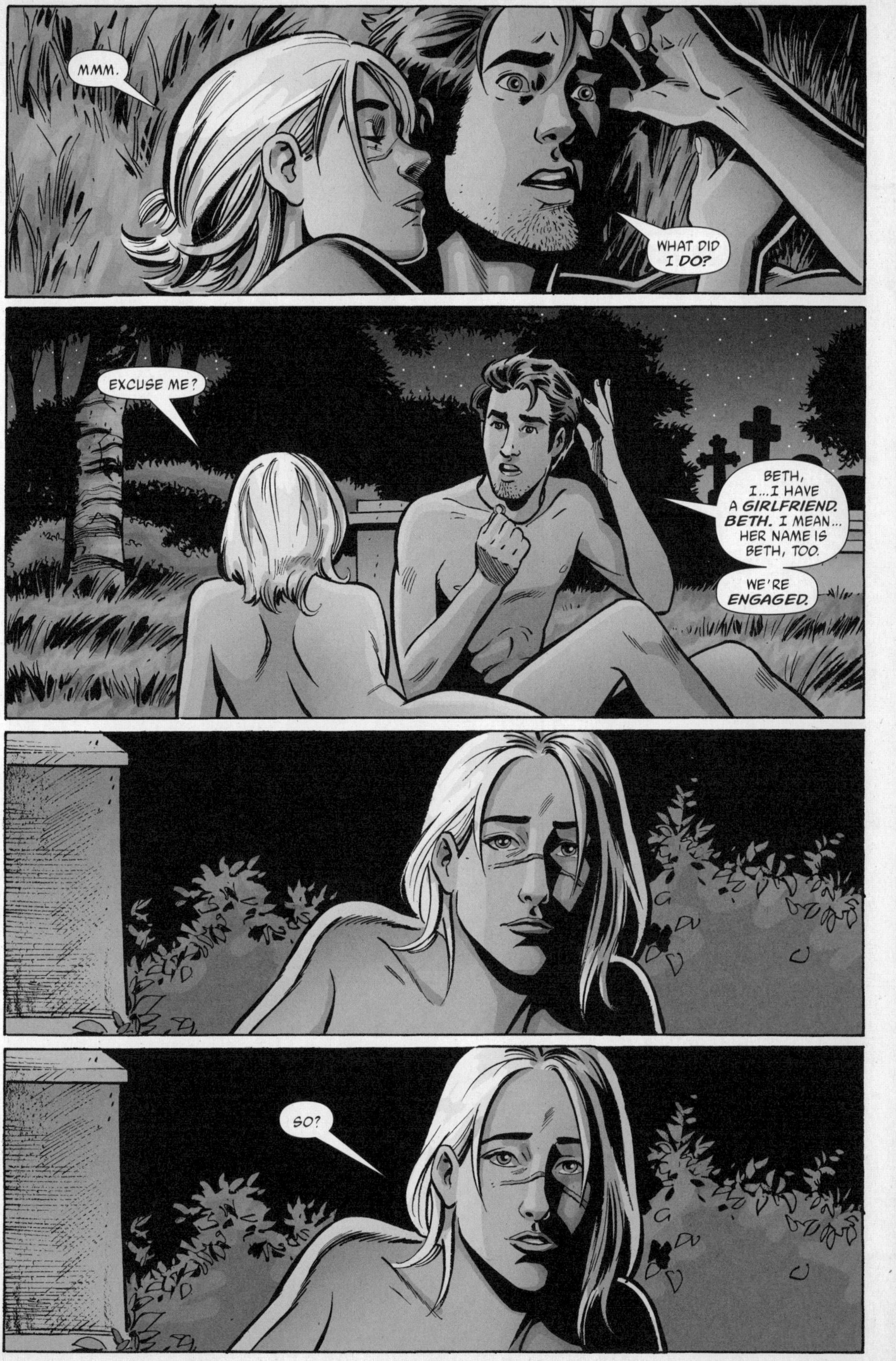
MMM.
WHAT DID I DO?
EXCUSE ME?
BETH, I...I HAVE A GIRLFRIEND. BETH. I MEAN... HER NAME IS BETH, TOO.
WE'RE ENGAGED.
SO?

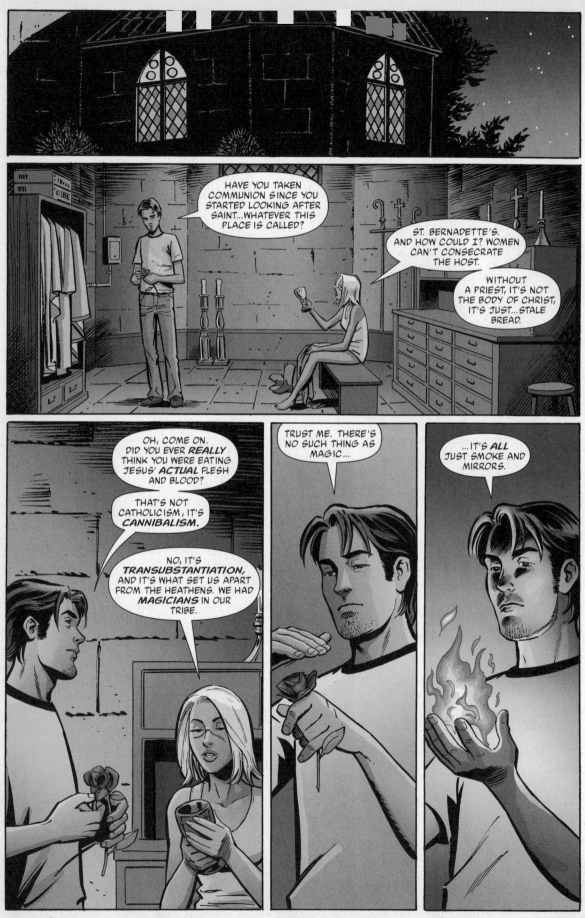

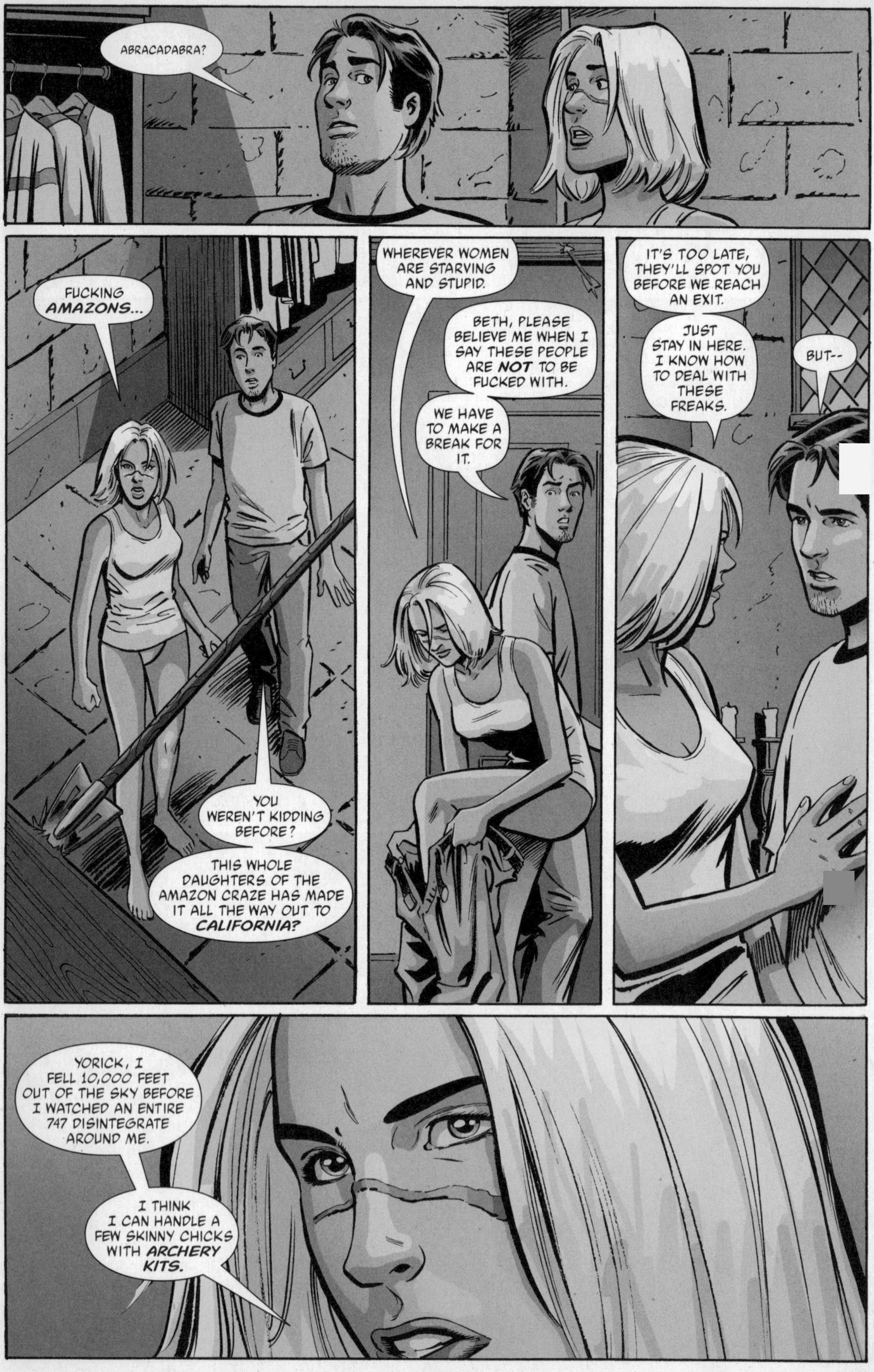
ABRACADABRA?
FUCKING AMAZONS...
YOU WEREN'T KIDDING BEFORE?
THIS WHOLE DAUGHTERS OF THE AMAZON CRAZE HAS MADE IT ALL THE WAY OUT TO CALIFORNIA?
WHEREVER WOMEN ARE STARVING AND STUPID.
BETH, PLEASE BELIEVE ME WHEN I SAY THESE PEOPLE ARE NOT TO BE FUCKED WITH.
WE HAVE TO MAKE A BREAK FOR IT.
IT'S TOO LATE, THEY'LL SPOT YOU BEFORE WE REACH AN EXIT.
JUST STAY IN HERE. I KNOW HOW TO DEAL WITH THESE FREAKS.
BUT--
YORICK, I FELL 10,000 FEET OUT OF THE SKY BEFORE I WATCHED AN ENTIRE 747 DISINTEGRATE AROUND ME.
I THINK I CAN HANDLE A FEW SKINNY CHICKS WITH ARCHERY KITS.

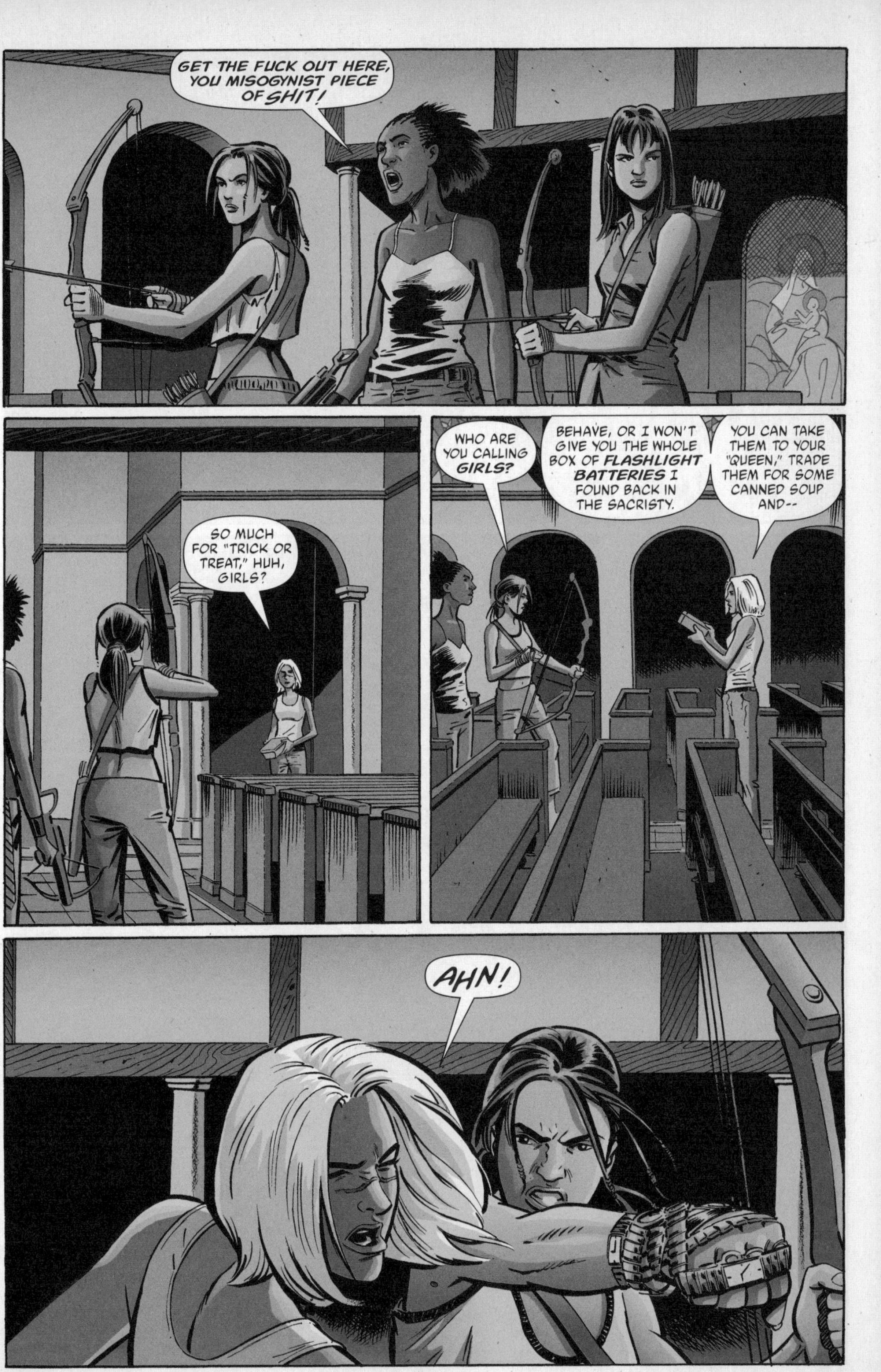
GET THE FUCK OUT HERE, YOU MISOGYNIST PIECE OF SHIT!
SO MUCH FOR "TRICK OR TREAT," HUH, GIRLS?
WHO ARE YOU CALLING GIRLS?
BEHAVE, OR I WON'T GIVE YOU THE WHOLE BOX OF FLASHLIGHT BATTERIES I FOUND BACK IN THE SACRISTY.
YOU CAN TAKE THEM TO YOUR "QUEEN," TRADE THEM FOR SOME CANNED SOUP AND--
AHN!

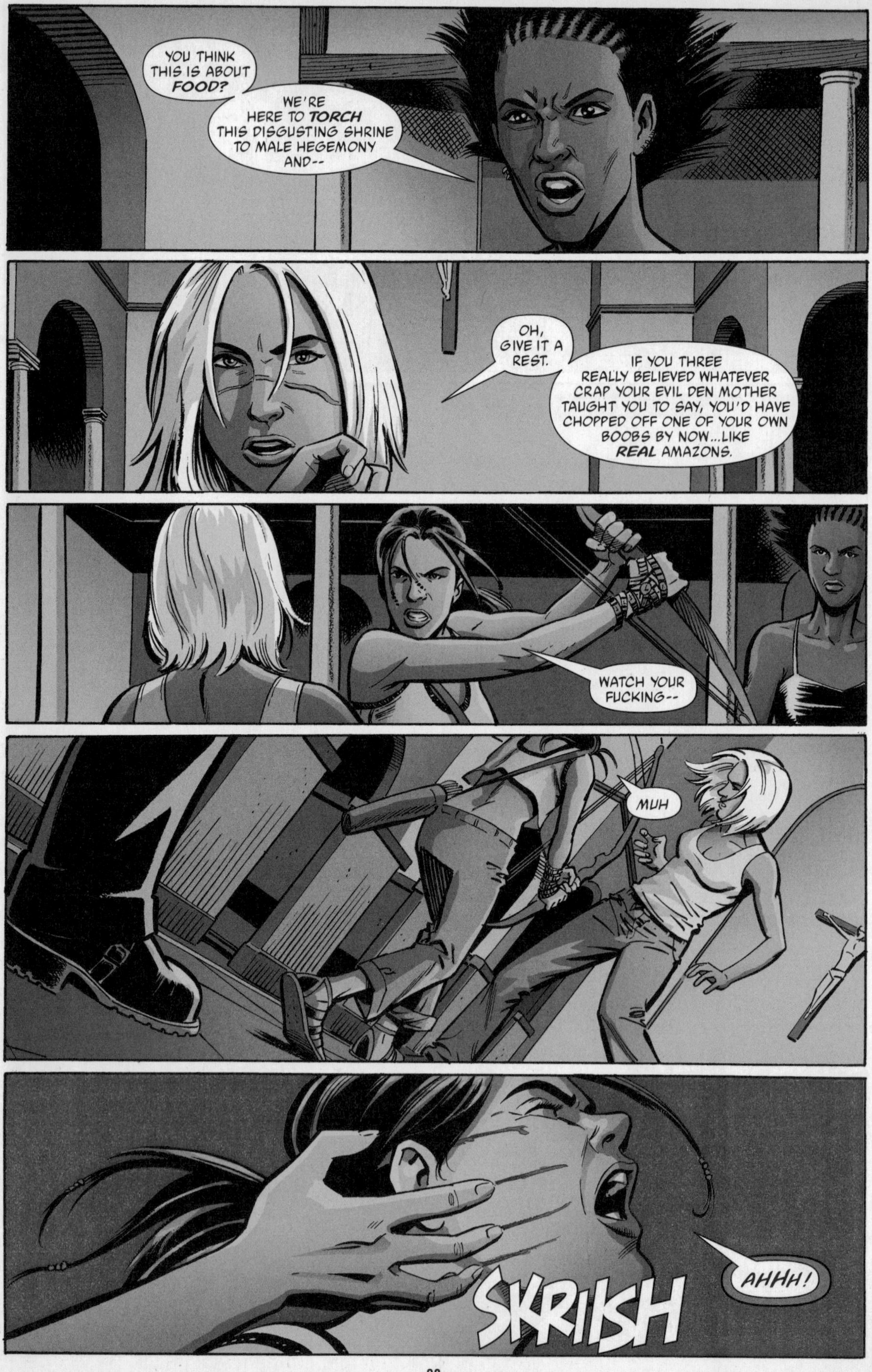

YOU THINK THIS IS ABOUT FOOD?
WE'RE HERE TO TORCH THIS DISGUSTING SHRINE TO MALE HEGEMONY AND--
OH, GIVE IT A REST.
IF YOU THREE REALLY BELIEVED WHATEVER CRAP YOUR EVIL DEN MOTHER TAUGHT YOU TO SAY, YOU'D HAVE CHOPPED OFF ONE OF YOUR OWN BOOBS BY NOW...LIKE REAL AMAZONS.
WATCH YOUR FUCKING--
MUH
SKRIISH
AHHH!

39

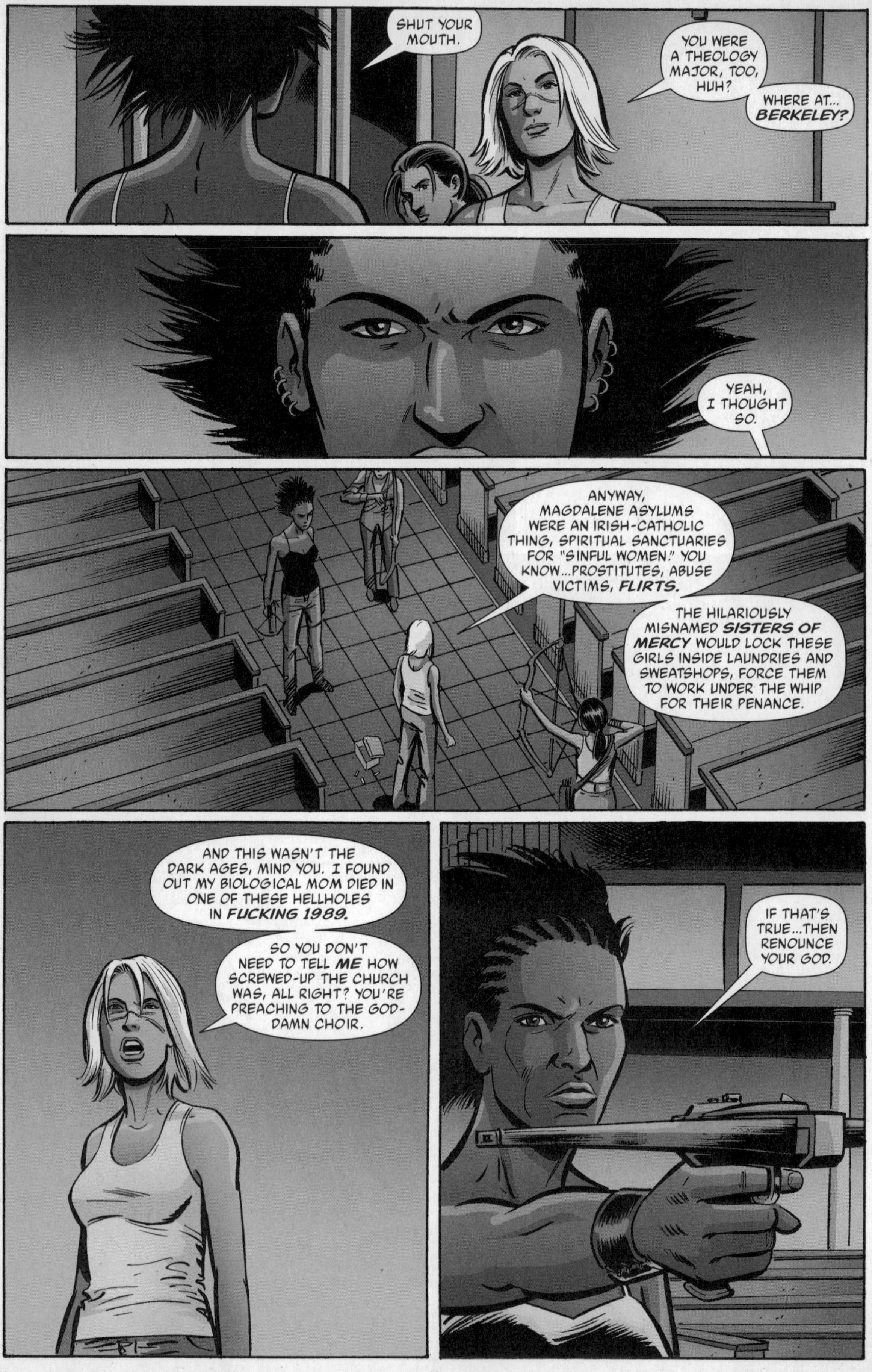

SHUT YOUR MOUTH.
YOU WERE A THEOLOGY MAJOR, TOO, HUH?
WHERE AT... BERKELEY?
YEAH, I THOUGHT SO.
ANYWAY, MAGDALENE ASYLUMS WERE AN IRISH-CATHOLIC THING, SPIRITUAL SANCTUARIES FOR "SINFUL WOMEN." YOU KNOW...PROSTITUTES, ABUSE VICTIMS, FLIRTS.
THE HILARIOUSLY MISNAMED SISTERS OF MERCY WOULD LOCK THESE GIRLS INSIDE LAUNDRIES AND SWEATSHOPS, FORCE THEM TO WORK UNDER THE WHIP FOR THEIR PENANCE.
AND THIS WASN'T THE DARK AGES, MIND YOU. I FOUND OUT MY BIOLOGICAL MOM DIED IN ONE OF THESE HELLHOLES IN FUCKING 1989.
SO YOU DON'T NEED TO TELL ME HOW SCREWED-UP THE CHURCH WAS, ALL RIGHT? YOU'RE PREACHING TO THE GOD-DAMN CHOIR.
IF THAT'S TRUE...THEN RENOUNCE YOUR GOD.

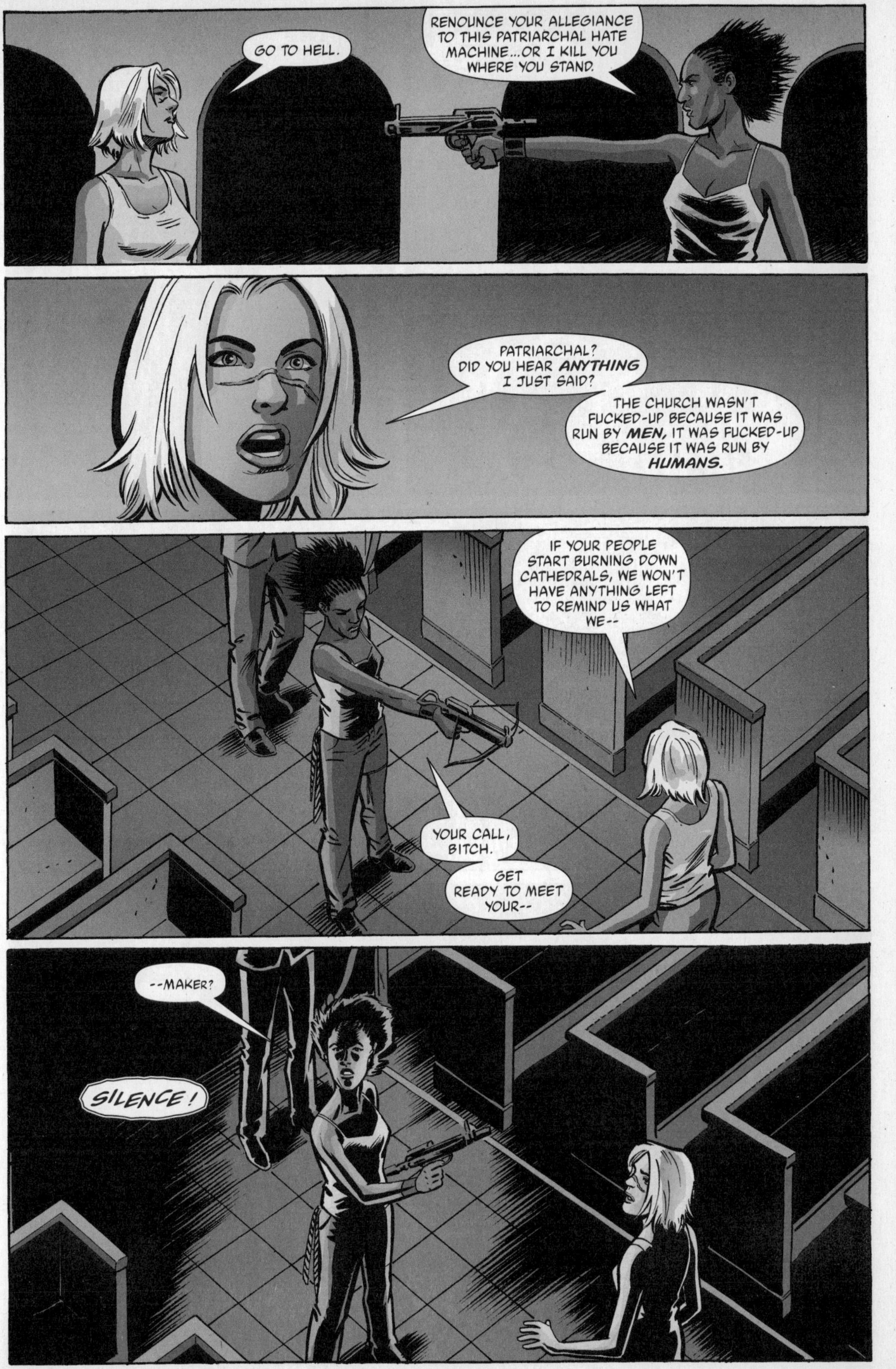
GO TO HELL.
RENOUNCE YOUR ALLEGIANCE TO THIS PATRIARCHAL HATE MACHINE...OR I KILL YOU WHERE YOU STAND.
PATRIARCHAL? DID YOU HEAR ANYTHING I JUST SAID?
THE CHURCH WASN'T FUCKED-UP BECAUSE IT WAS RUN BY MEN, IT WAS FUCKED-UP BECAUSE IT WAS RUN BY HUMANS.
IF YOUR PEOPLE START BURNING DOWN CATHEDRALS, WE WON'T HAVE ANYTHING LEFT TO REMIND US WHAT WE--
YOUR CALL, BITCH.
GET READY TO MEET YOUR--
--MAKER?
SILENCE!

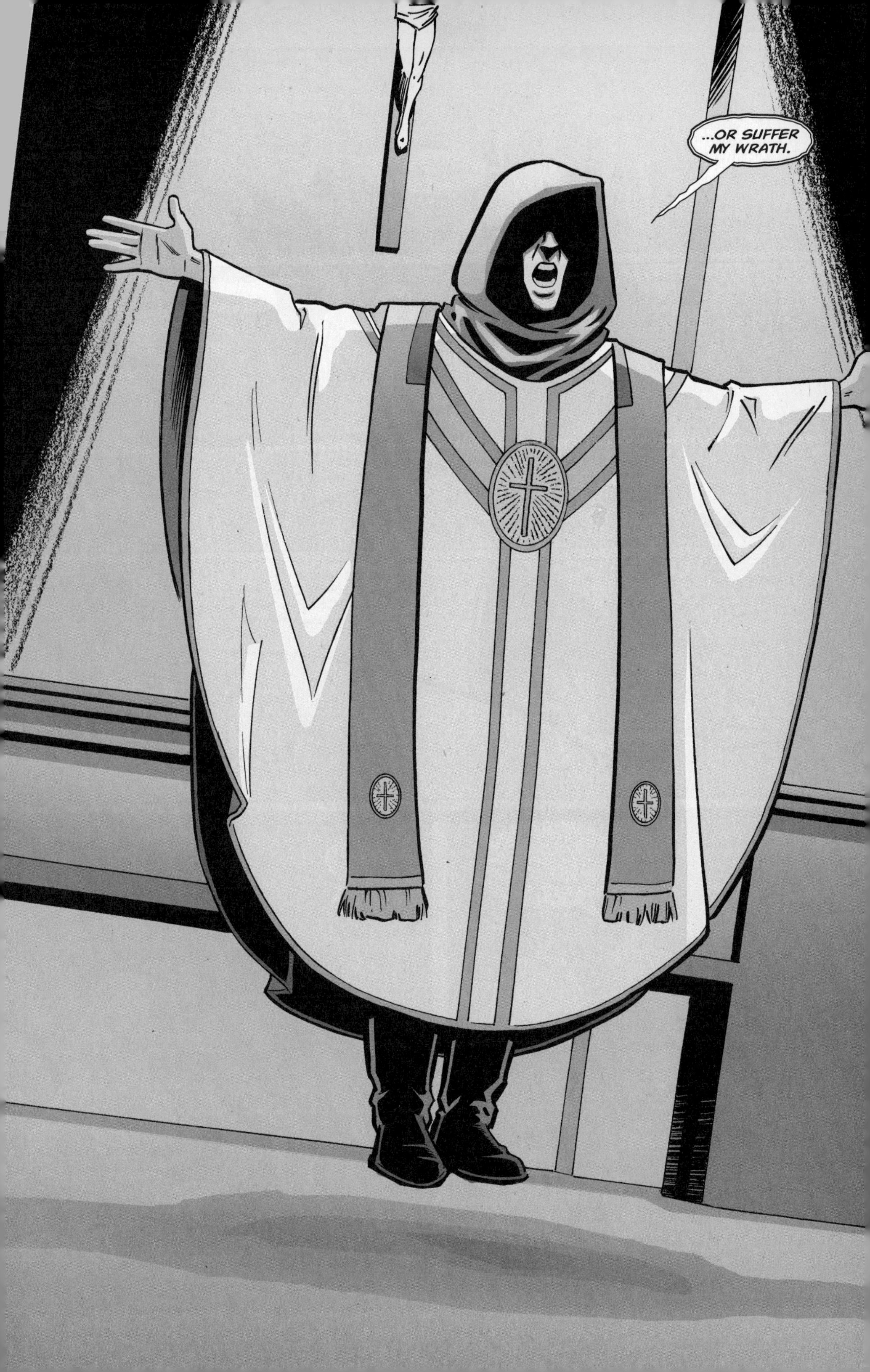
...OR SUFFER
MY WRATH.

44

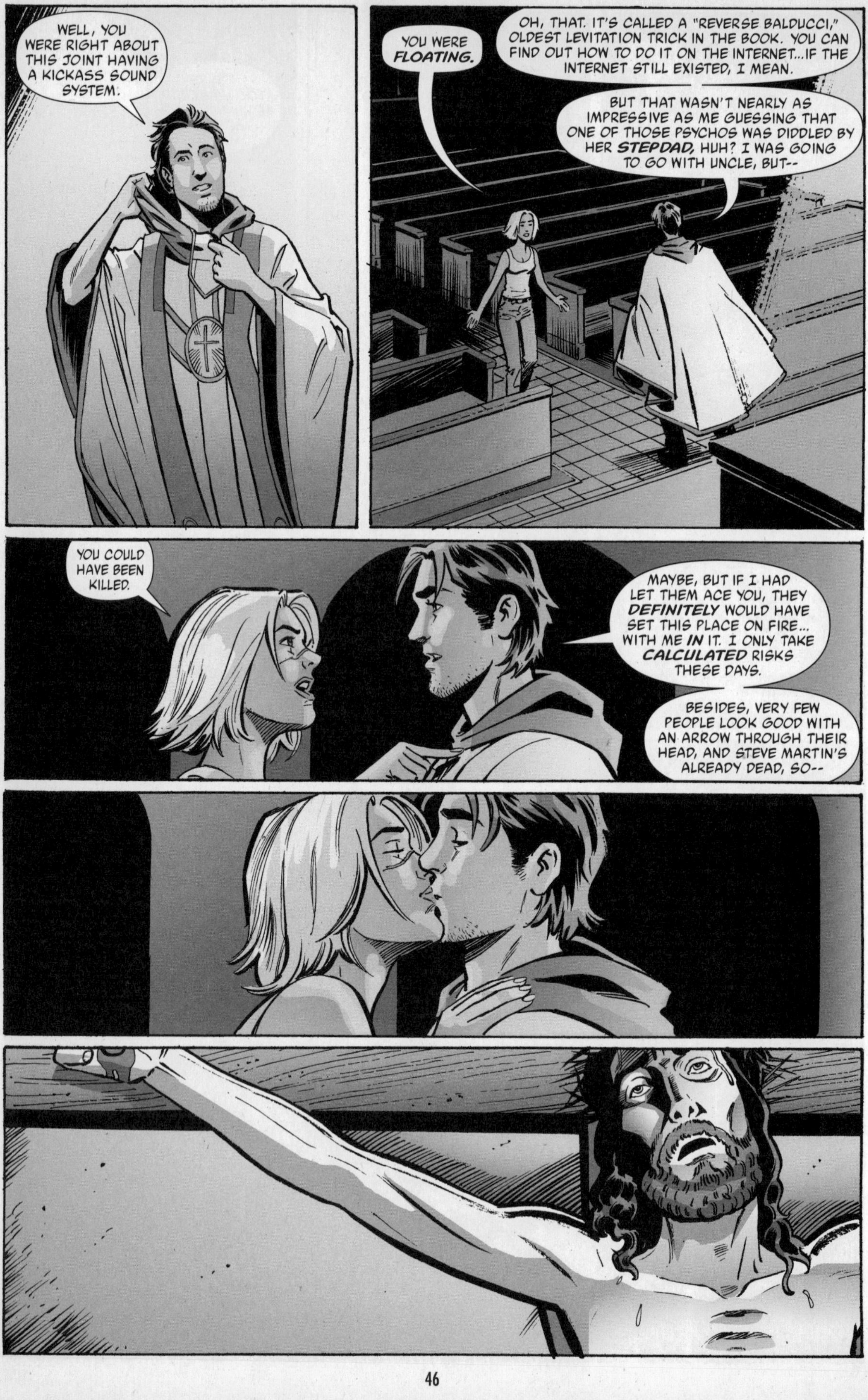
WELL, YOU WERE RIGHT ABOUT THIS JOINT HAVING A KICKASS SOUND SYSTEM.
YOU WERE FLOATING.
OH, THAT. IT'S CALLED A "REVERSE BALDUCCI," OLDEST LEVITATION TRICK IN THE BOOK. YOU CAN FIND OUT HOW TO DO IT ON THE INTERNET...IF THE INTERNET STILL EXISTED, I MEAN.
BUT THAT WASN'T NEARLY AS IMPRESSIVE AS ME GUESSING THAT ONE OF THOSE PSYCHOS WAS DIDDLED BY HER STEPDAD, HUH? I WAS GOING TO GO WITH UNCLE, BUT--
YOU COULD HAVE BEEN KILLED.
MAYBE, BUT IF I HAD LET THEM ACE YOU, THEY DEFINITELY WOULD HAVE SET THIS PLACE ON FIRE... WITH ME IN IT. I ONLY TAKE CALCULATED RISKS THESE DAYS.
BESIDES, VERY FEW PEOPLE LOOK GOOD WITH AN ARROW THROUGH THEIR HEAD, AND STEVE MARTIN'S ALREADY DEAD, SO--

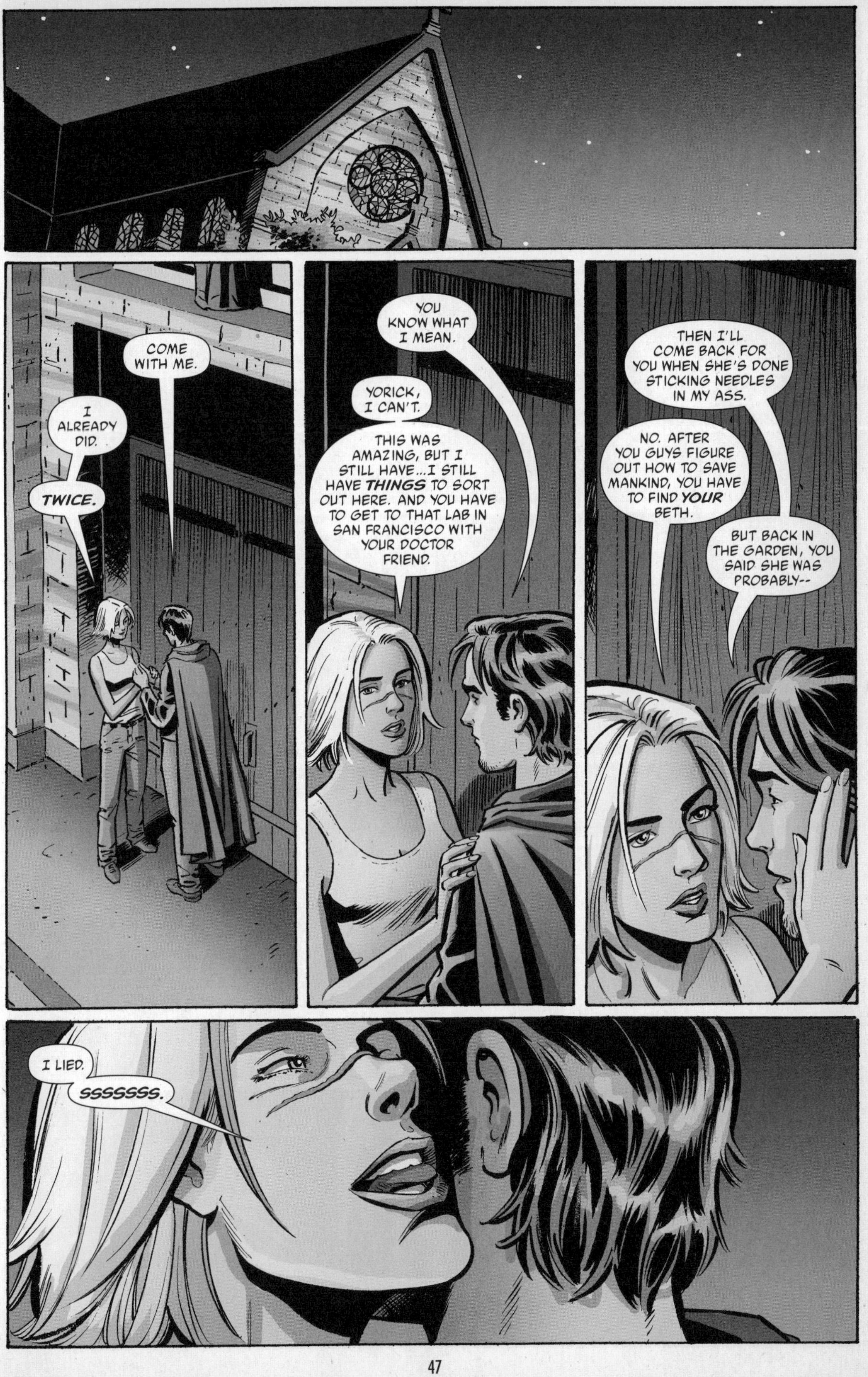
COME WITH ME.
I ALREADY DID.
TWICE.
YOU KNOW WHAT I MEAN.
YORICK, I CAN'T.
THIS WAS AMAZING, BUT I STILL HAVE...I STILL HAVE THINGS TO SORT OUT HERE. AND YOU HAVE TO GET TO THAT LAB IN SAN FRANCISCO WITH YOUR DOCTOR FRIEND.
THEN I'LL COME BACK FOR YOU WHEN SHE'S DONE STICKING NEEDLES IN MY ASS.
NO. AFTER YOU GUYS FIGURE OUT HOW TO SAVE MANKIND, YOU HAVE TO FIND YOUR BETH.
BUT BACK IN THE GARDEN, YOU SAID SHE WAS PROBABLY--
I LIED.
SSSSSSS.

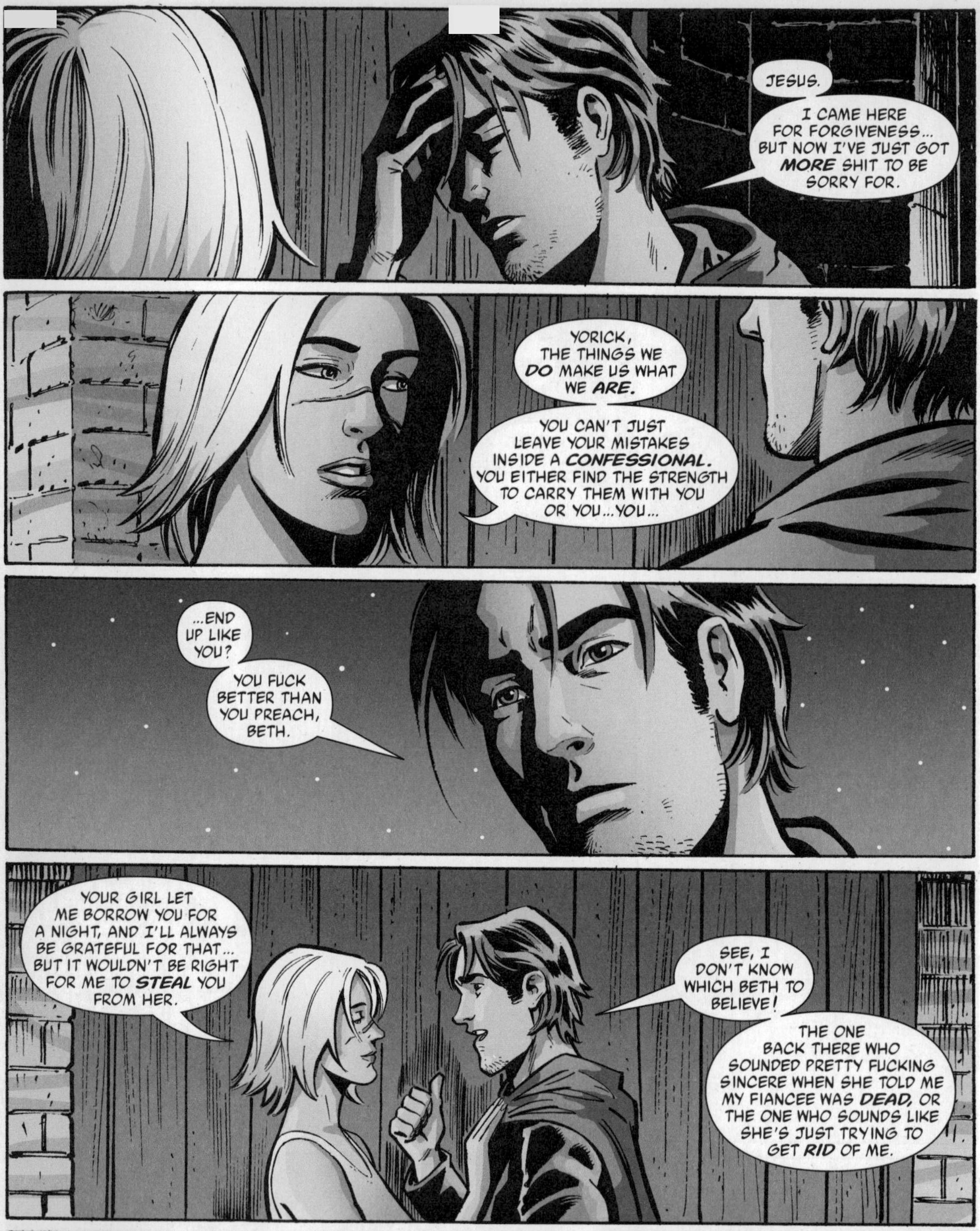
JESUS.
I CAME HERE FOR FORGIVENESS... BUT NOW I'VE JUST GOT MORE SHIT TO BE SORRY FOR.
YORICK, THE THINGS WE DO MAKE US WHAT WE ARE.
YOU CAN'T JUST LEAVE YOUR MISTAKES INSIDE A CONFESSIONAL. YOU EITHER FIND THE STRENGTH TO CARRY THEM WITH YOU OR YOU...YOU...
...END UP LIKE YOU?
YOU FUCK BETTER THAN YOU PREACH, BETH.
YOUR GIRL LET ME BORROW YOU FOR A NIGHT, AND I'LL ALWAYS BE GRATEFUL FOR THAT... BUT IT WOULDN'T BE RIGHT FOR ME TO STEAL YOU FROM HER.
SEE, I DON'T KNOW WHICH BETH TO BELIEVE!
THE ONE BACK THERE WHO SOUNDED PRETTY FUCKING SINCERE WHEN SHE TOLD ME MY FIANCEE WAS DEAD, OR THE ONE WHO SOUNDS LIKE SHE'S JUST TRYING TO GET RID OF ME.
THERE'S ONLY ONE BETH FOR YOU, AND SHE'S STILL ALIVE.
YOU HAVE TO HAVE FAITH IN THAT.

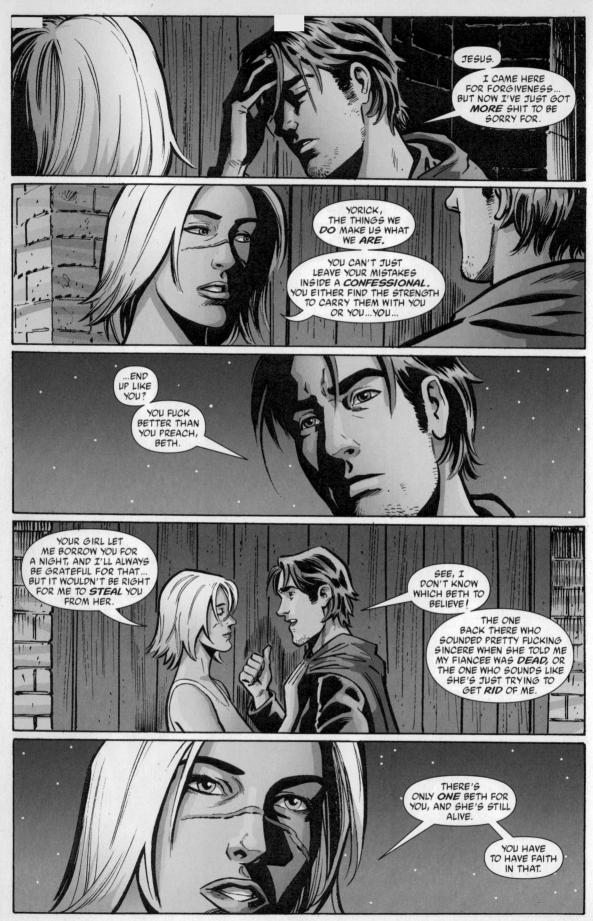

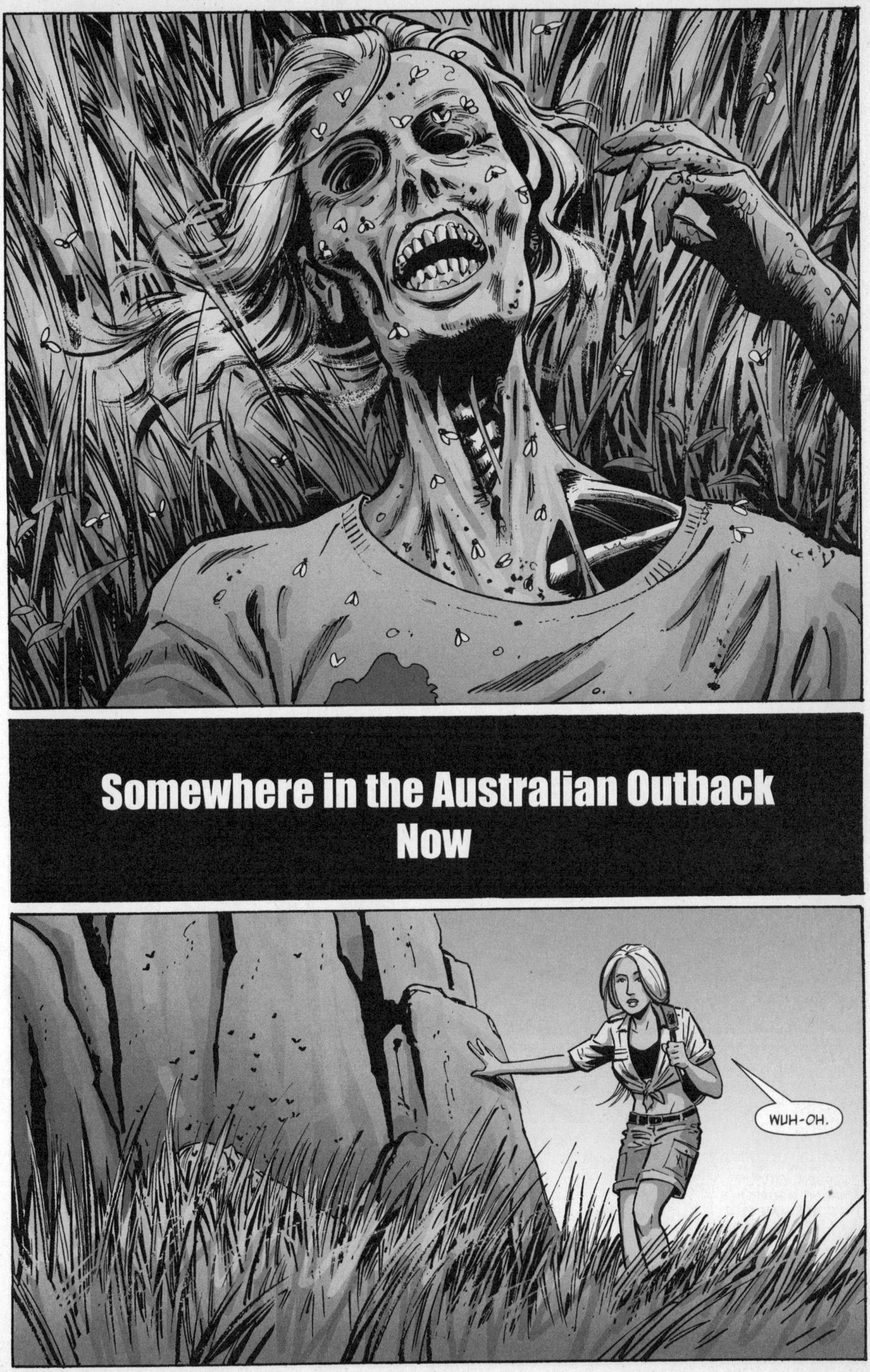
Somewhere in the Australian Outback
Now
WUH-OH.

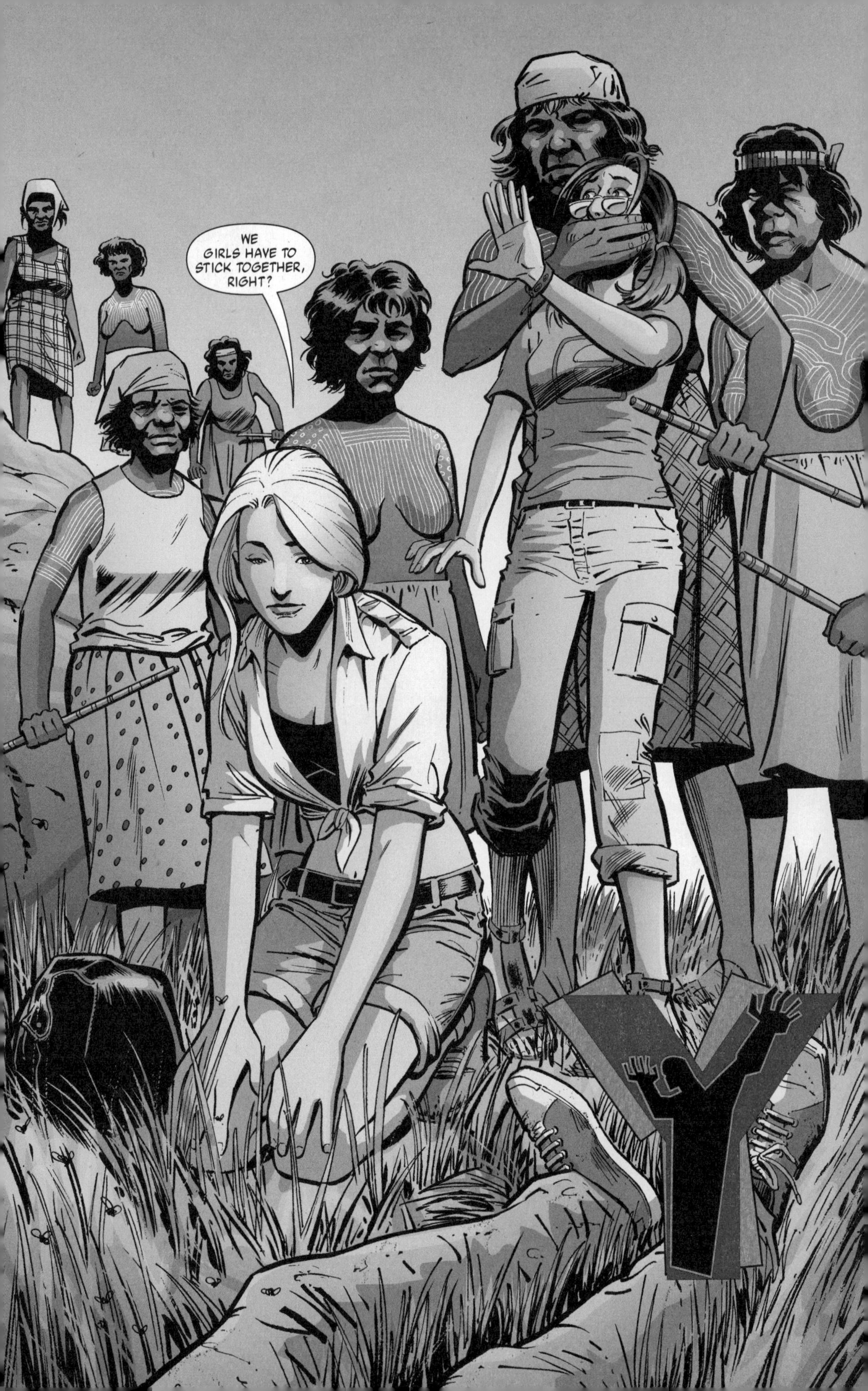
WE GIRLS HAVE TO STICK TOGETHER, RIGHT?

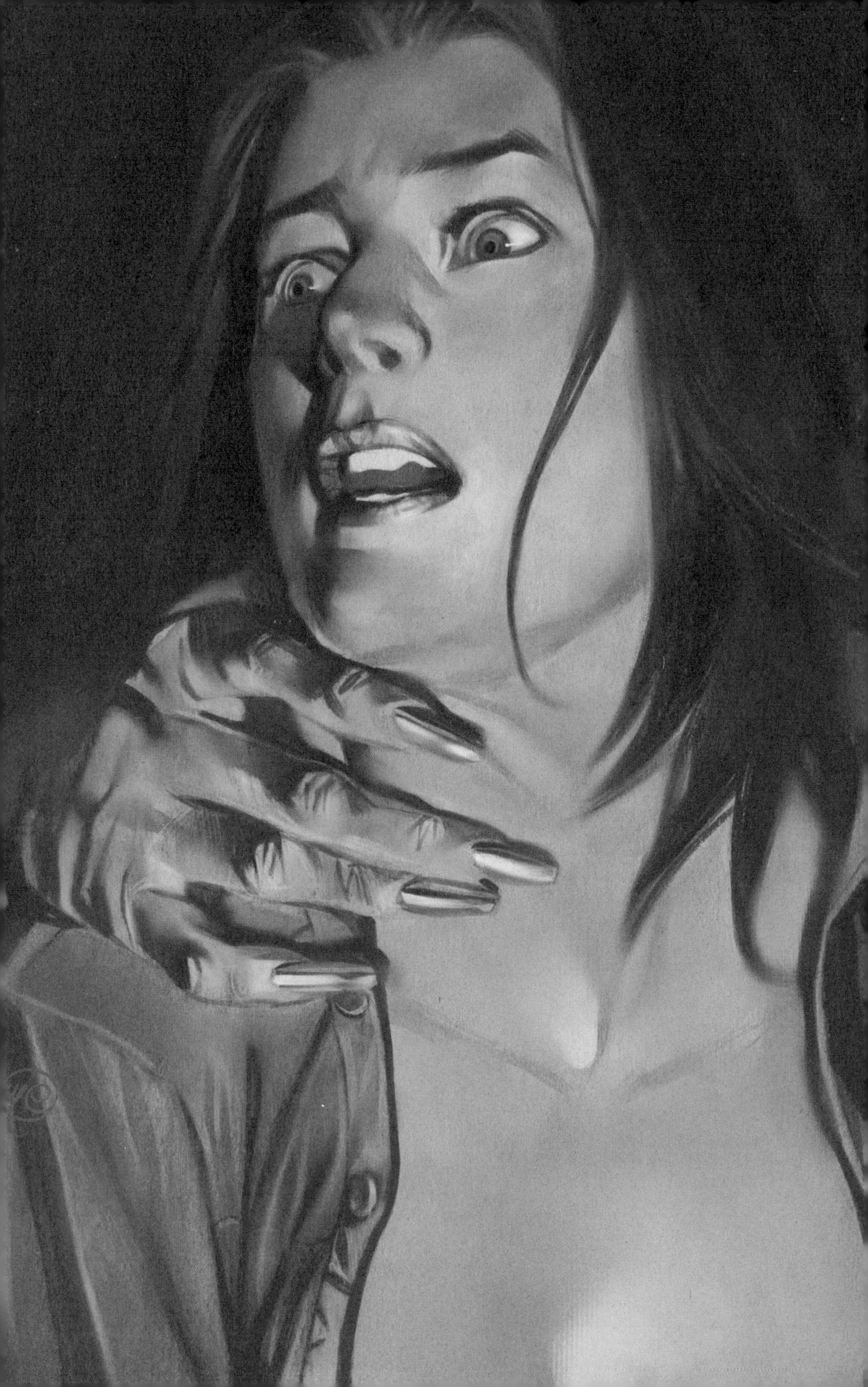

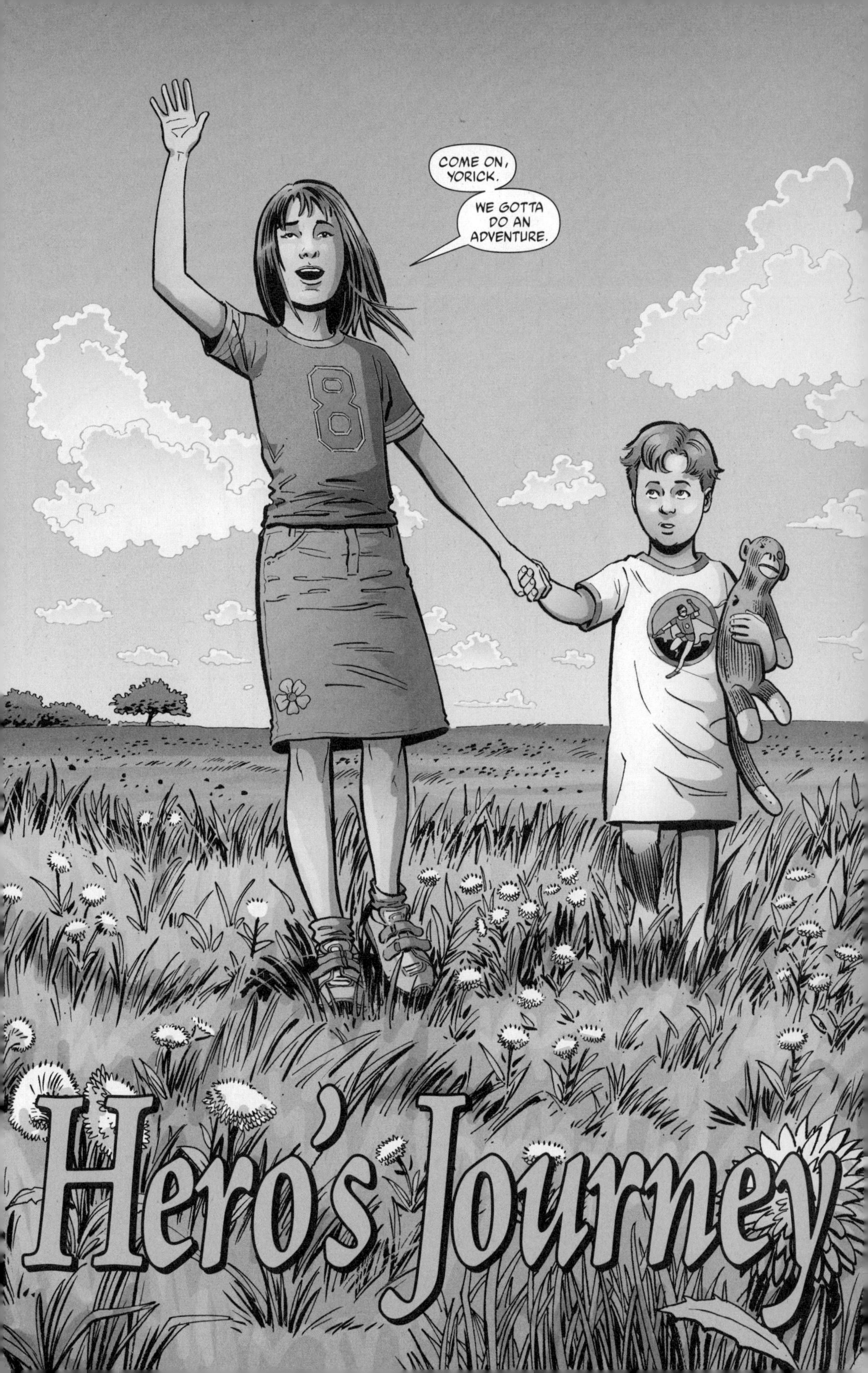
COME ON, YORICK.
WE GOTTA DO AN ADVENTURE.
Hero's Journey

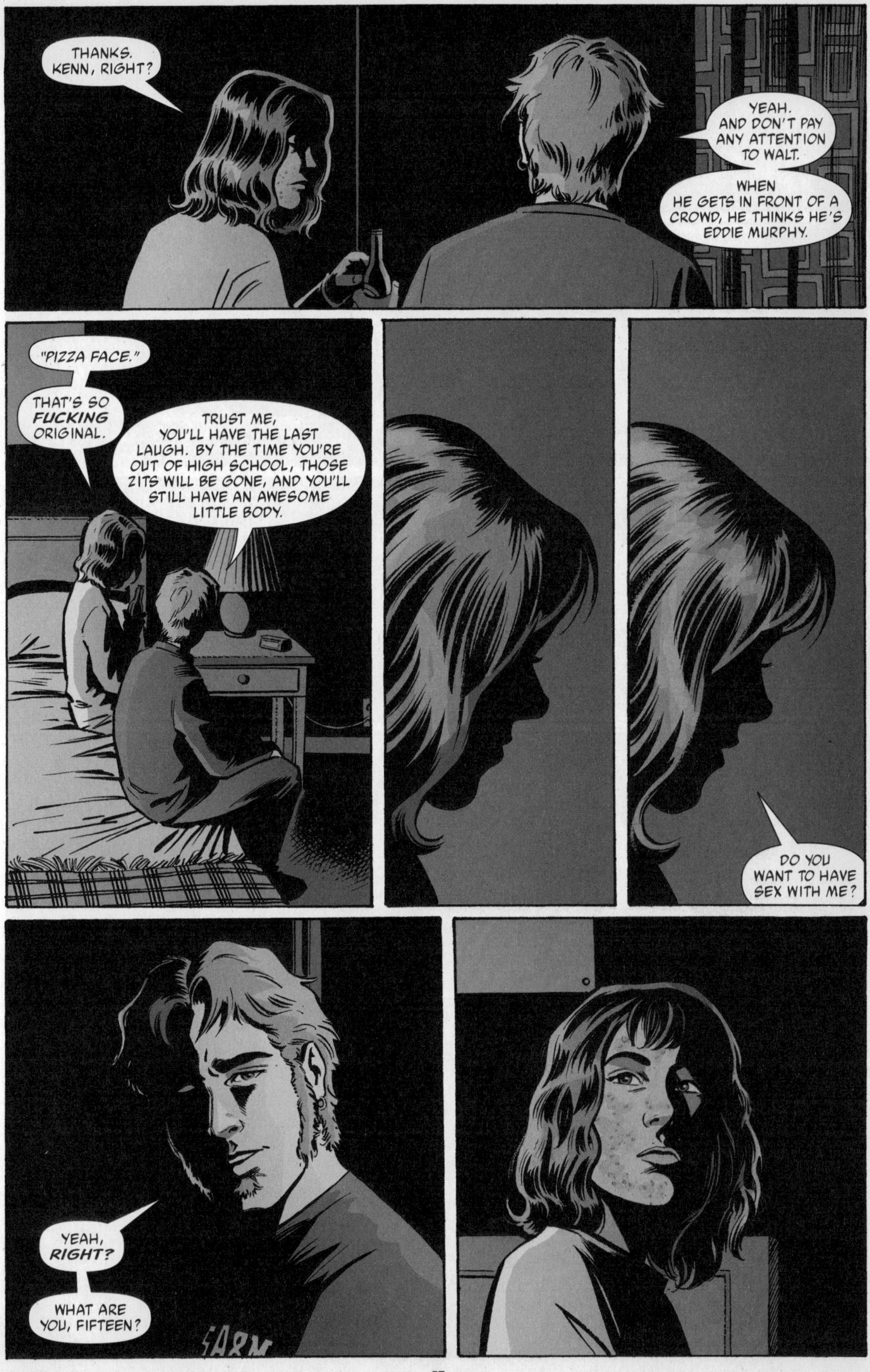
THANKS. KENN, RIGHT?
YEAH. AND DON'T PAY ANY ATTENTION TO WALT.
WHEN HE GETS IN FRONT OF A CROWD, HE THINKS HE'S EDDIE MURPHY.
"PIZZA FACE."
THAT'S SO **FUCKING** ORIGINAL.
TRUST ME, YOU'LL HAVE THE LAST LAUGH. BY THE TIME YOU'RE OUT OF HIGH SCHOOL, THOSE ZITS WILL BE GONE, AND YOU'LL STILL HAVE AN AWESOME LITTLE BODY.
DO YOU WANT TO HAVE SEX WITH ME?
YEAH, **RIGHT?**
WHAT ARE YOU, FIFTEEN?

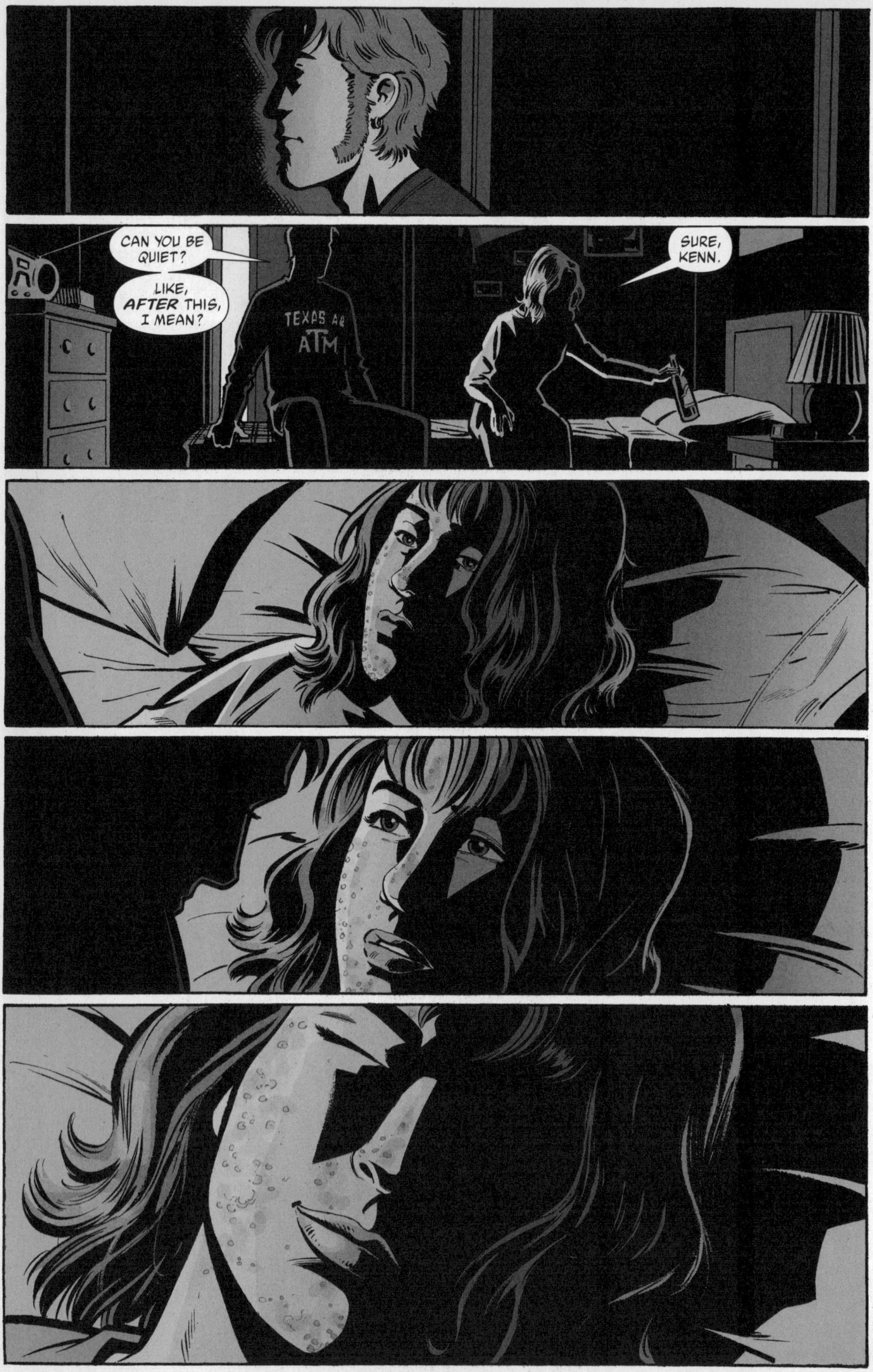
CAN YOU BE QUIET?
LIKE, AFTER THIS, I MEAN?
SURE, KENN.
TEXAS A&M

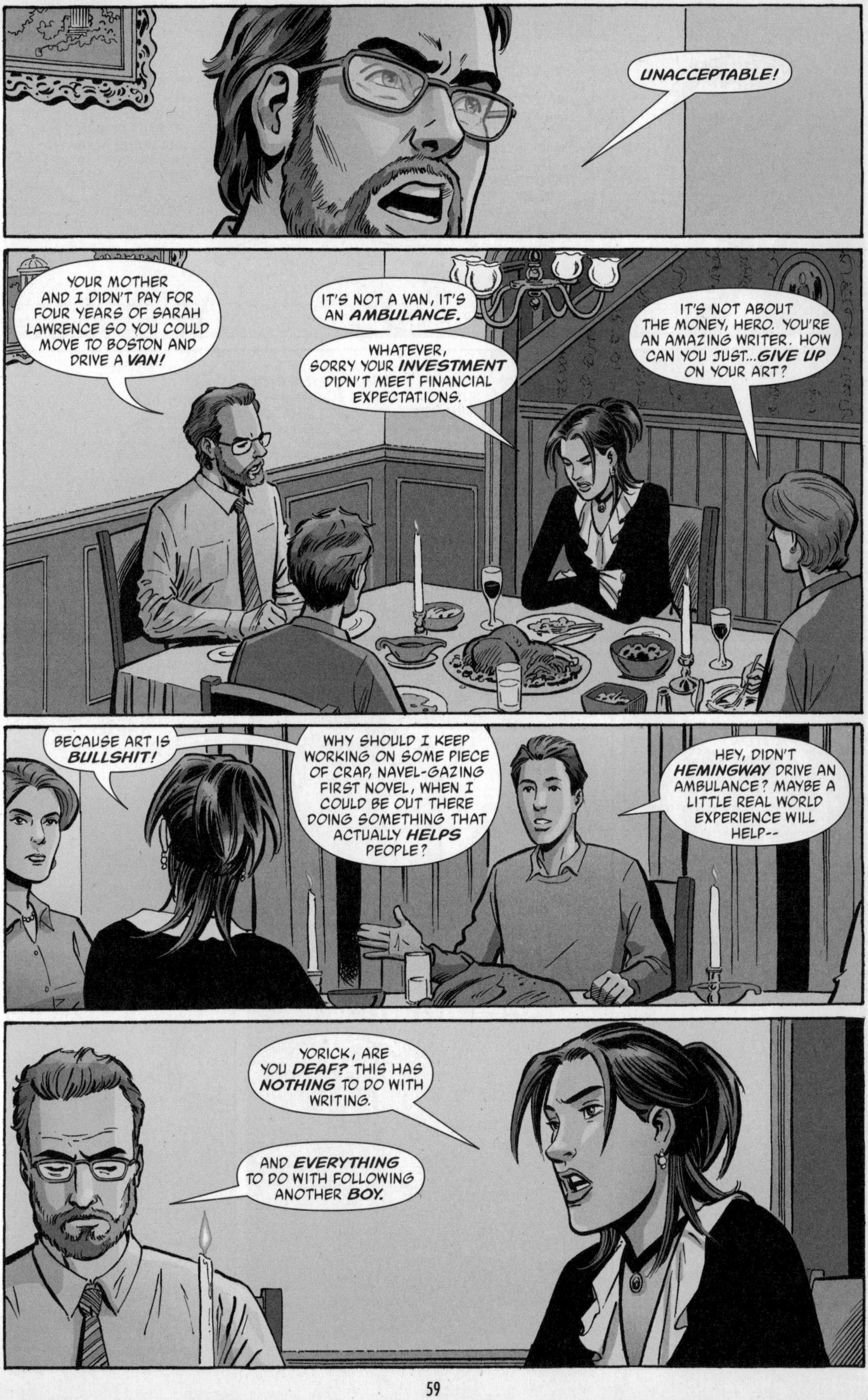
UNACCEPTABLE!
YOUR MOTHER AND I DIDN'T PAY FOR FOUR YEARS OF SARAH LAWRENCE SO YOU COULD MOVE TO BOSTON AND DRIVE A VAN!
IT'S NOT A VAN, IT'S AN AMBULANCE.
WHATEVER, SORRY YOUR INVESTMENT DIDN'T MEET FINANCIAL EXPECTATIONS.
IT'S NOT ABOUT THE MONEY, HERO. YOU'RE AN AMAZING WRITER. HOW CAN YOU JUST...GIVE UP ON YOUR ART?
BECAUSE ART IS BULLSHIT!
WHY SHOULD I KEEP WORKING ON SOME PIECE OF CRAP, NAVEL-GAZING FIRST NOVEL, WHEN I COULD BE OUT THERE DOING SOMETHING THAT ACTUALLY HELPS PEOPLE?
HEY, DIDN'T HEMINGWAY DRIVE AN AMBULANCE? MAYBE A LITTLE REAL WORLD EXPERIENCE WILL HELP--
YORICK, ARE YOU DEAF? THIS HAS NOTHING TO DO WITH WRITING.
AND EVERYTHING TO DO WITH FOLLOWING ANOTHER BOY.

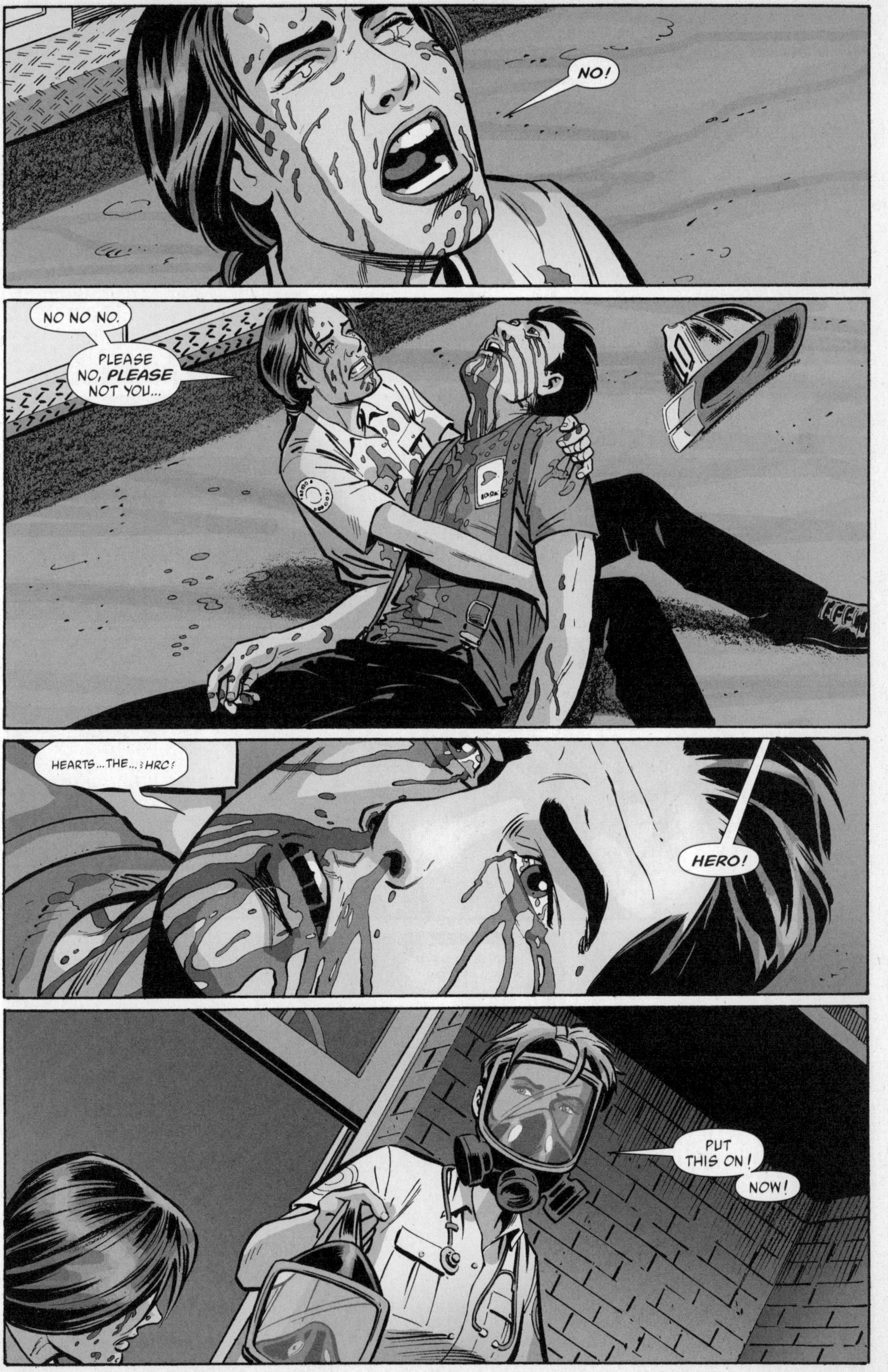
NO!
NO NO NO.
PLEASE NO, PLEASE NOT YOU...
HEARTS...THE...HRC!
HERO!
PUT THIS ON!
NOW!

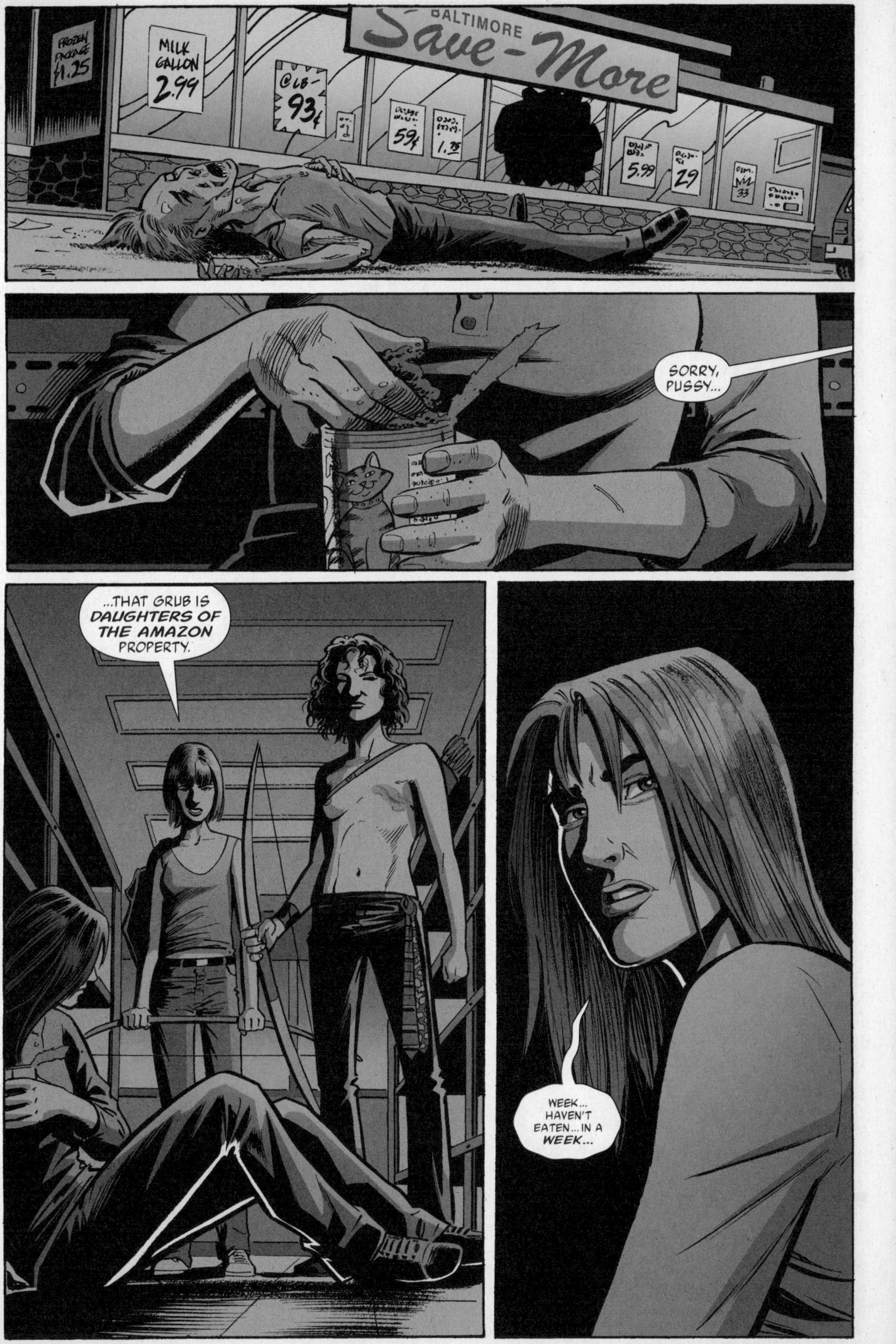

FROZEN PACKAGE $1.25
MILK GALLON 2.99
@LB- 93¢
59¢
1.35
5.99
29
33
BALTIMORE
Save-More
SORRY, PUSSY...
...THAT GRUB IS DAUGHTERS OF THE AMAZON PROPERTY.
WEEK... HAVEN'T EATEN... IN A WEEK...

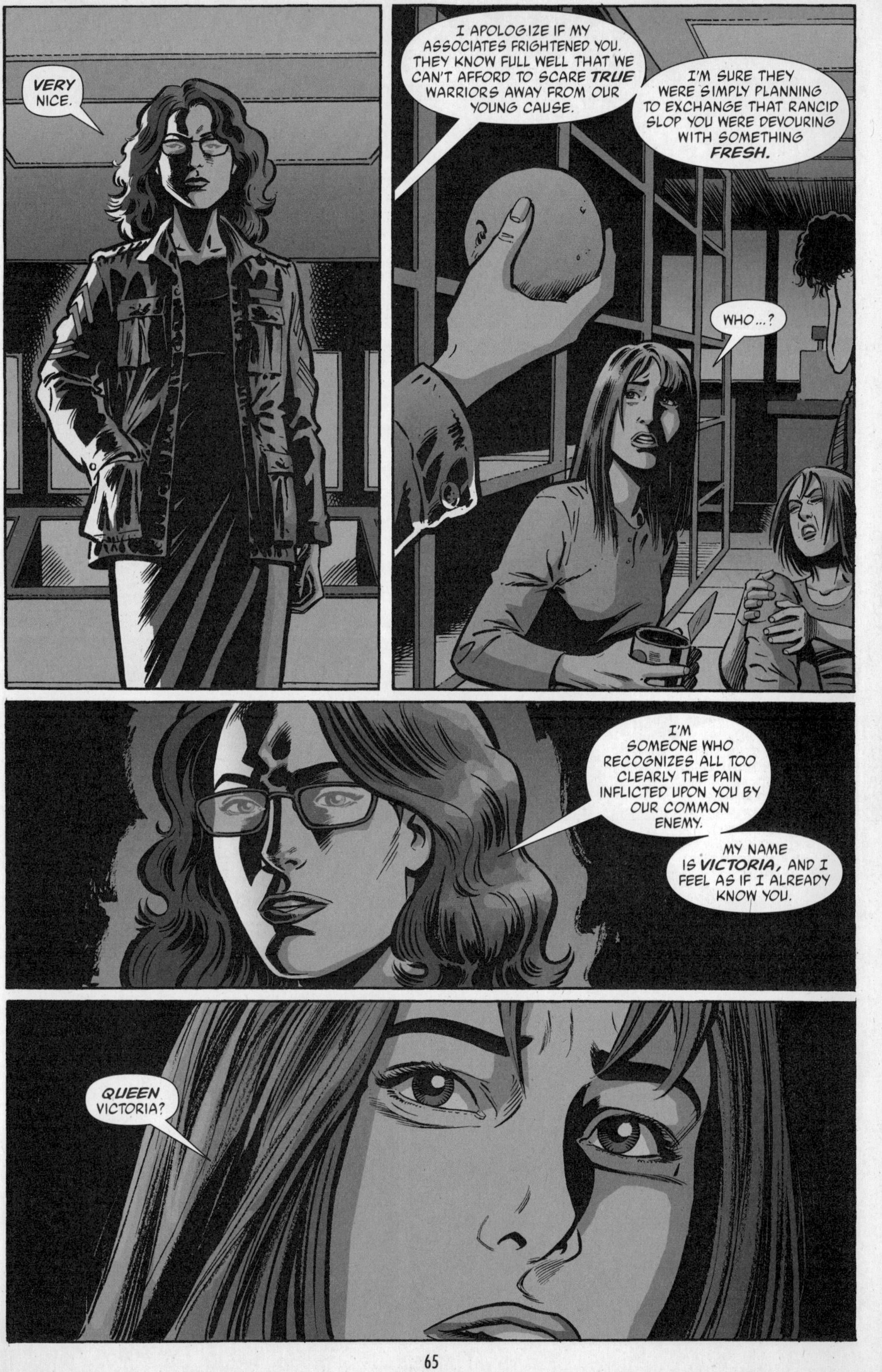
VERY NICE.
I APOLOGIZE IF MY ASSOCIATES FRIGHTENED YOU. THEY KNOW FULL WELL THAT WE CAN'T AFFORD TO SCARE TRUE WARRIORS AWAY FROM OUR YOUNG CAUSE.
I'M SURE THEY WERE SIMPLY PLANNING TO EXCHANGE THAT RANCID SLOP YOU WERE DEVOURING WITH SOMETHING FRESH.
WHO...?
I'M SOMEONE WHO RECOGNIZES ALL TOO CLEARLY THE PAIN INFLICTED UPON YOU BY OUR COMMON ENEMY.
MY NAME IS VICTORIA, AND I FEEL AS IF I ALREADY KNOW YOU.
QUEEN VICTORIA?

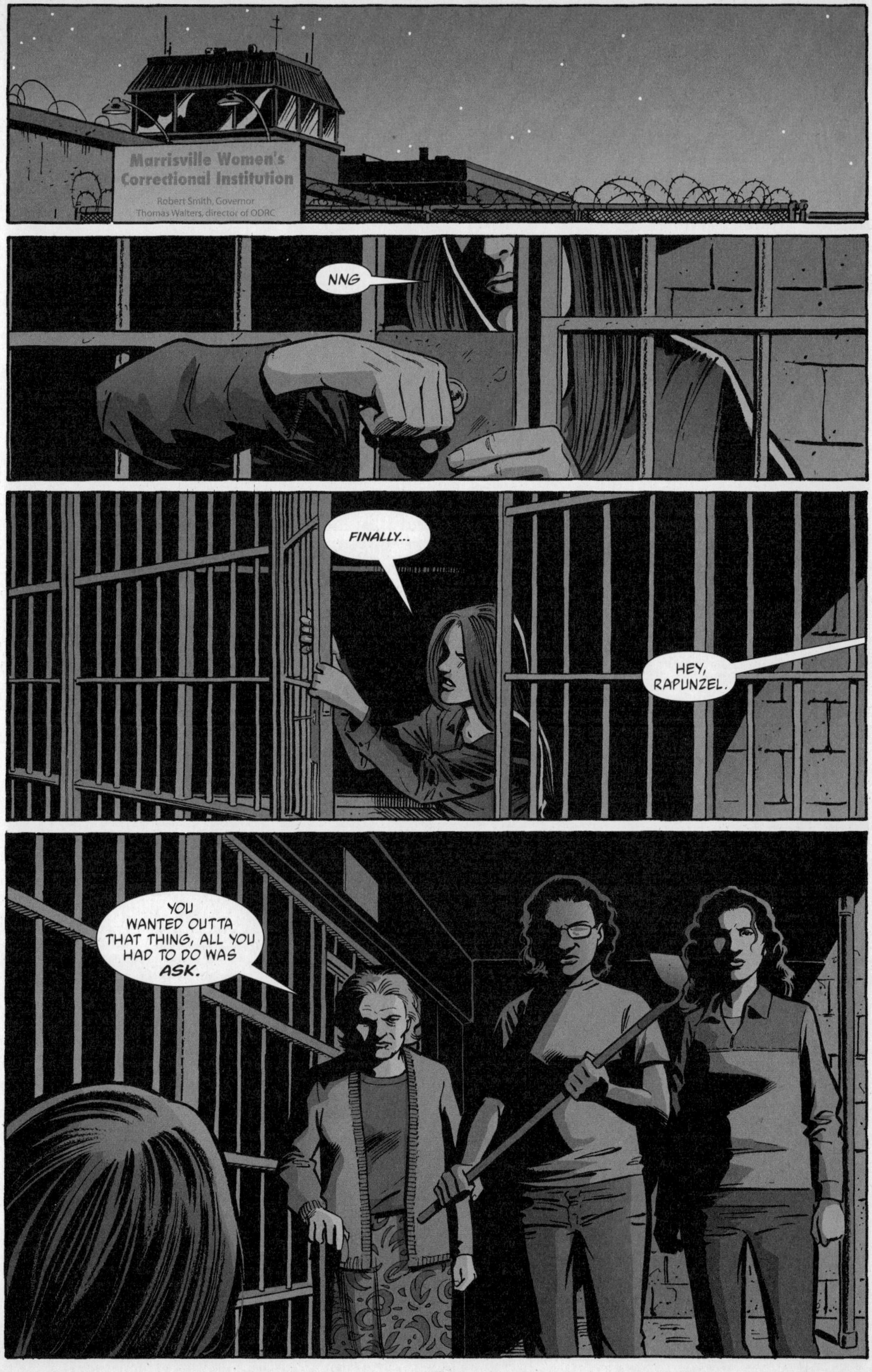
Marrisville Women's Correctional Institution
Robert Smith, Governor
Thomas Walters, director of ODRC
NNG
FINALLY...
HEY, RAPUNZEL.
YOU WANTED OUTTA THAT THING, ALL YOU HAD TO DO WAS ASK.

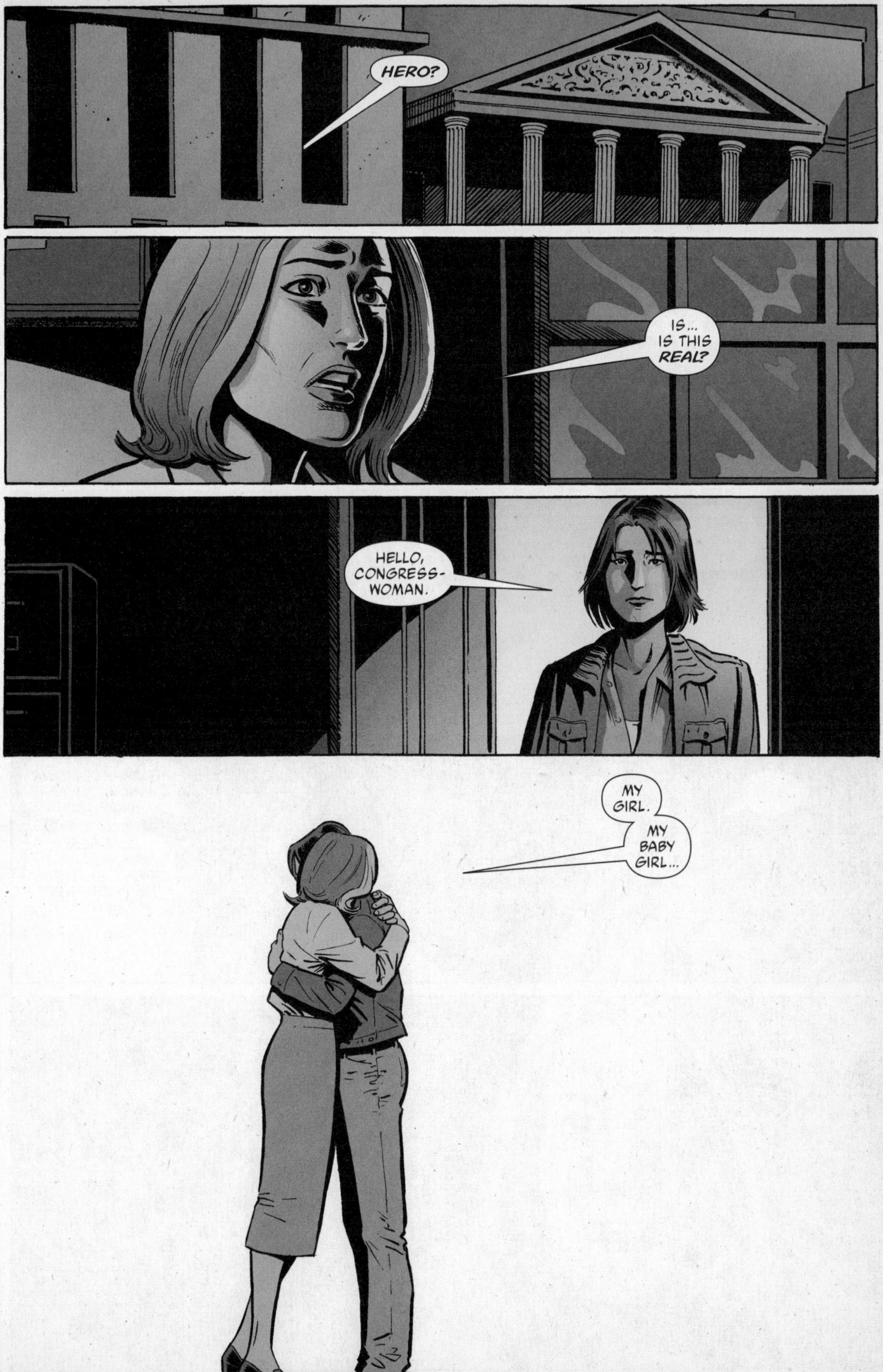
HERO?
IS... IS THIS REAL?
HELLO, CONGRESS-WOMAN.
MY GIRL.
MY BABY GIRL...

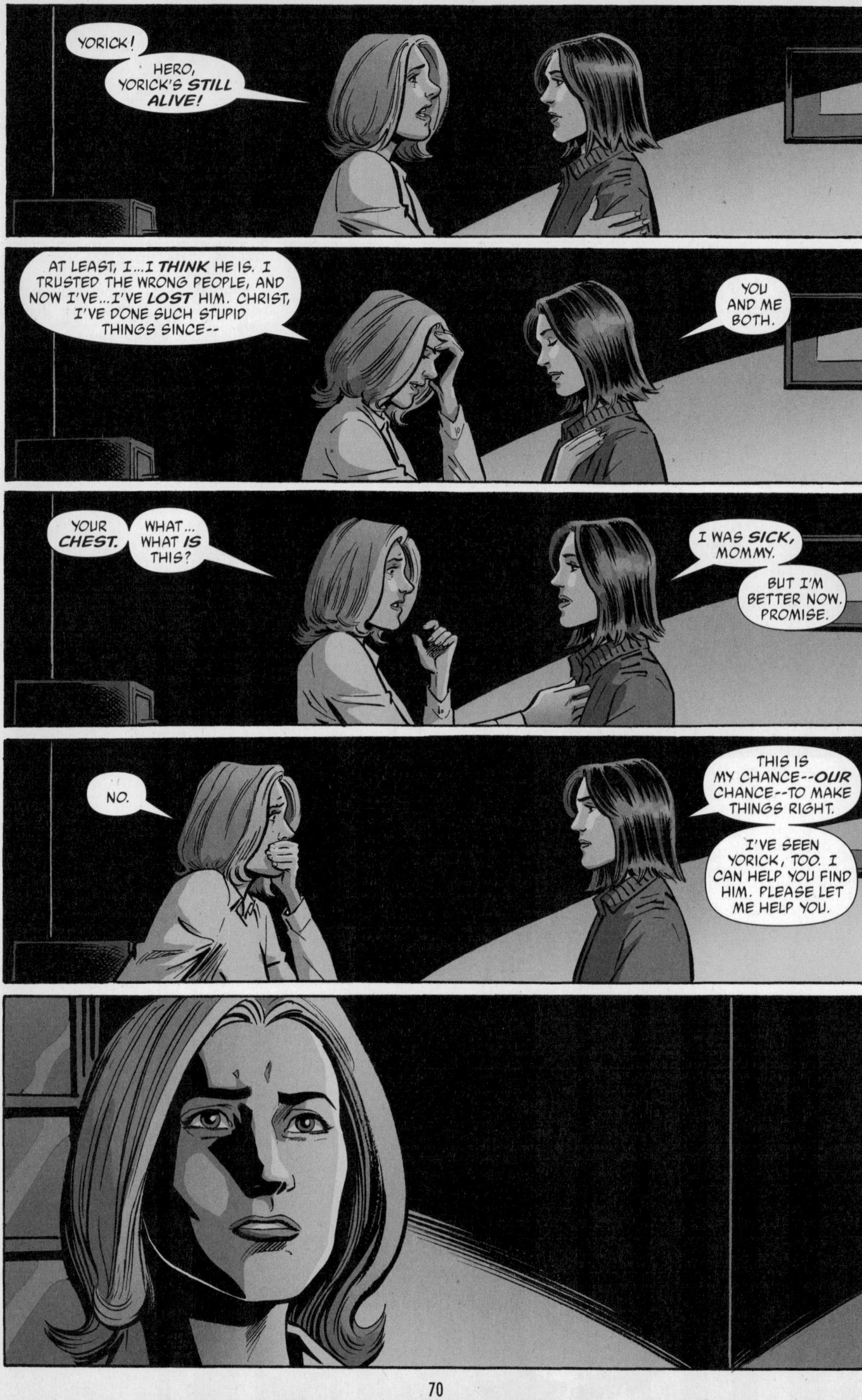
YORICK!
HERO, YORICK'S STILL ALIVE!
AT LEAST, I...I THINK HE IS. I TRUSTED THE WRONG PEOPLE, AND NOW I'VE...I'VE LOST HIM. CHRIST, I'VE DONE SUCH STUPID THINGS SINCE--
YOU AND ME BOTH.
YOUR CHEST.
WHAT... WHAT IS THIS?
I WAS SICK, MOMMY.
BUT I'M BETTER NOW. PROMISE.
NO.
THIS IS MY CHANCE--OUR CHANCE--TO MAKE THINGS RIGHT.
I'VE SEEN YORICK, TOO. I CAN HELP YOU FIND HIM. PLEASE LET ME HELP YOU.

71

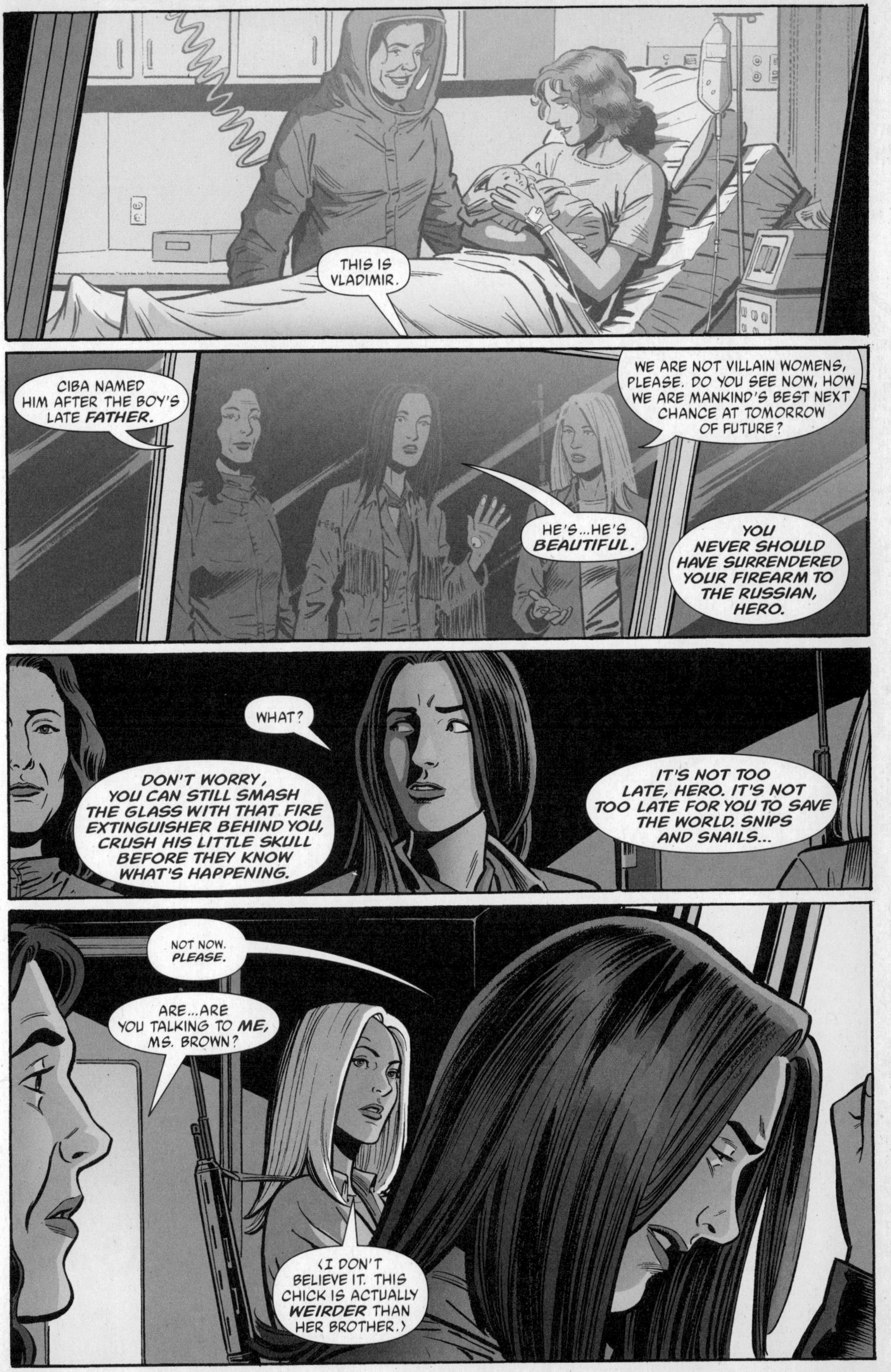
THIS IS VLADIMIR.
CIBA NAMED HIM AFTER THE BOY'S LATE FATHER.
WE ARE NOT VILLAIN WOMENS, PLEASE. DO YOU SEE NOW, HOW WE ARE MANKIND'S BEST NEXT CHANCE AT TOMORROW OF FUTURE?
HE'S...HE'S BEAUTIFUL.
YOU NEVER SHOULD HAVE SURRENDERED YOUR FIREARM TO THE RUSSIAN, HERO.
WHAT?
DON'T WORRY, YOU CAN STILL SMASH THE GLASS WITH THAT FIRE EXTINGUISHER BEHIND YOU, CRUSH HIS LITTLE SKULL BEFORE THEY KNOW WHAT'S HAPPENING.
IT'S NOT TOO LATE, HERO. IT'S NOT TOO LATE FOR YOU TO SAVE THE WORLD. SNIPS AND SNAILS...
NOT NOW. PLEASE.
ARE...ARE YOU TALKING TO ME, MS. BROWN?
‹I DON'T BELIEVE IT. THIS CHICK IS ACTUALLY WEIRDER THAN HER BROTHER.›

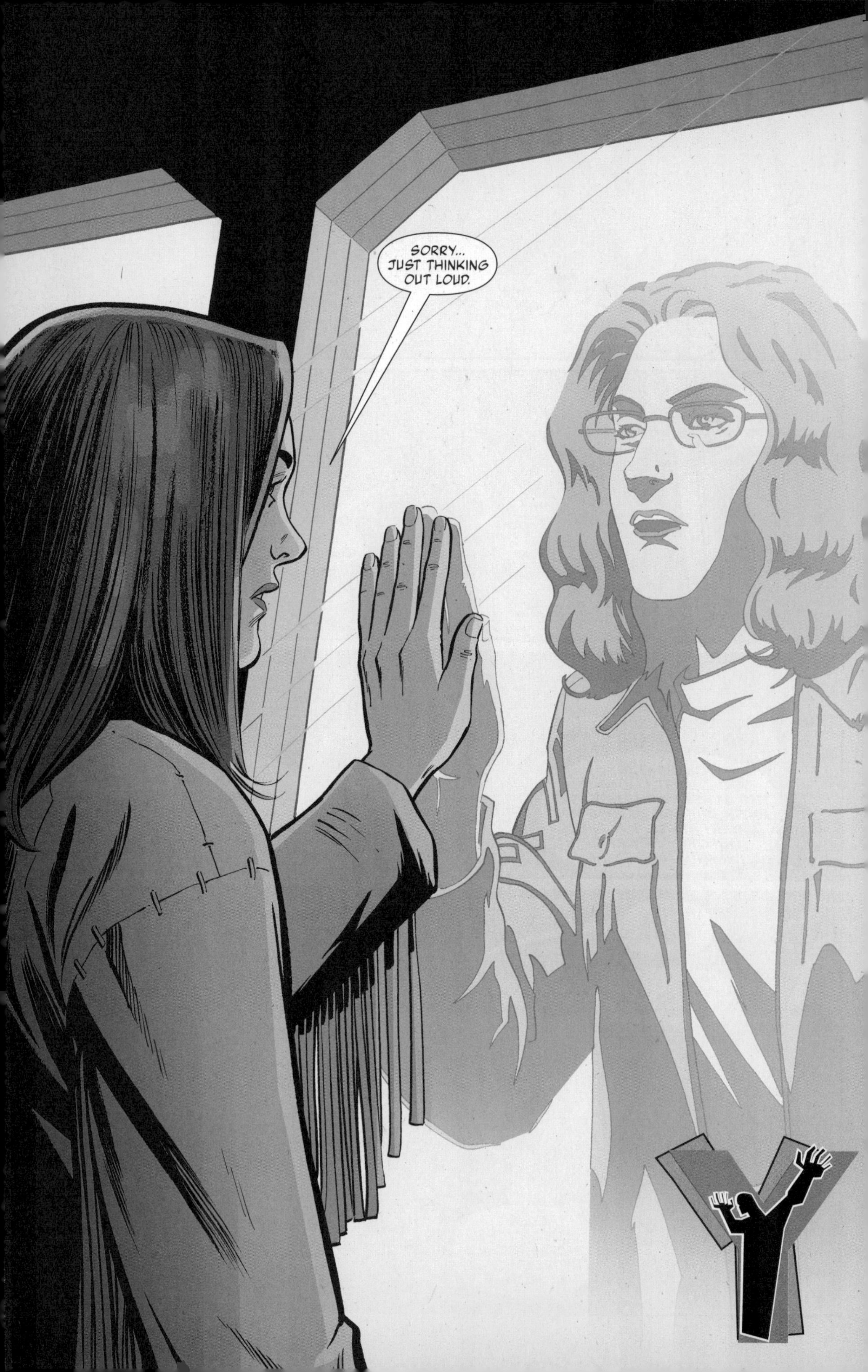
SORRY... JUST THINKING OUT LOUD.

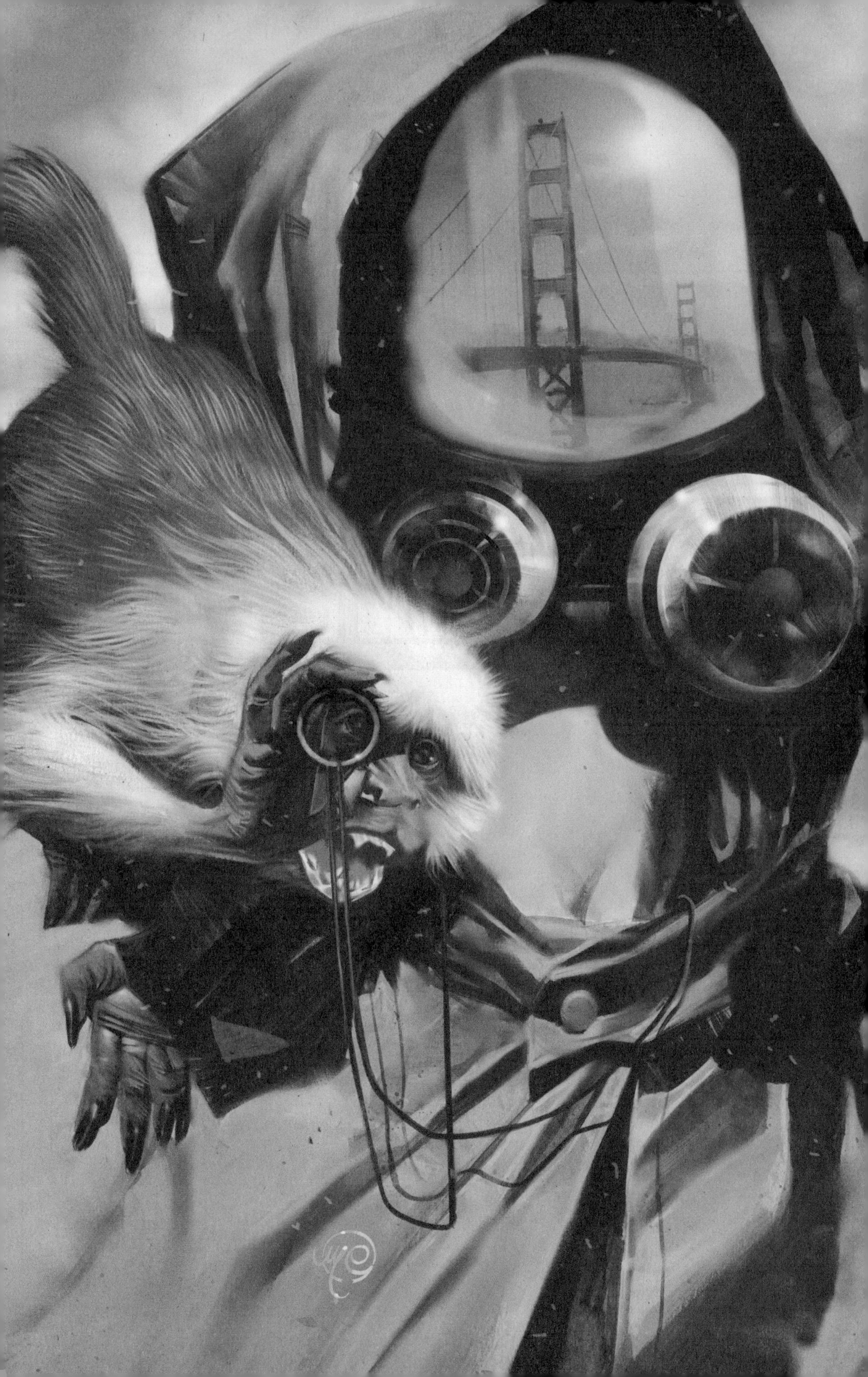

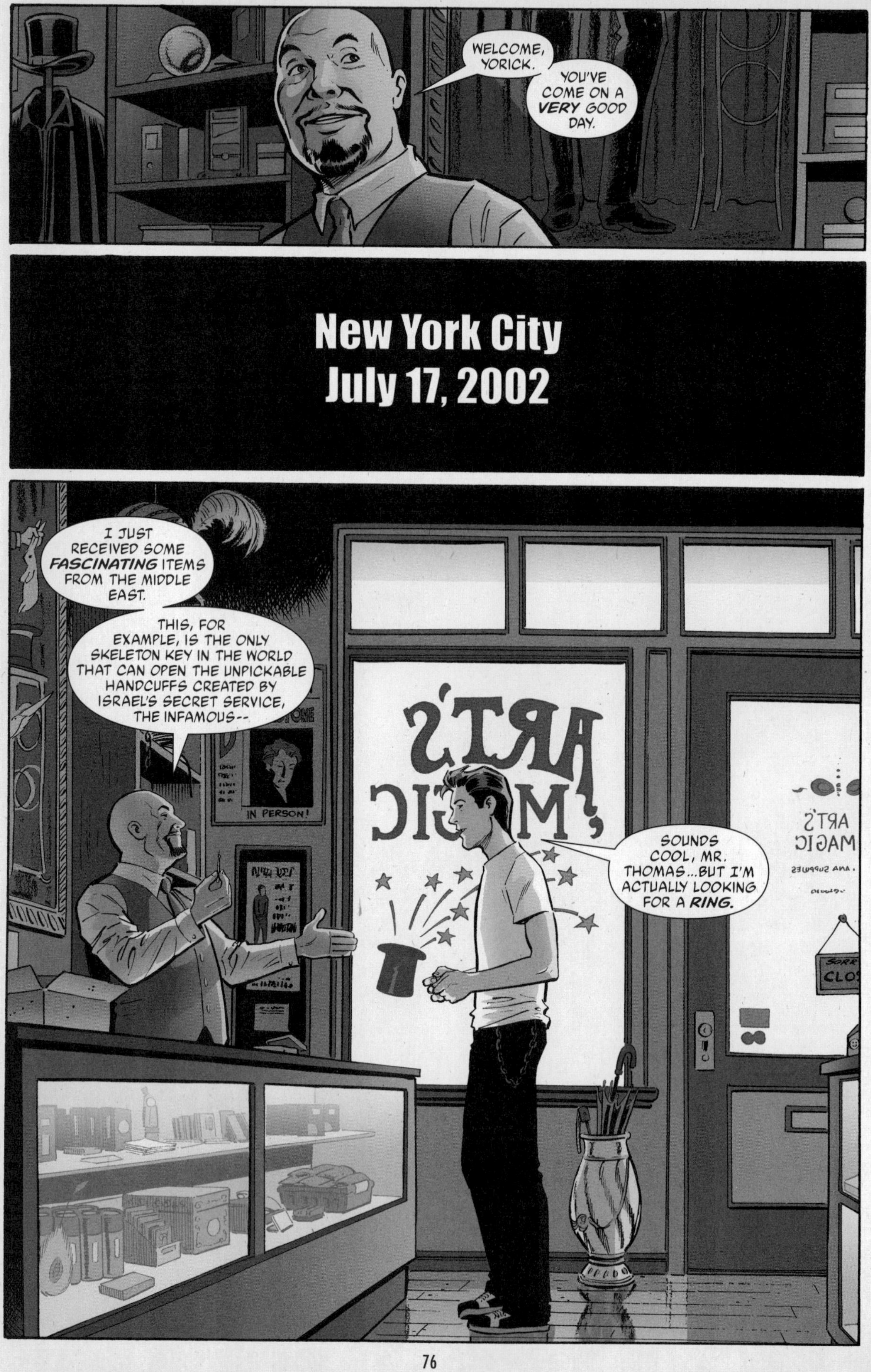
WELCOME, YORICK.
YOU'VE COME ON A VERY GOOD DAY.
New York City
July 17, 2002
I JUST RECEIVED SOME FASCINATING ITEMS FROM THE MIDDLE EAST.
THIS, FOR EXAMPLE, IS THE ONLY SKELETON KEY IN THE WORLD THAT CAN OPEN THE UNPICKABLE HANDCUFFS CREATED BY ISRAEL'S SECRET SERVICE, THE INFAMOUS--
IN PERSON!
SOUNDS COOL, MR. THOMAS...BUT I'M ACTUALLY LOOKING FOR A RING.

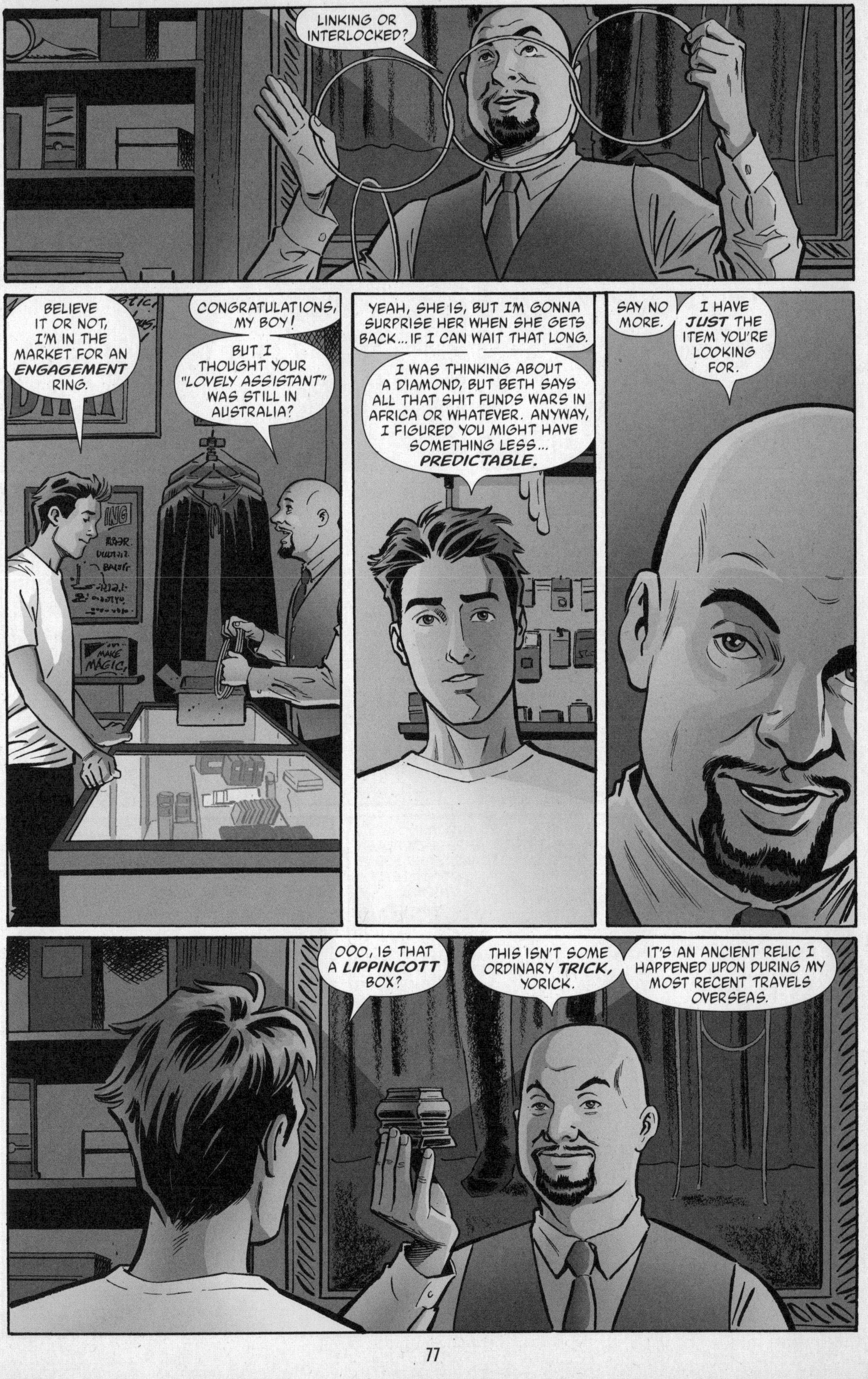

LINKING OR INTERLOCKED?
BELIEVE IT OR NOT, I'M IN THE MARKET FOR AN ENGAGEMENT RING.
CONGRATULATIONS, MY BOY!
BUT I THOUGHT YOUR "LOVELY ASSISTANT" WAS STILL IN AUSTRALIA?
MAKE MAGIC
YEAH, SHE IS, BUT I'M GONNA SURPRISE HER WHEN SHE GETS BACK... IF I CAN WAIT THAT LONG.
I WAS THINKING ABOUT A DIAMOND, BUT BETH SAYS ALL THAT SHIT FUNDS WARS IN AFRICA OR WHATEVER. ANYWAY, I FIGURED YOU MIGHT HAVE SOMETHING LESS... PREDICTABLE.
SAY NO MORE.
I HAVE JUST THE ITEM YOU'RE LOOKING FOR.
OOO, IS THAT A LIPPINCOTT BOX?
THIS ISN'T SOME ORDINARY TRICK, YORICK.
IT'S AN ANCIENT RELIC I HAPPENED UPON DURING MY MOST RECENT TRAVELS OVERSEAS.

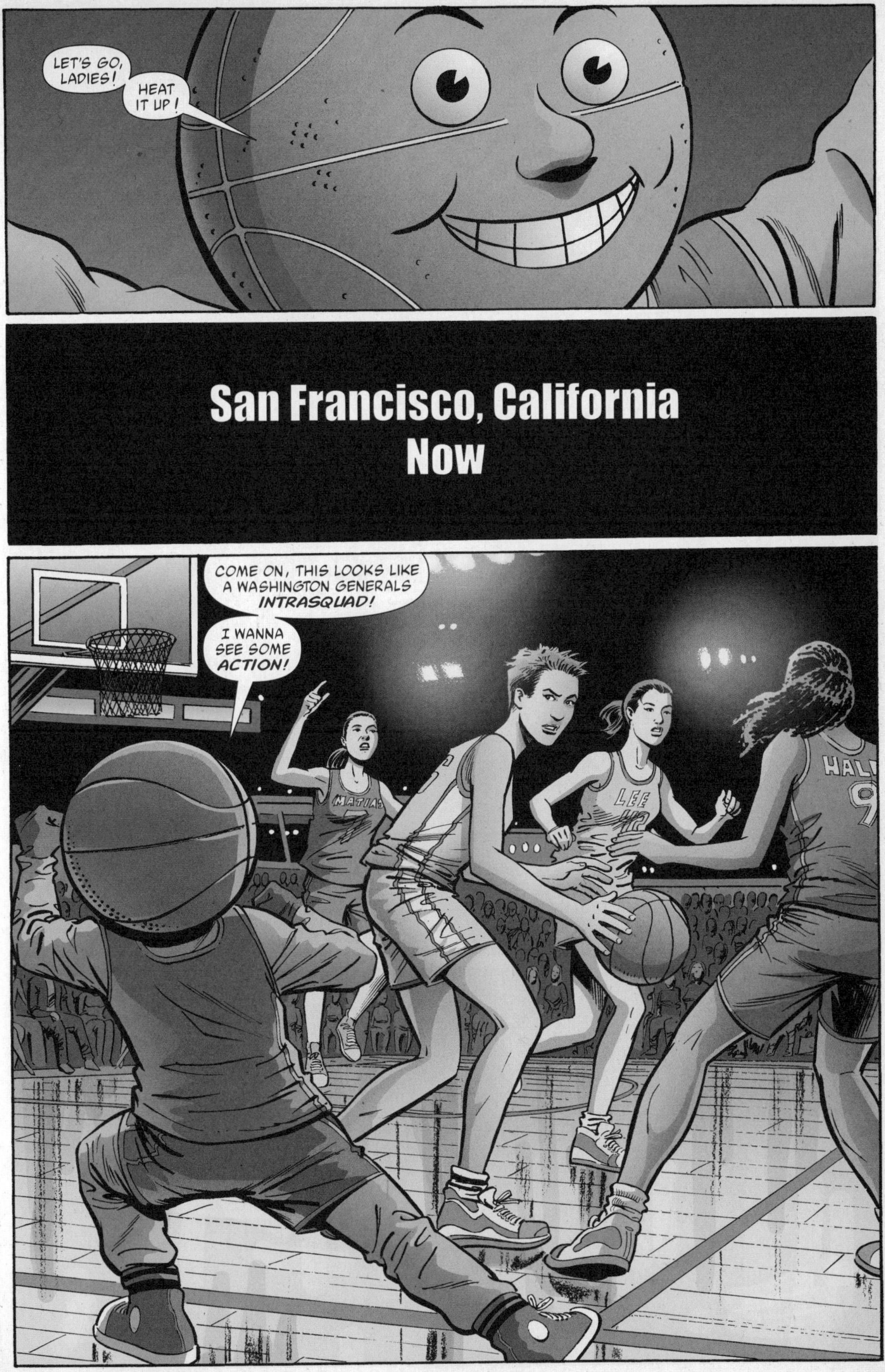
LET'S GO, LADIES!
HEAT IT UP!
San Francisco, California
Now
COME ON, THIS LOOKS LIKE A WASHINGTON GENERALS *INTRASQUAD!*
I WANNA SEE SOME *ACTION!*
MATIAS
LEE

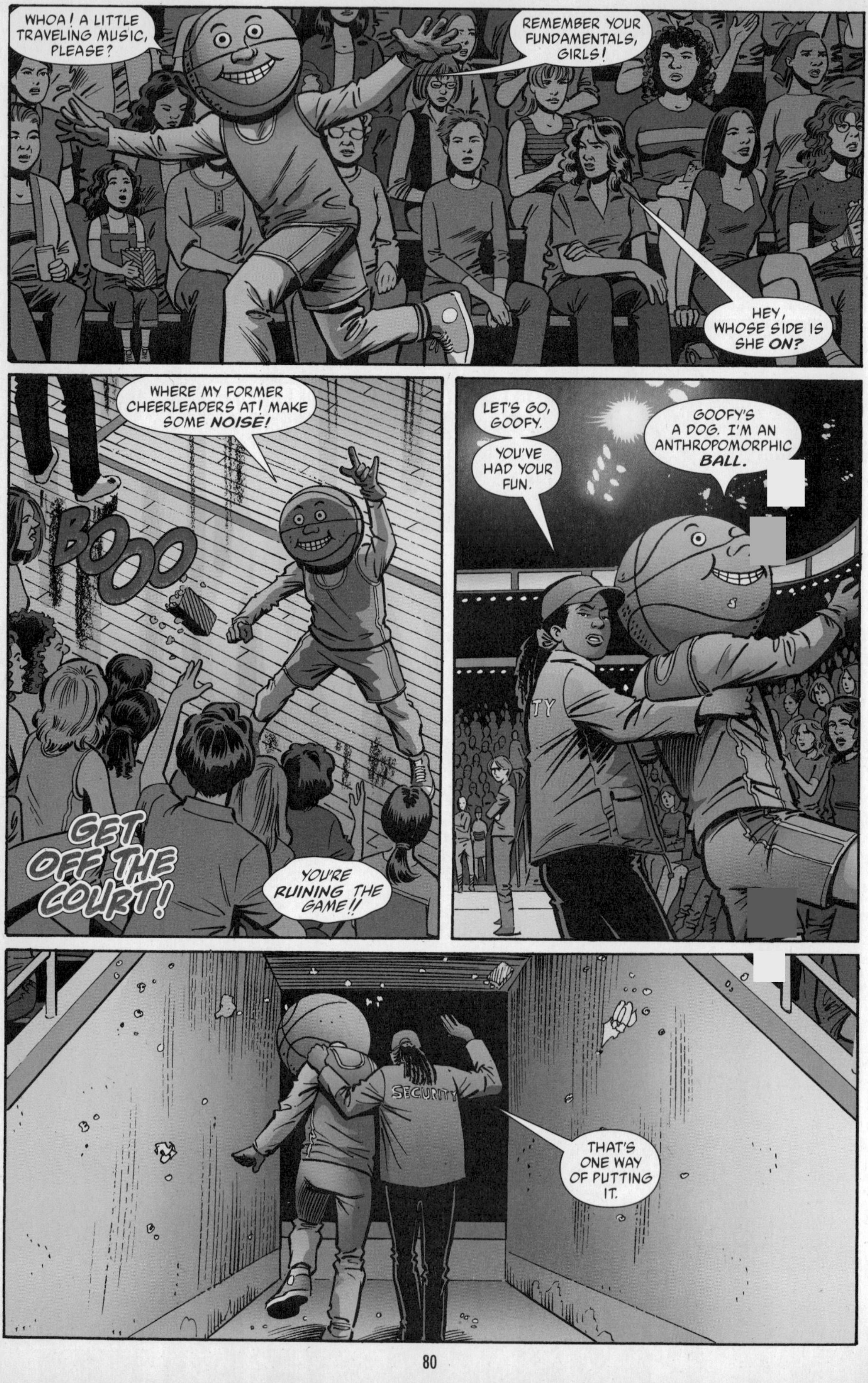
WHOA! A LITTLE TRAVELING MUSIC, PLEASE?
REMEMBER YOUR FUNDAMENTALS, GIRLS!
HEY, WHOSE SIDE IS SHE ON?
WHERE MY FORMER CHEERLEADERS AT! MAKE SOME NOISE!
BOOO
GET OFF THE COURT!
YOU'RE RUINING THE GAME!!
LET'S GO, GOOFY.
YOU'VE HAD YOUR FUN.
GOOFY'S A DOG. I'M AN ANTHROPOMORPHIC BALL.
SECURITY
THAT'S ONE WAY OF PUTTING IT.

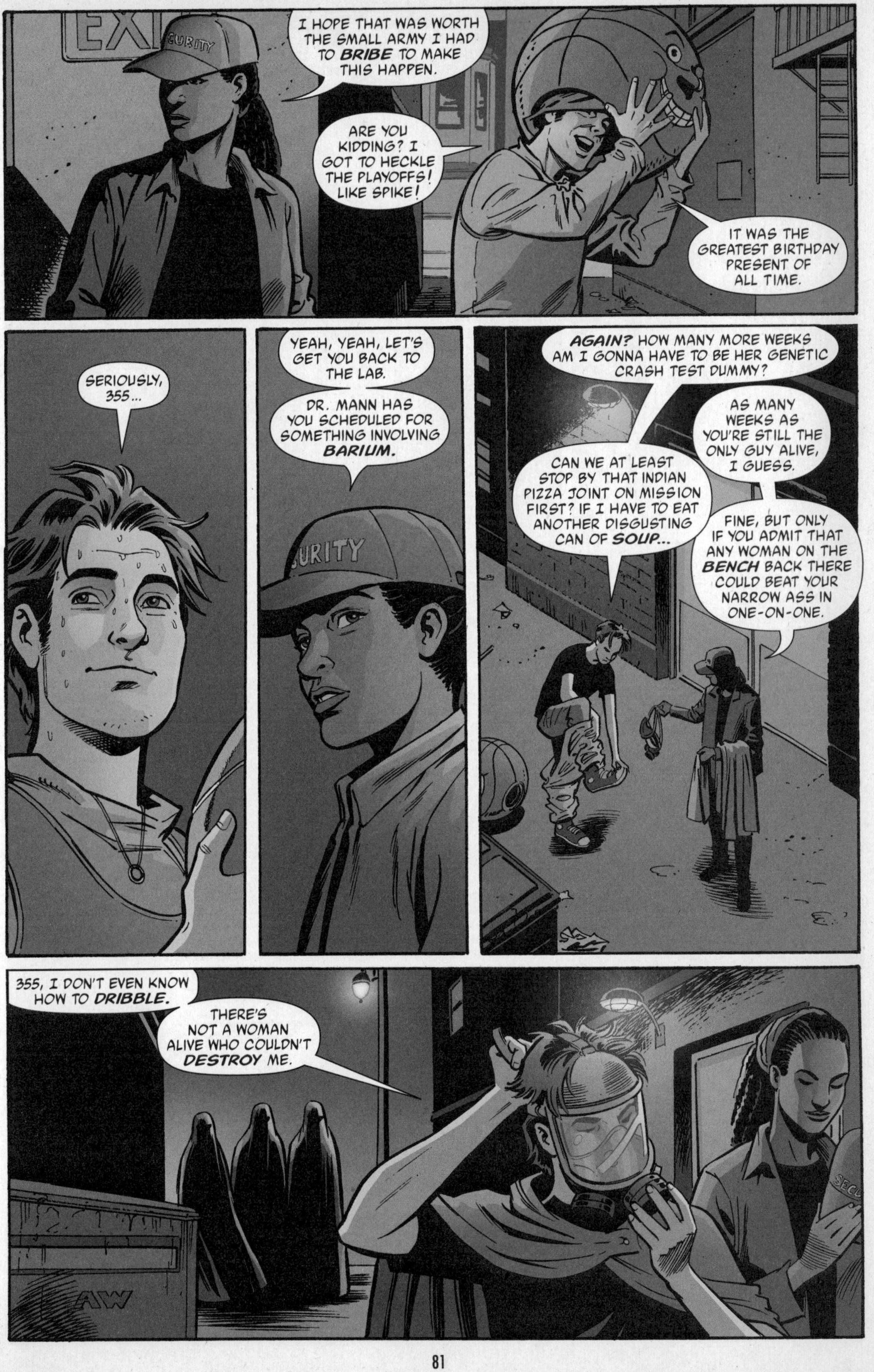
EXIT
SECURITY
I HOPE THAT WAS WORTH THE SMALL ARMY I HAD TO BRIBE TO MAKE THIS HAPPEN.
ARE YOU KIDDING? I GOT TO HECKLE THE PLAYOFFS! LIKE SPIKE!
IT WAS THE GREATEST BIRTHDAY PRESENT OF ALL TIME.
SERIOUSLY, 355...
YEAH, YEAH, LET'S GET YOU BACK TO THE LAB.
DR. MANN HAS YOU SCHEDULED FOR SOMETHING INVOLVING BARIUM.
CURITY
AGAIN? HOW MANY MORE WEEKS AM I GONNA HAVE TO BE HER GENETIC CRASH TEST DUMMY?
AS MANY WEEKS AS YOU'RE STILL THE ONLY GUY ALIVE, I GUESS.
CAN WE AT LEAST STOP BY THAT INDIAN PIZZA JOINT ON MISSION FIRST? IF I HAVE TO EAT ANOTHER DISGUSTING CAN OF SOUP...
FINE, BUT ONLY IF YOU ADMIT THAT ANY WOMAN ON THE BENCH BACK THERE COULD BEAT YOUR NARROW ASS IN ONE-ON-ONE.
355, I DON'T EVEN KNOW HOW TO DRIBBLE.
THERE'S NOT A WOMAN ALIVE WHO COULDN'T DESTROY ME.
AW

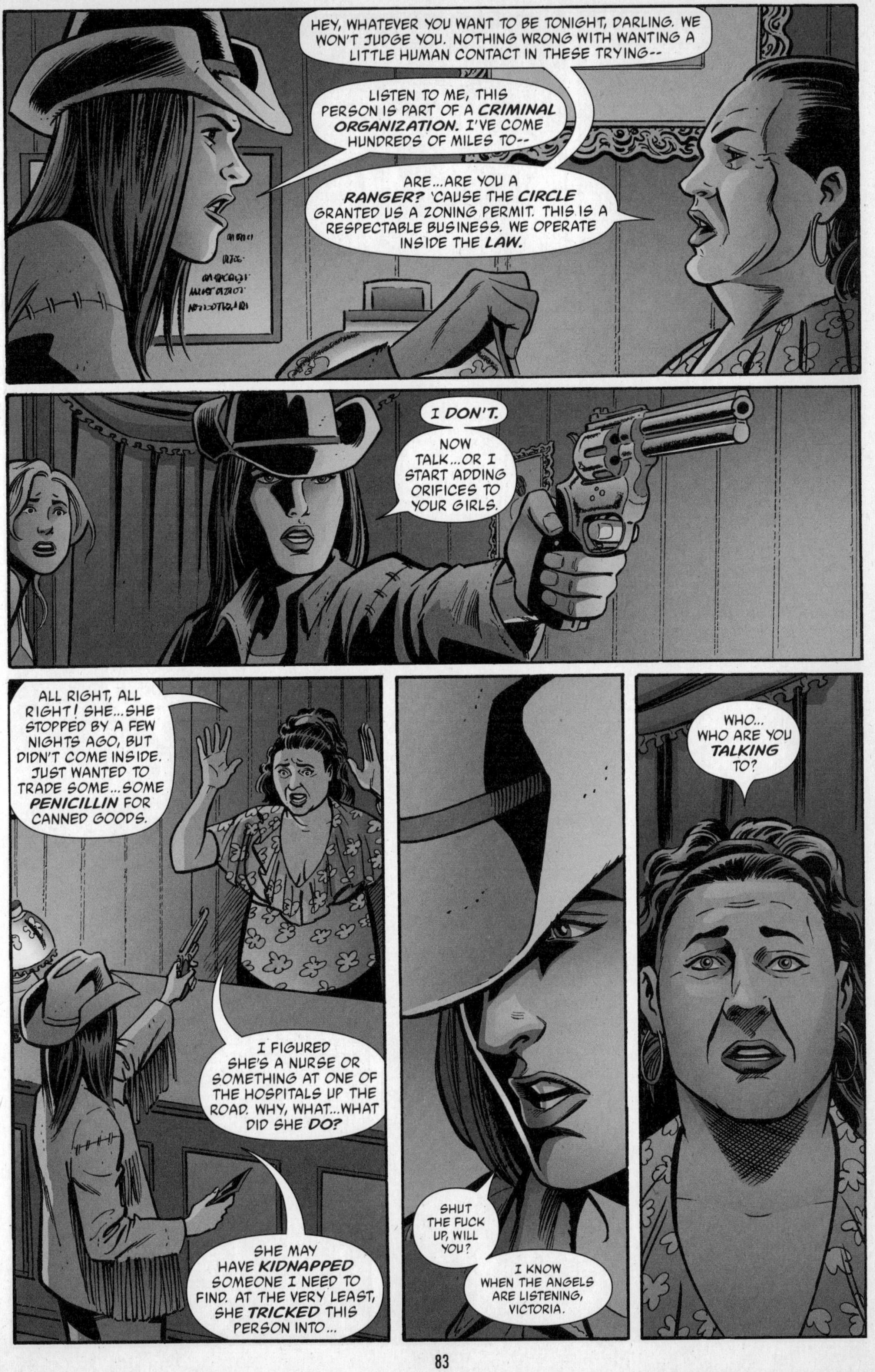
HEY, WHATEVER YOU WANT TO BE TONIGHT, DARLING. WE WON'T JUDGE YOU. NOTHING WRONG WITH WANTING A LITTLE HUMAN CONTACT IN THESE TRYING--
LISTEN TO ME, THIS PERSON IS PART OF A CRIMINAL ORGANIZATION. I'VE COME HUNDREDS OF MILES TO--
ARE...ARE YOU A RANGER? 'CAUSE THE CIRCLE GRANTED US A ZONING PERMIT. THIS IS A RESPECTABLE BUSINESS. WE OPERATE INSIDE THE LAW.
I DON'T.
NOW TALK...OR I START ADDING ORIFICES TO YOUR GIRLS.
ALL RIGHT, ALL RIGHT! SHE...SHE STOPPED BY A FEW NIGHTS AGO, BUT DIDN'T COME INSIDE. JUST WANTED TO TRADE SOME...SOME PENICILLIN FOR CANNED GOODS.
I FIGURED SHE'S A NURSE OR SOMETHING AT ONE OF THE HOSPITALS UP THE ROAD. WHY, WHAT...WHAT DID SHE DO?
SHE MAY HAVE KIDNAPPED SOMEONE I NEED TO FIND. AT THE VERY LEAST, SHE TRICKED THIS PERSON INTO...
SHUT THE FUCK UP, WILL YOU?
I KNOW WHEN THE ANGELS ARE LISTENING, VICTORIA.
WHO... WHO ARE YOU TALKING TO?

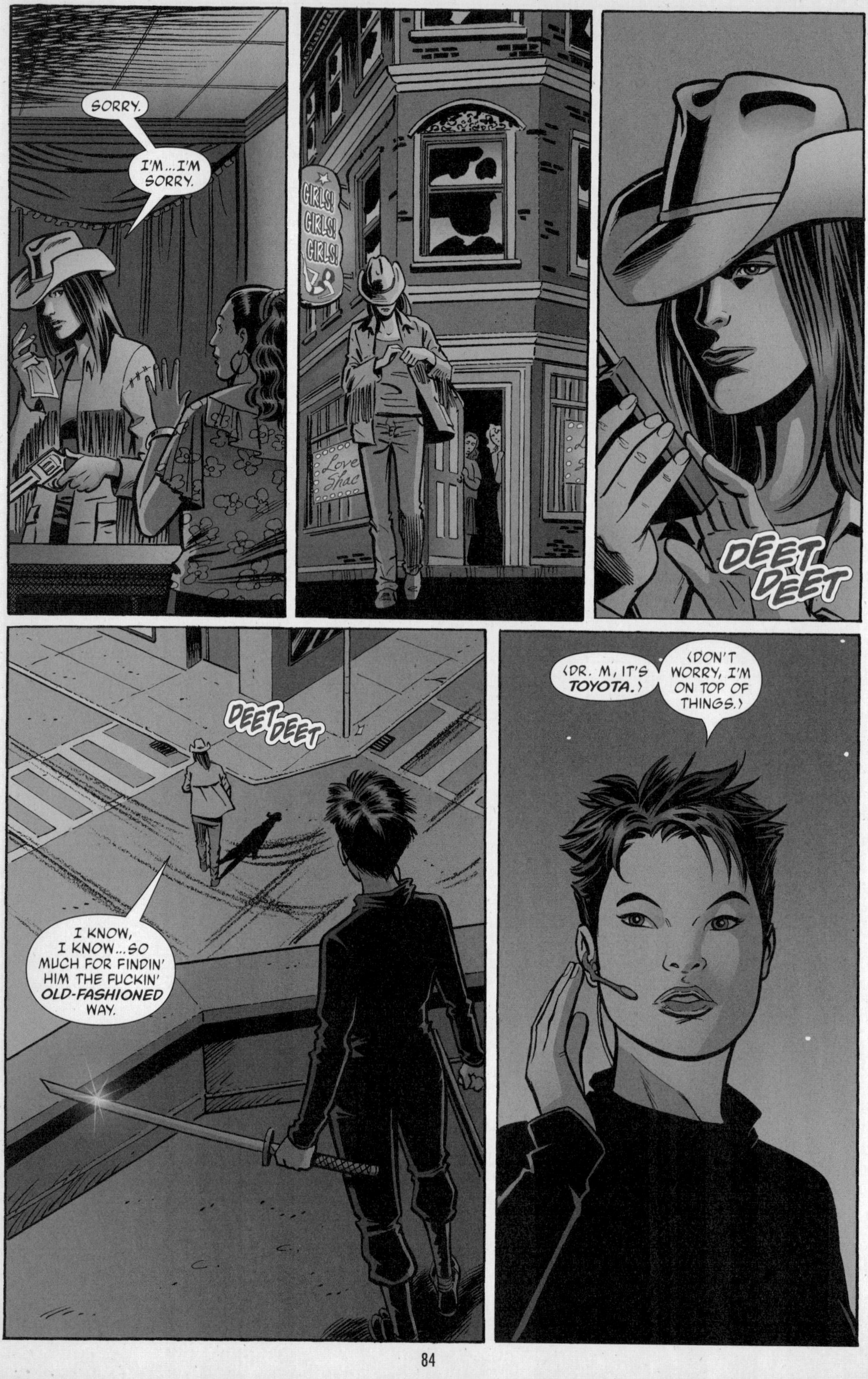

SORRY.
I'M...I'M SORRY.
GIRLS! GIRLS! GIRLS!
Love Shac
DEET DEET
DEET DEET
I KNOW, I KNOW...SO MUCH FOR FINDIN' HIM THE FUCKIN' **OLD-FASHIONED** WAY.
‹DR. M, IT'S **TOYOTA.**›
‹DON'T WORRY, I'M ON TOP OF THINGS.›

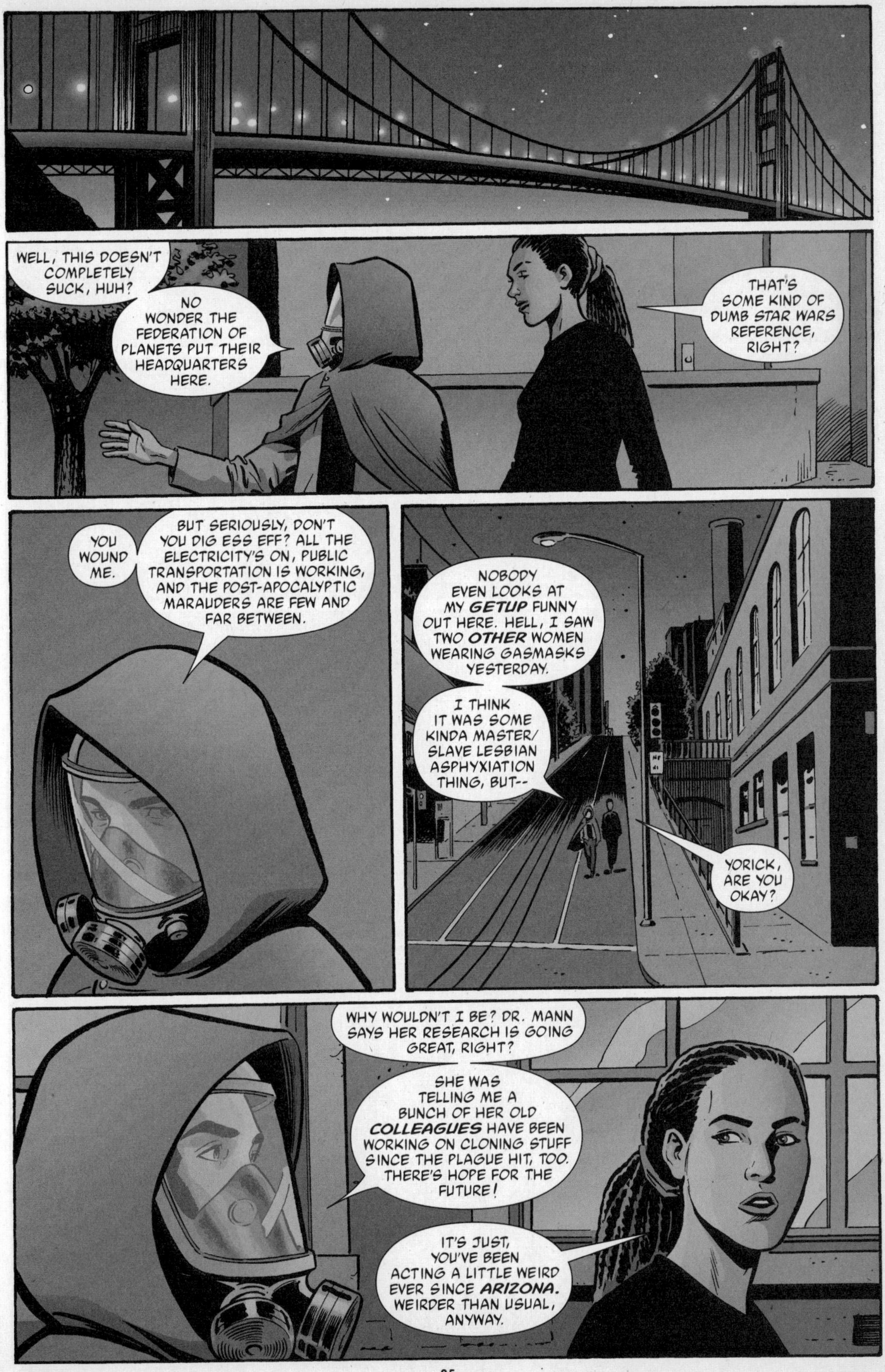
WELL, THIS DOESN'T COMPLETELY SUCK, HUH?
NO WONDER THE FEDERATION OF PLANETS PUT THEIR HEADQUARTERS HERE.
THAT'S SOME KIND OF DUMB STAR WARS REFERENCE, RIGHT?
YOU WOUND ME.
BUT SERIOUSLY, DON'T YOU DIG ESS EFF? ALL THE ELECTRICITY'S ON, PUBLIC TRANSPORTATION IS WORKING, AND THE POST-APOCALYPTIC MARAUDERS ARE FEW AND FAR BETWEEN.
NOBODY EVEN LOOKS AT MY **GETUP** FUNNY OUT HERE. HELL, I SAW TWO **OTHER** WOMEN WEARING GASMASKS YESTERDAY.
I THINK IT WAS SOME KINDA MASTER/ SLAVE LESBIAN ASPHYXIATION THING, BUT--
YORICK, ARE YOU OKAY?
WHY WOULDN'T I BE? DR. MANN SAYS HER RESEARCH IS GOING GREAT, RIGHT?
SHE WAS TELLING ME A BUNCH OF HER OLD **COLLEAGUES** HAVE BEEN WORKING ON CLONING STUFF SINCE THE PLAGUE HIT, TOO. THERE'S HOPE FOR THE FUTURE!
IT'S JUST, YOU'VE BEEN ACTING A LITTLE WEIRD EVER SINCE **ARIZONA.** WEIRDER THAN USUAL, ANYWAY.

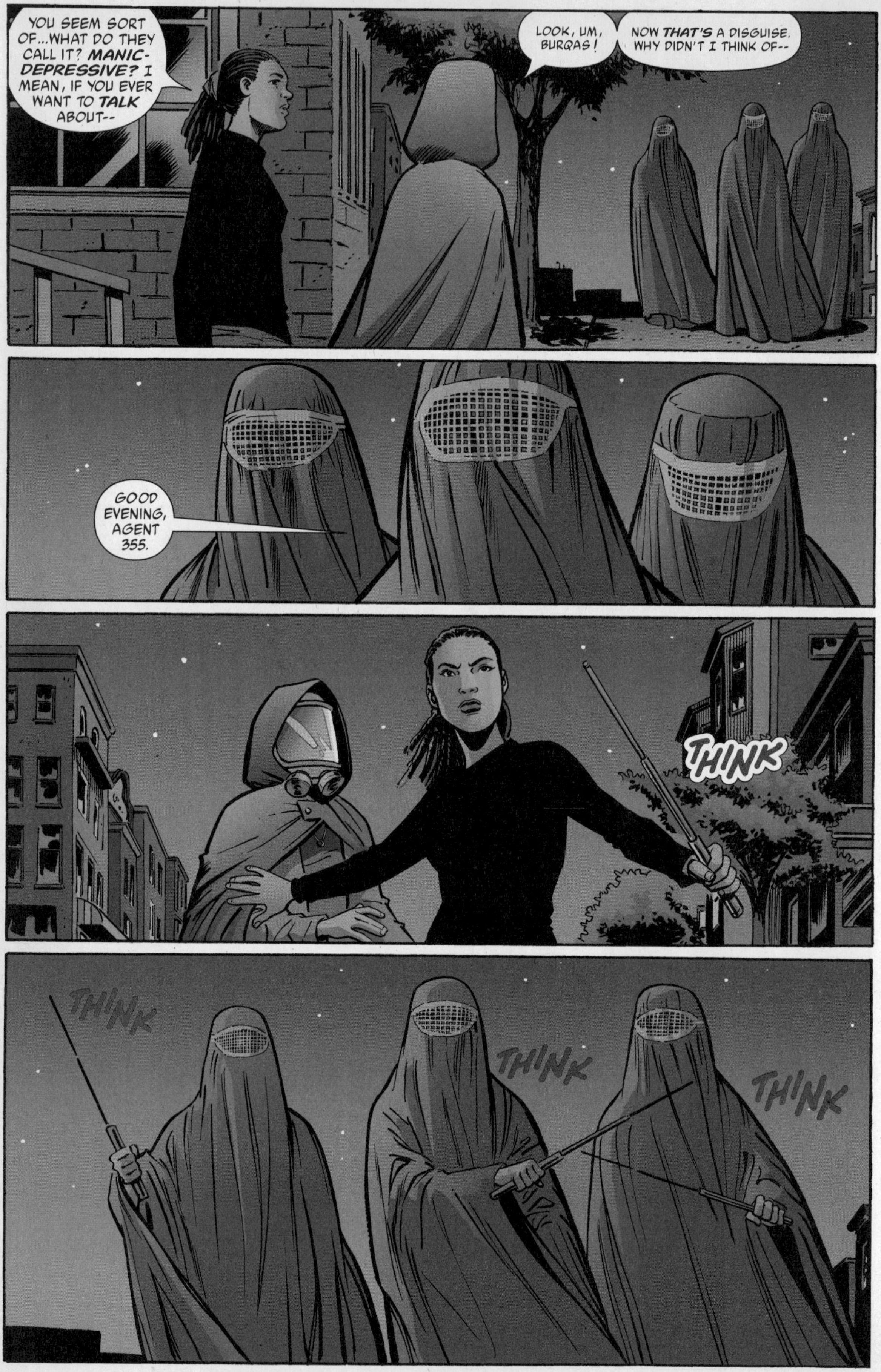
YOU SEEM SORT OF...WHAT DO THEY CALL IT? MANIC-DEPRESSIVE? I MEAN, IF YOU EVER WANT TO TALK ABOUT--
LOOK, UM, BURQAS!
NOW THAT'S A DISGUISE. WHY DIDN'T I THINK OF--
GOOD EVENING, AGENT 355.
THINK
THINK
THINK
THINK

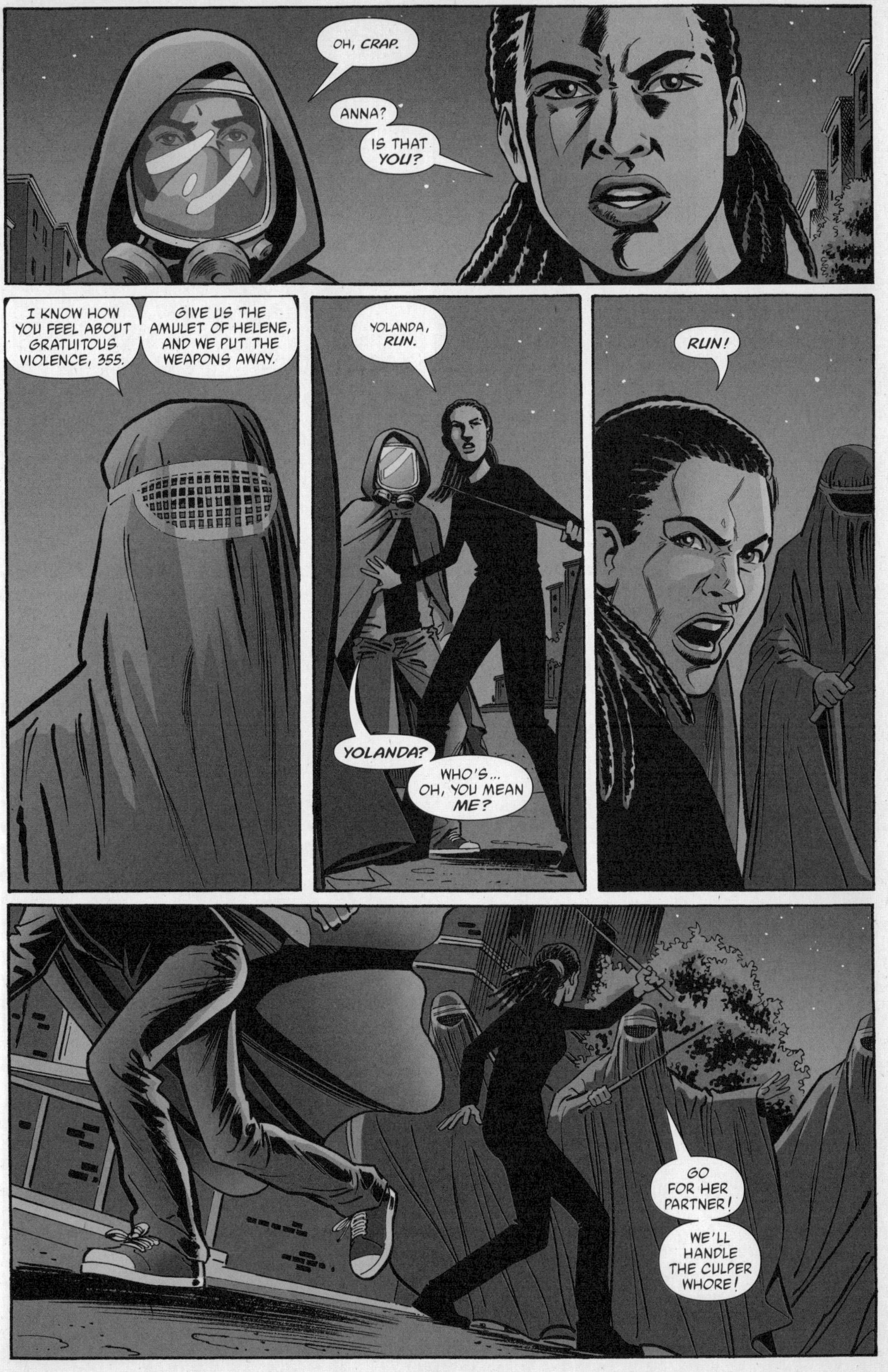
OH, CRAP.
ANNA?
IS THAT YOU?
I KNOW HOW YOU FEEL ABOUT GRATUITOUS VIOLENCE, 355.
GIVE US THE AMULET OF HELENE, AND WE PUT THE WEAPONS AWAY.
YOLANDA, RUN.
YOLANDA?
WHO'S... OH, YOU MEAN ME?
RUN!
GO FOR HER PARTNER!
WE'LL HANDLE THE CULPER WHORE!

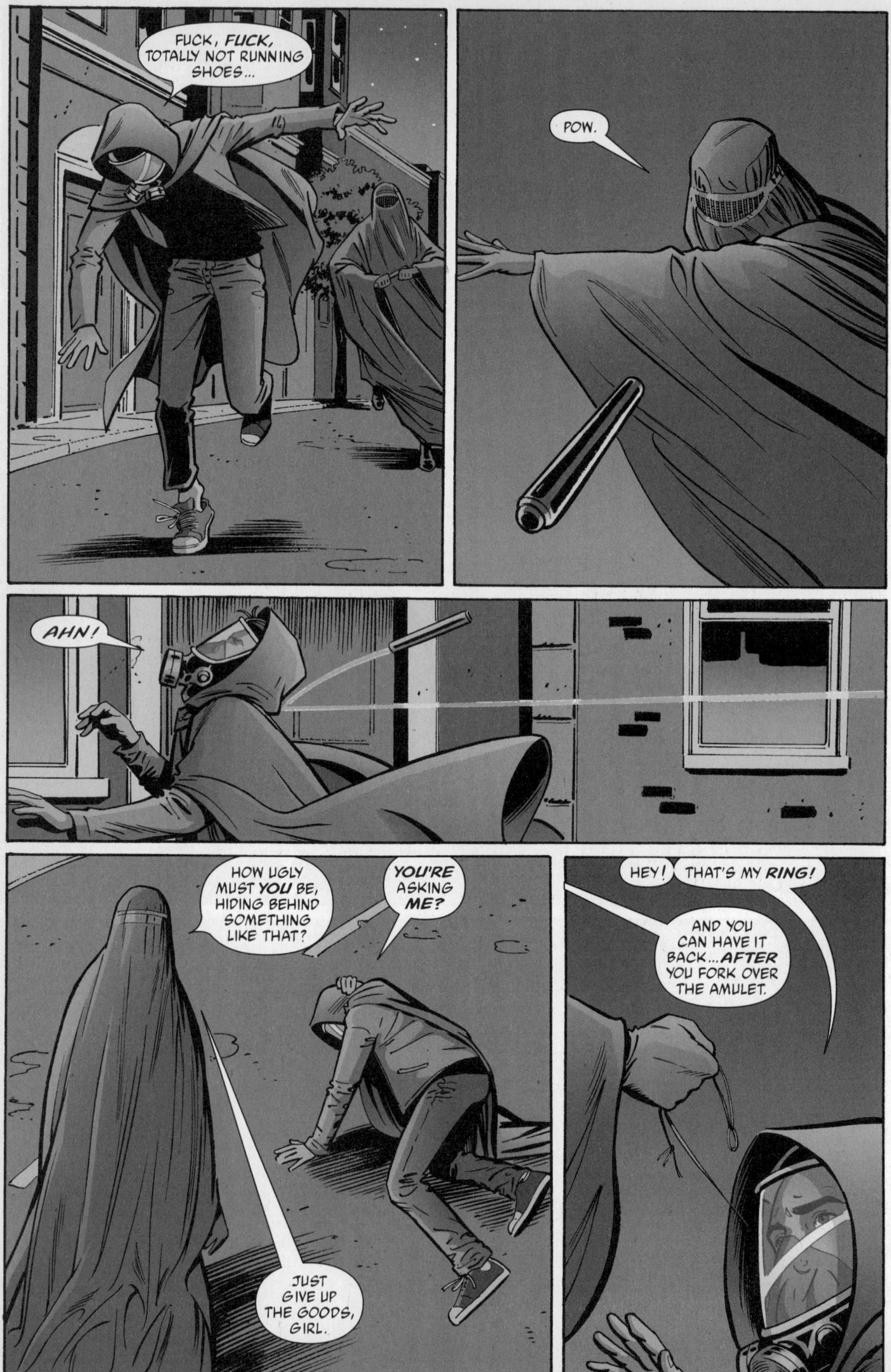
FUCK, FUCK, TOTALLY NOT RUNNING SHOES...
POW.
AHN!
HOW UGLY MUST YOU BE, HIDING BEHIND SOMETHING LIKE THAT?
YOU'RE ASKING ME?
JUST GIVE UP THE GOODS, GIRL.
HEY!
THAT'S MY RING!
AND YOU CAN HAVE IT BACK...AFTER YOU FORK OVER THE AMULET.

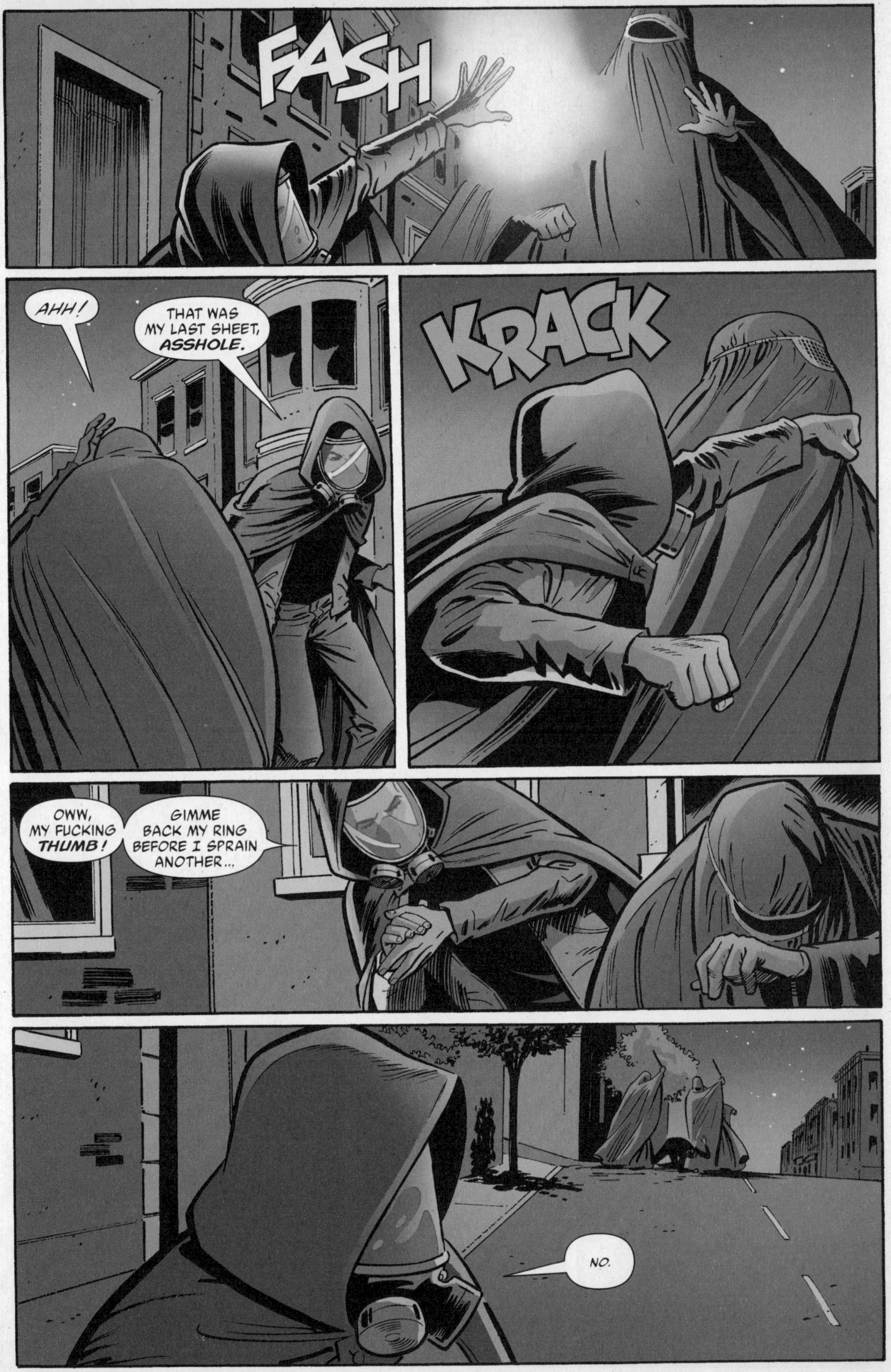
FASH
AHH!
THAT WAS MY LAST SHEET, ASSHOLE.
KRACK
OWW, MY FUCKING THUMB!
GIMME BACK MY RING BEFORE I SPRAIN ANOTHER...
NO.

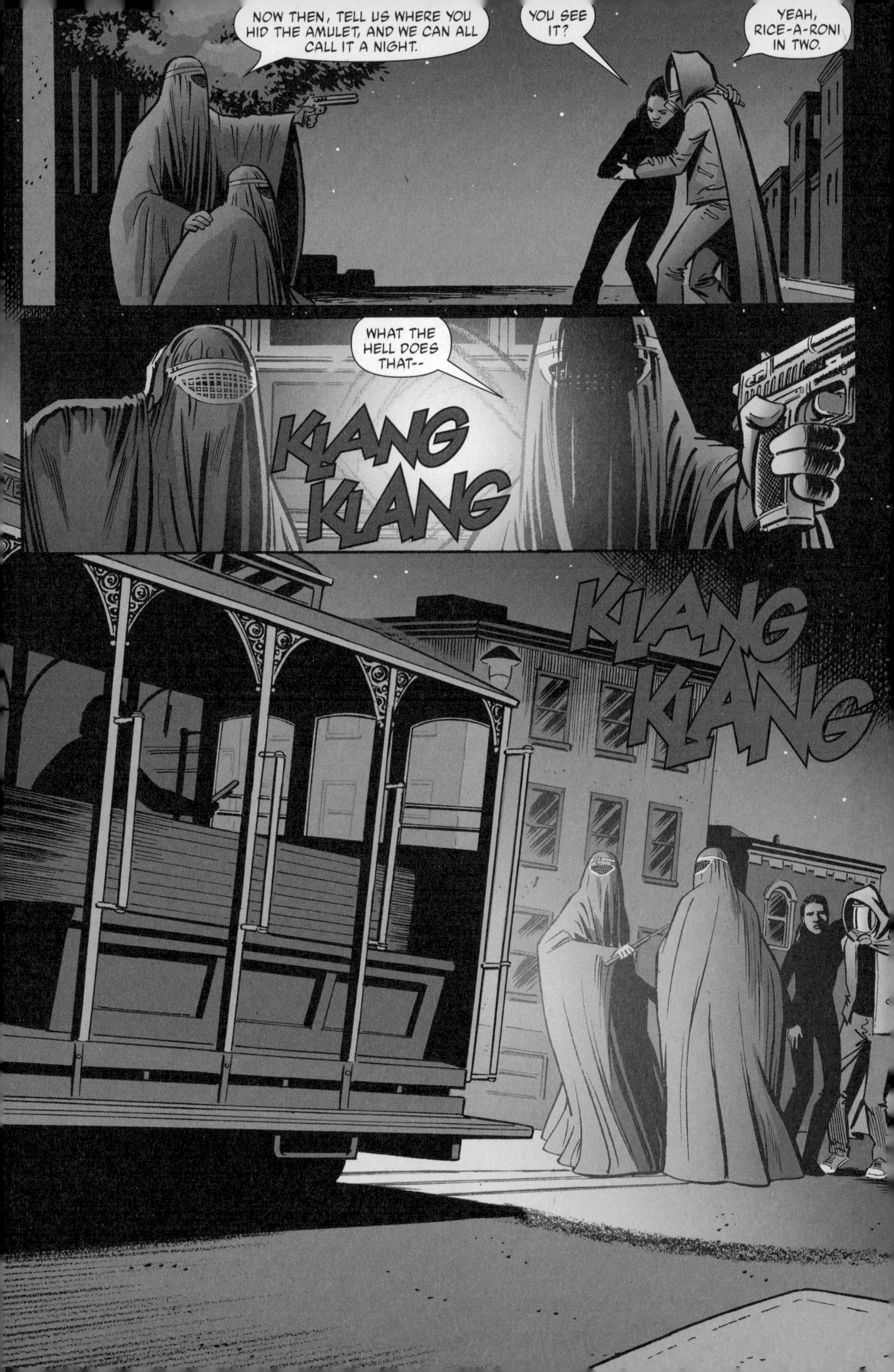
NOW THEN, TELL US WHERE YOU HID THE AMULET, AND WE CAN ALL CALL IT A NIGHT.
YOU SEE IT?
YEAH, RICE-A-RONI IN TWO.
WHAT THE HELL DOES THAT--
KLANG KLANG
KLANG KLANG

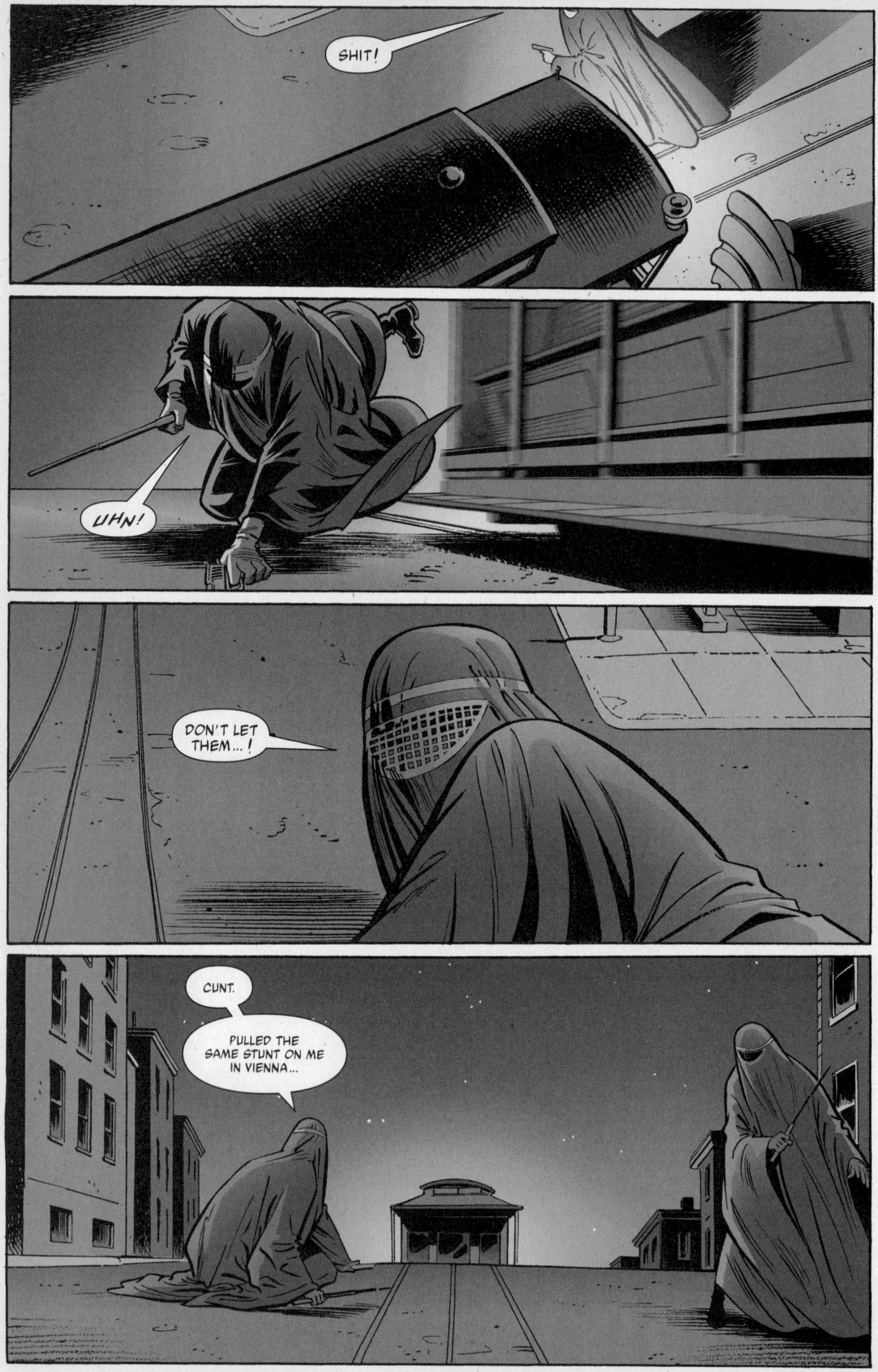
SHIT!
UHN!
DON'T LET THEM...!
CUNT.
PULLED THE SAME STUNT ON ME IN VIENNA...

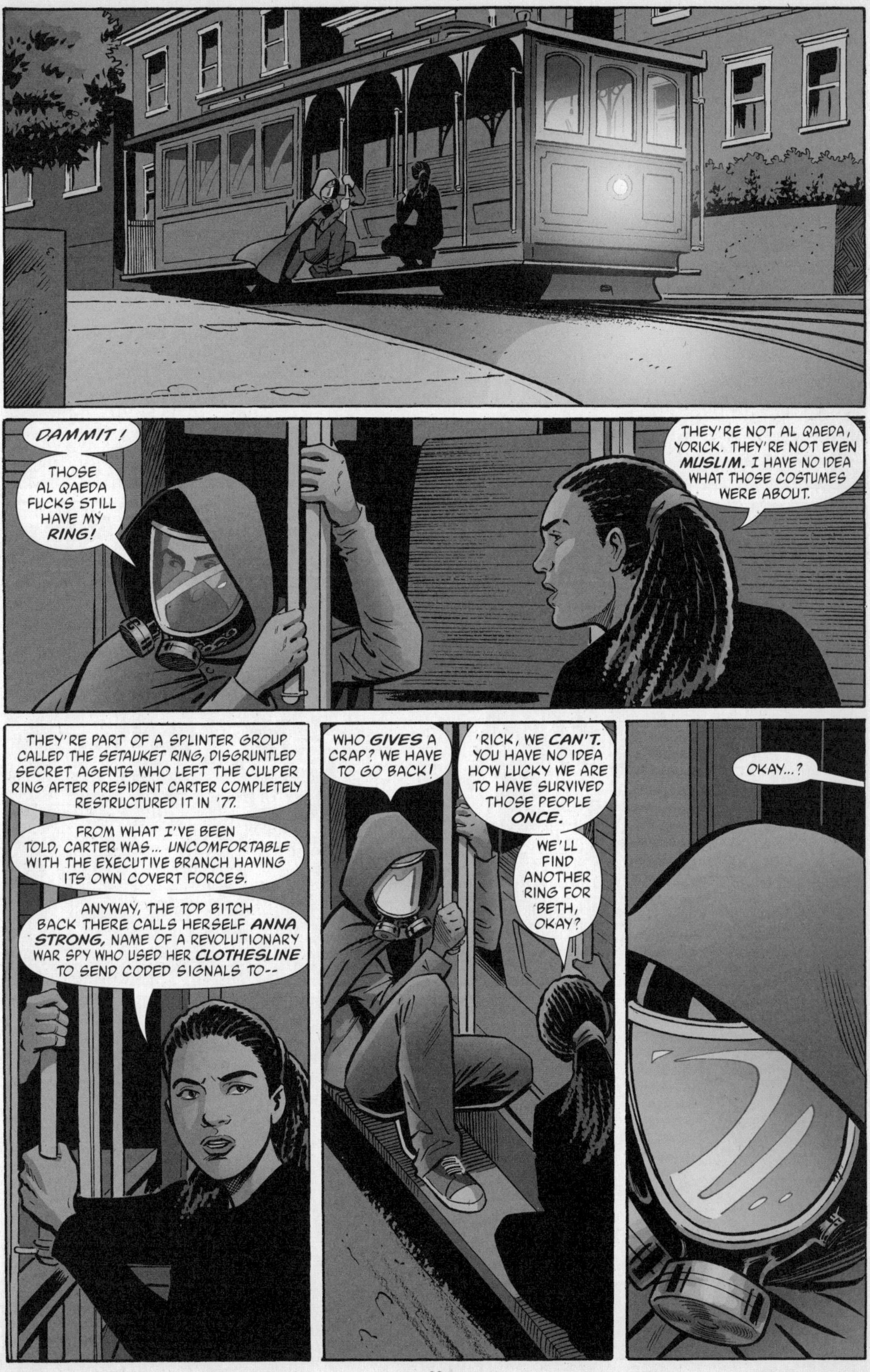
DAMMIT!
THOSE AL QAEDA FUCKS STILL HAVE MY RING!
THEY'RE NOT AL QAEDA, YORICK. THEY'RE NOT EVEN MUSLIM. I HAVE NO IDEA WHAT THOSE COSTUMES WERE ABOUT.
THEY'RE PART OF A SPLINTER GROUP CALLED THE SETAUKET RING, DISGRUNTLED SECRET AGENTS WHO LEFT THE CULPER RING AFTER PRESIDENT CARTER COMPLETELY RESTRUCTURED IT IN '77.
FROM WHAT I'VE BEEN TOLD, CARTER WAS... UNCOMFORTABLE WITH THE EXECUTIVE BRANCH HAVING ITS OWN COVERT FORCES.
ANYWAY, THE TOP BITCH BACK THERE CALLS HERSELF ANNA STRONG, NAME OF A REVOLUTIONARY WAR SPY WHO USED HER CLOTHESLINE TO SEND CODED SIGNALS TO--
WHO GIVES A CRAP? WE HAVE TO GO BACK!
'RICK, WE CAN'T. YOU HAVE NO IDEA HOW LUCKY WE ARE TO HAVE SURVIVED THOSE PEOPLE ONCE.
WE'LL FIND ANOTHER RING FOR BETH, OKAY?
OKAY...?

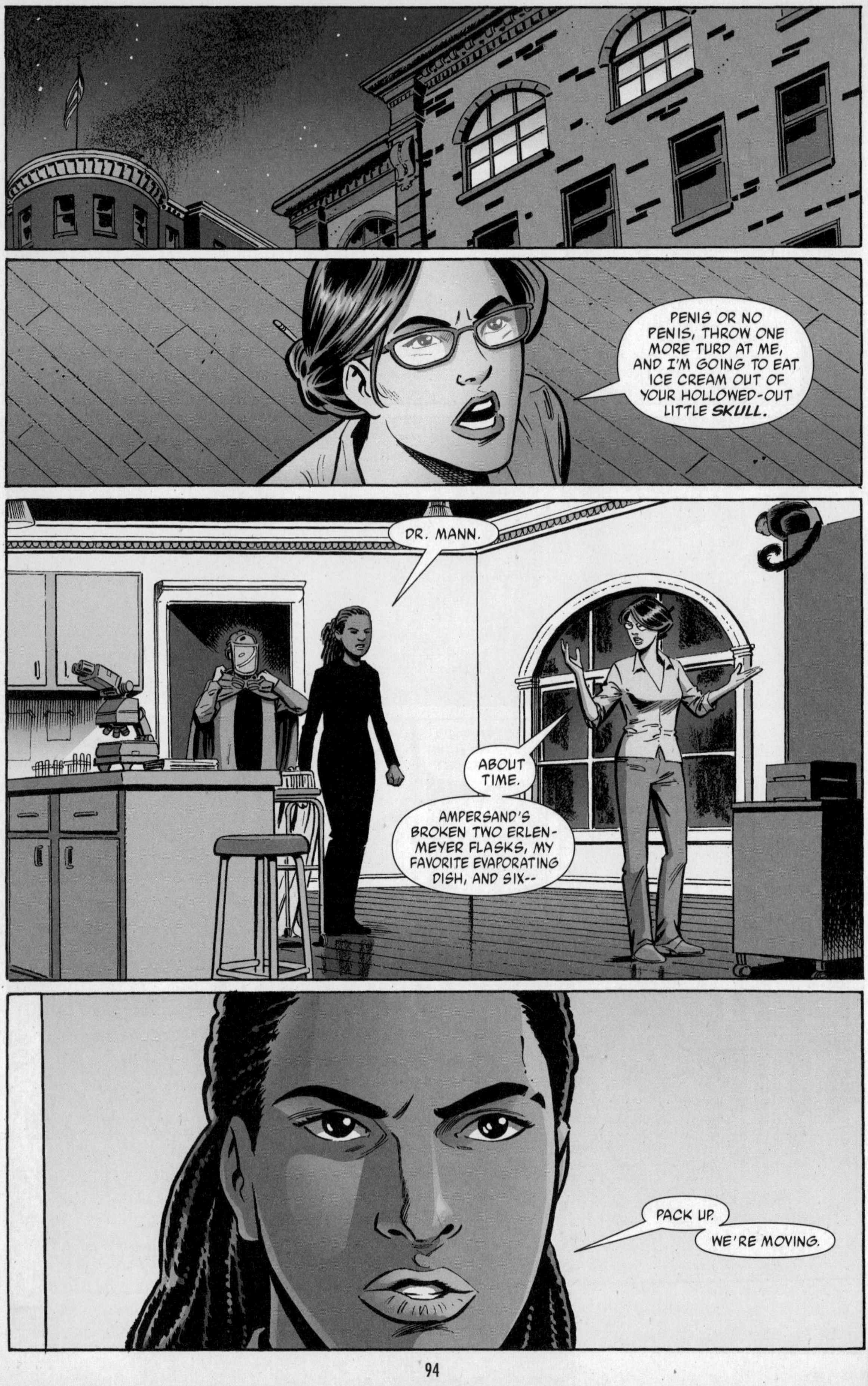
PENIS OR NO PENIS, THROW ONE MORE TURD AT ME, AND I'M GOING TO EAT ICE CREAM OUT OF YOUR HOLLOWED-OUT LITTLE SKULL.
DR. MANN.
ABOUT TIME.
AMPERSAND'S BROKEN TWO ERLEN-MEYER FLASKS, MY FAVORITE EVAPORATING DISH, AND SIX--
PACK UP.
WE'RE MOVING.

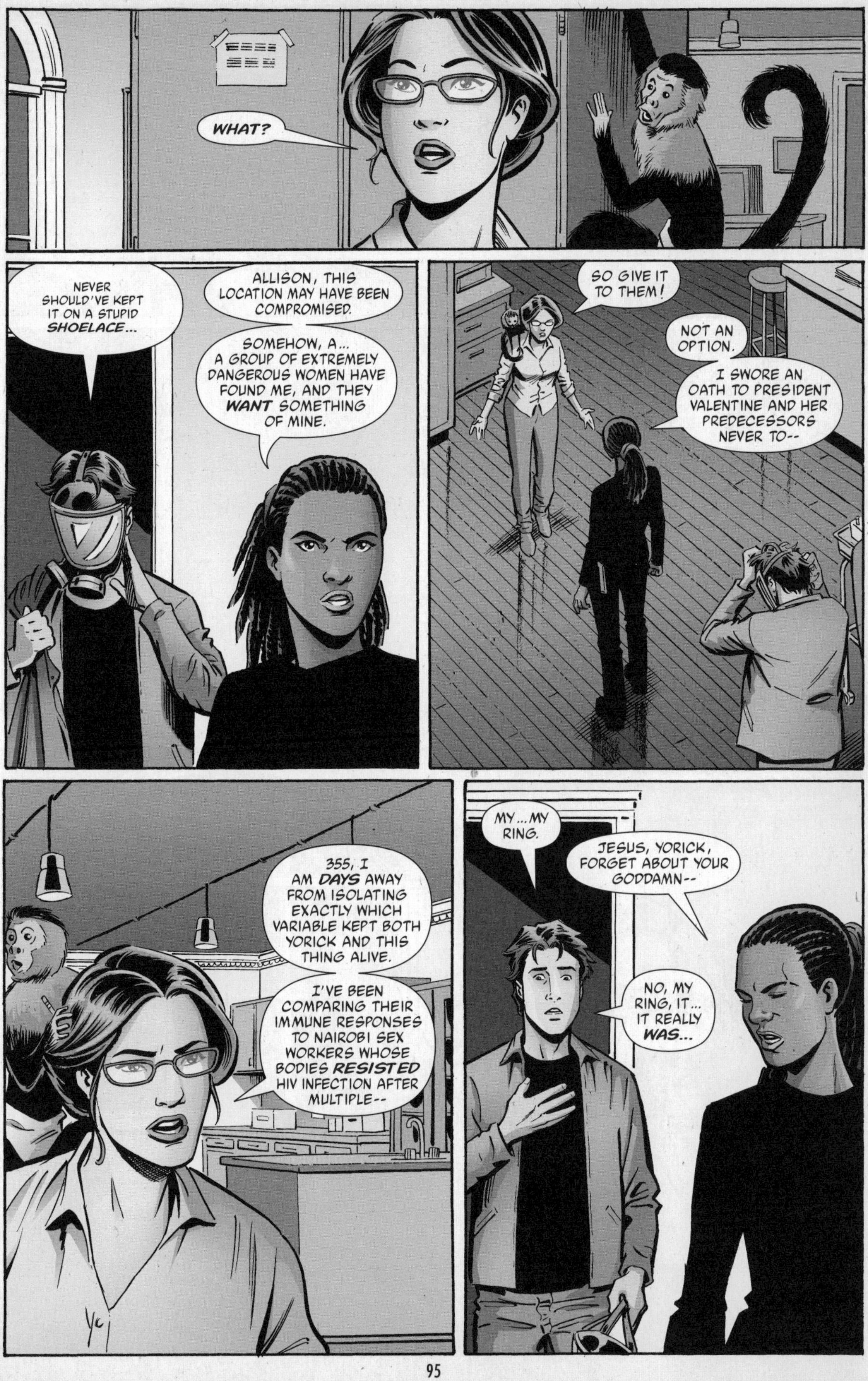
WHAT?
NEVER SHOULD'VE KEPT IT ON A STUPID SHOELACE...
ALLISON, THIS LOCATION MAY HAVE BEEN COMPROMISED.
SOMEHOW, A... A GROUP OF EXTREMELY DANGEROUS WOMEN HAVE FOUND ME, AND THEY WANT SOMETHING OF MINE.
SO GIVE IT TO THEM!
NOT AN OPTION.
I SWORE AN OATH TO PRESIDENT VALENTINE AND HER PREDECESSORS NEVER TO--
355, I AM DAYS AWAY FROM ISOLATING EXACTLY WHICH VARIABLE KEPT BOTH YORICK AND THIS THING ALIVE.
I'VE BEEN COMPARING THEIR IMMUNE RESPONSES TO NAIROBI SEX WORKERS WHOSE BODIES RESISTED HIV INFECTION AFTER MULTIPLE--
MY... MY RING.
JESUS, YORICK, FORGET ABOUT YOUR GODDAMN--
NO, MY RING, IT... IT REALLY WAS...

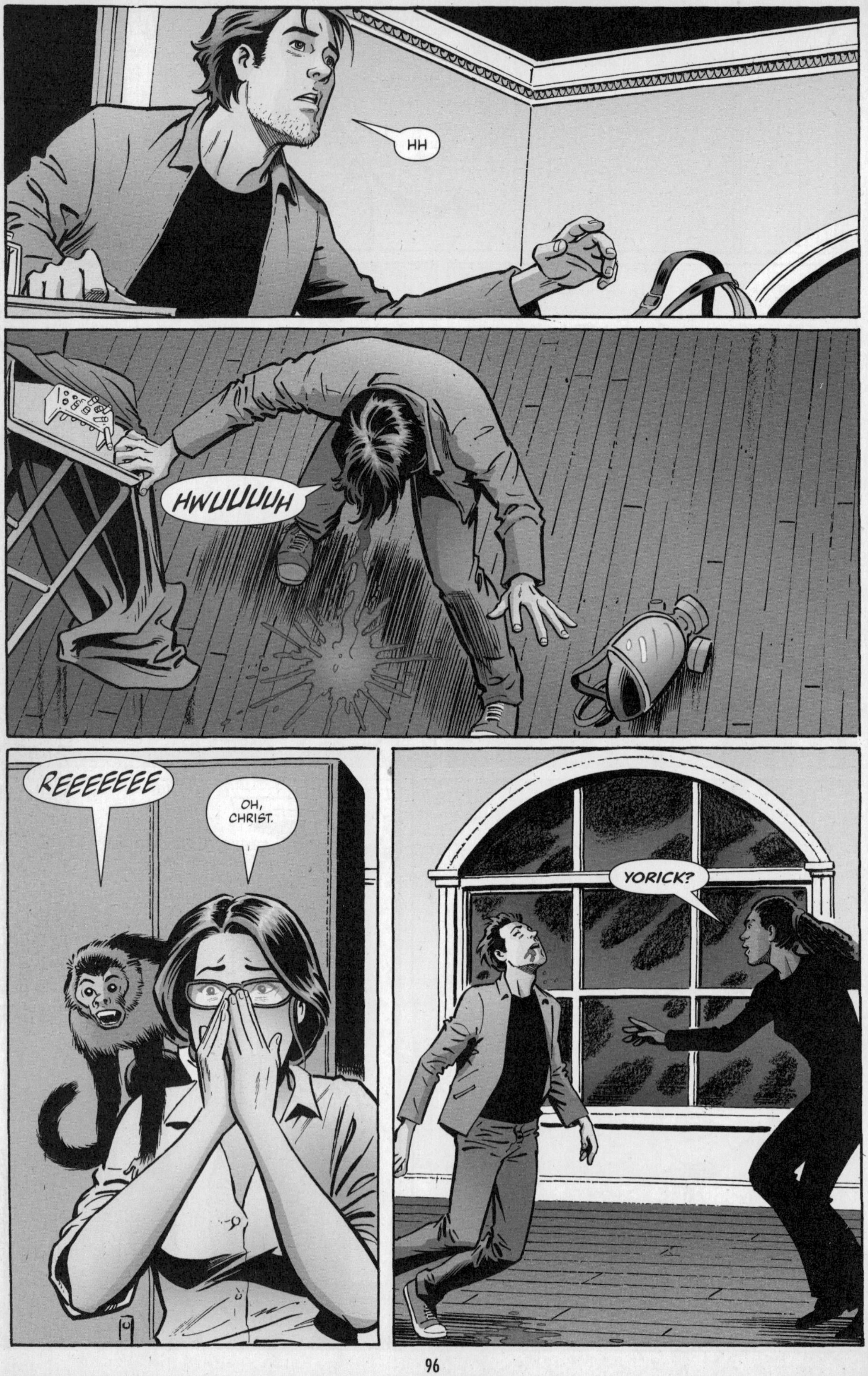
HH
HWUUUUUH
REEEEEEE
OH, CHRIST.
YORICK?

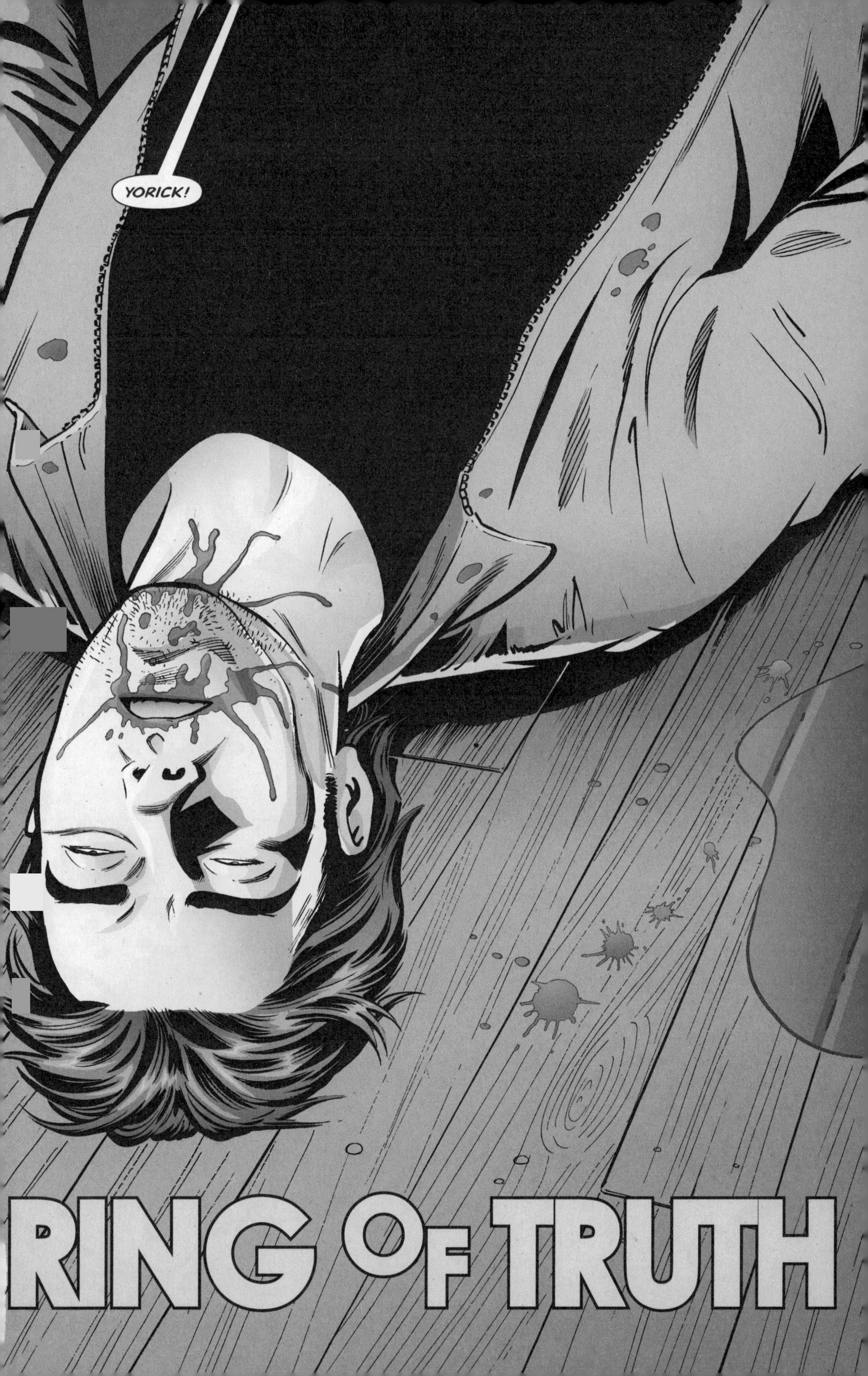
YORICK!
RING OF TRUTH

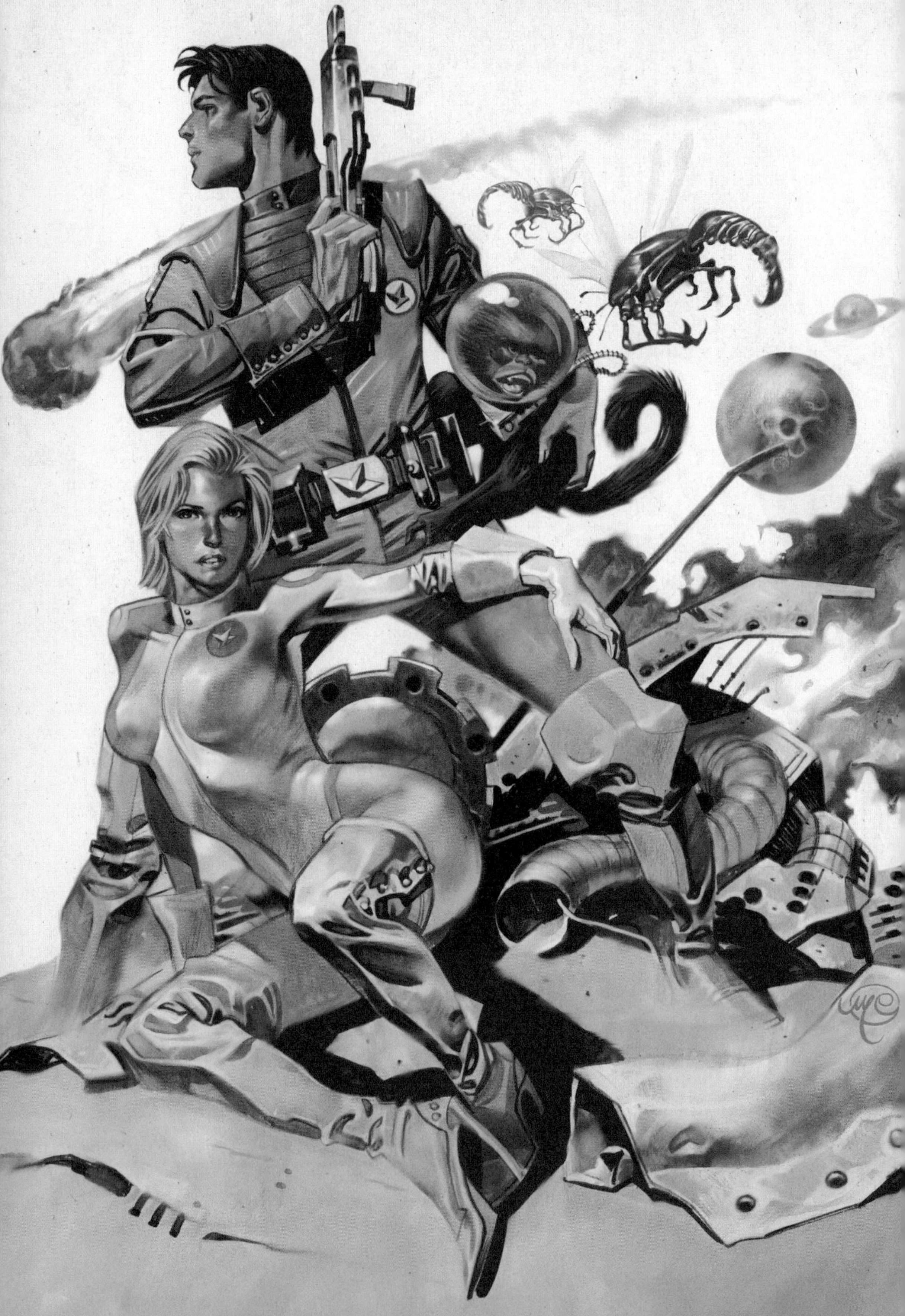

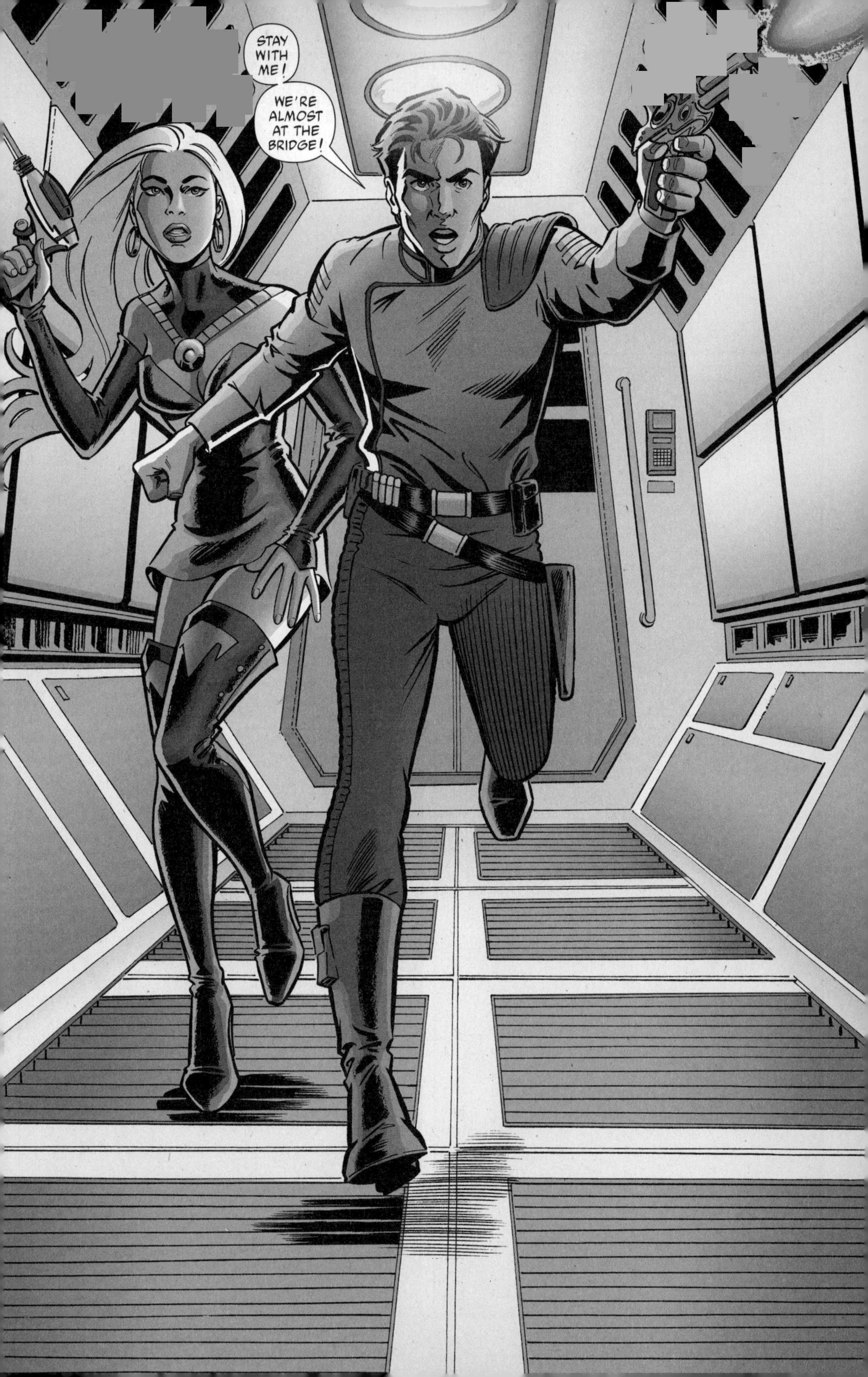
STAY WITH ME!
WE'RE ALMOST AT THE BRIDGE!

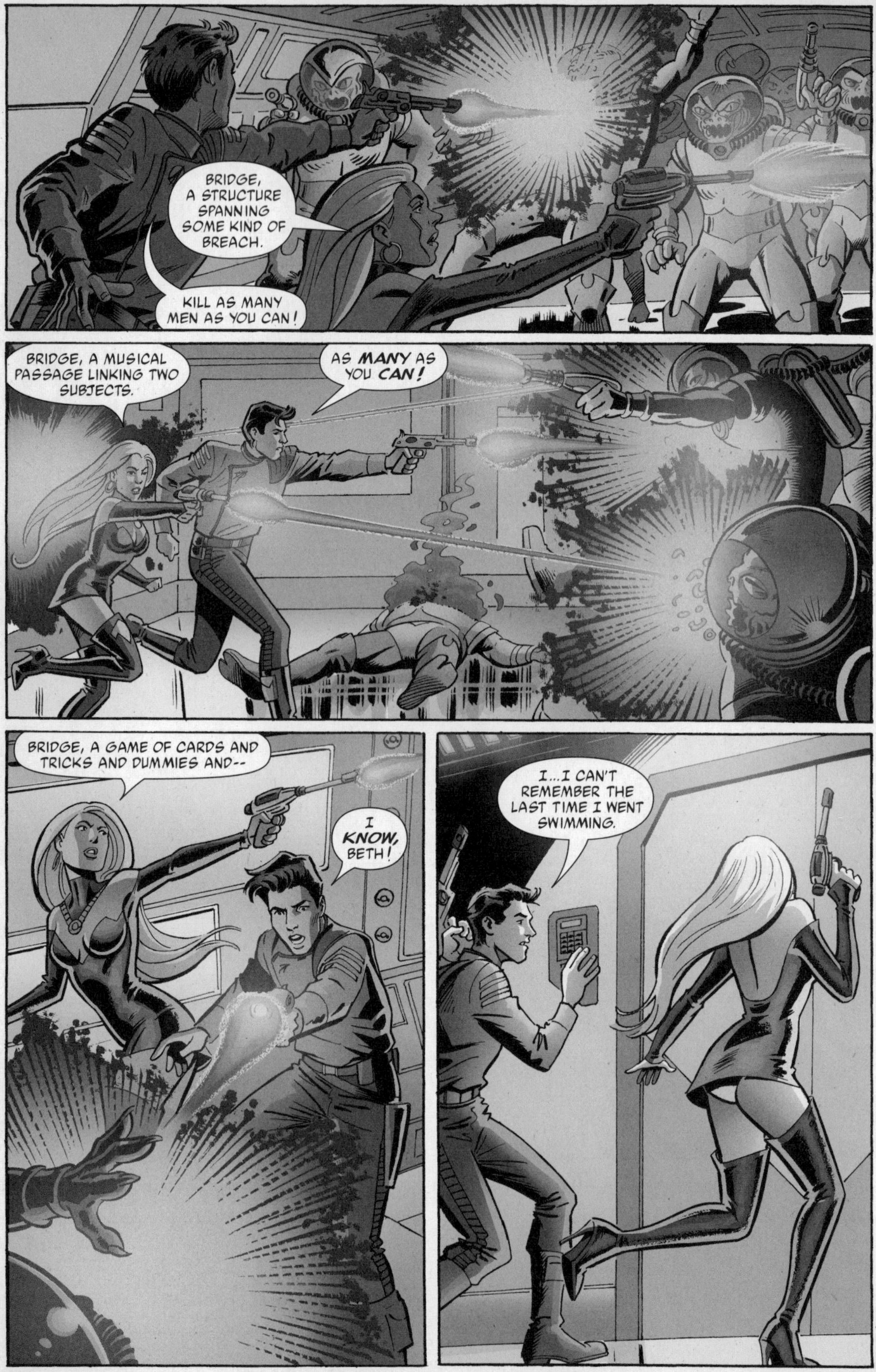
BRIDGE, A STRUCTURE SPANNING SOME KIND OF BREACH.
KILL AS MANY MEN AS YOU CAN!
BRIDGE, A MUSICAL PASSAGE LINKING TWO SUBJECTS.
AS MANY AS YOU CAN!
BRIDGE, A GAME OF CARDS AND TRICKS AND DUMMIES AND--
I KNOW, BETH!
I...I CAN'T REMEMBER THE LAST TIME I WENT SWIMMING.

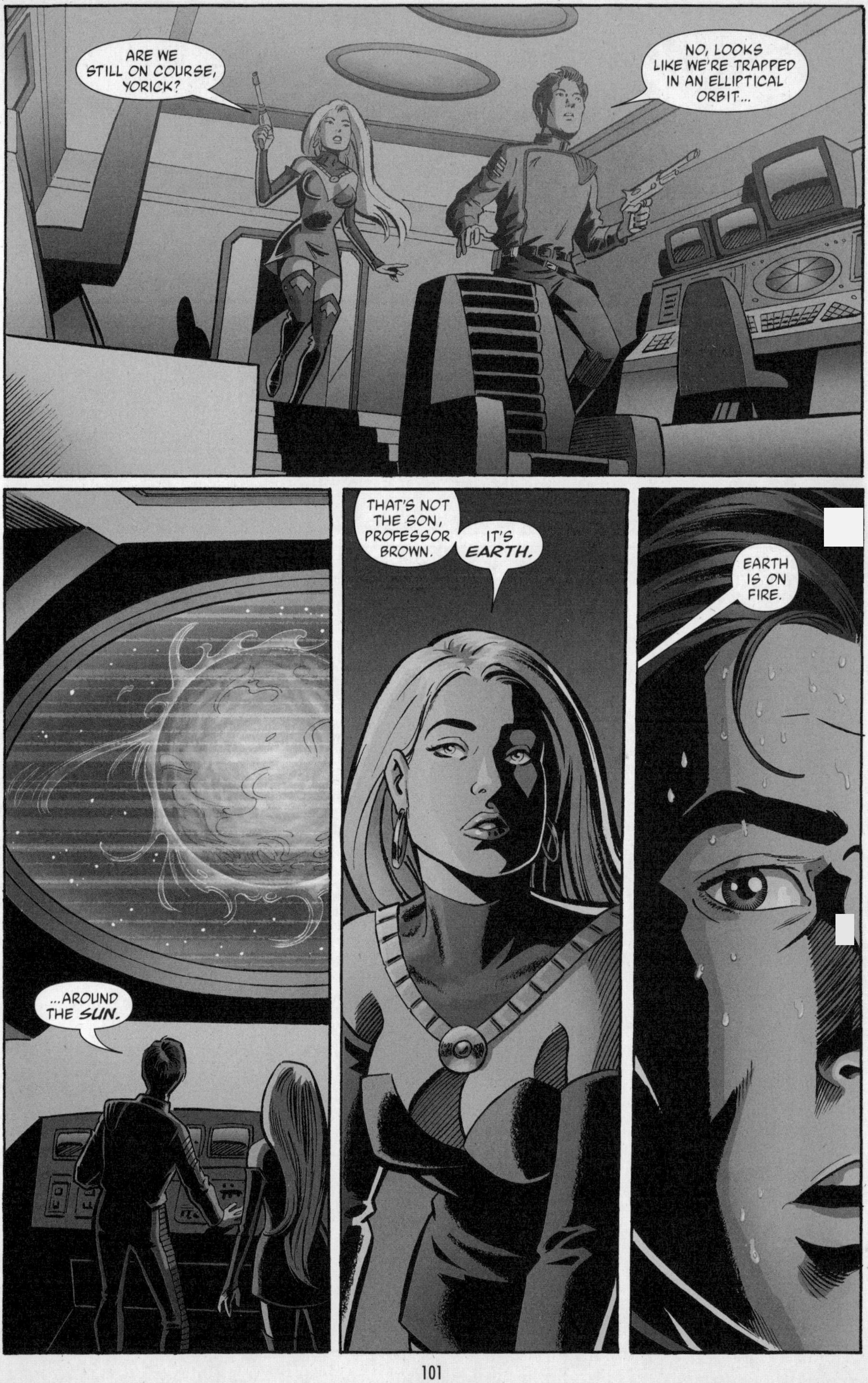
ARE WE STILL ON COURSE, YORICK?
NO, LOOKS LIKE WE'RE TRAPPED IN AN ELLIPTICAL ORBIT...
...AROUND THE SUN.
THAT'S NOT THE SON, PROFESSOR BROWN.
IT'S EARTH.
EARTH IS ON FIRE.

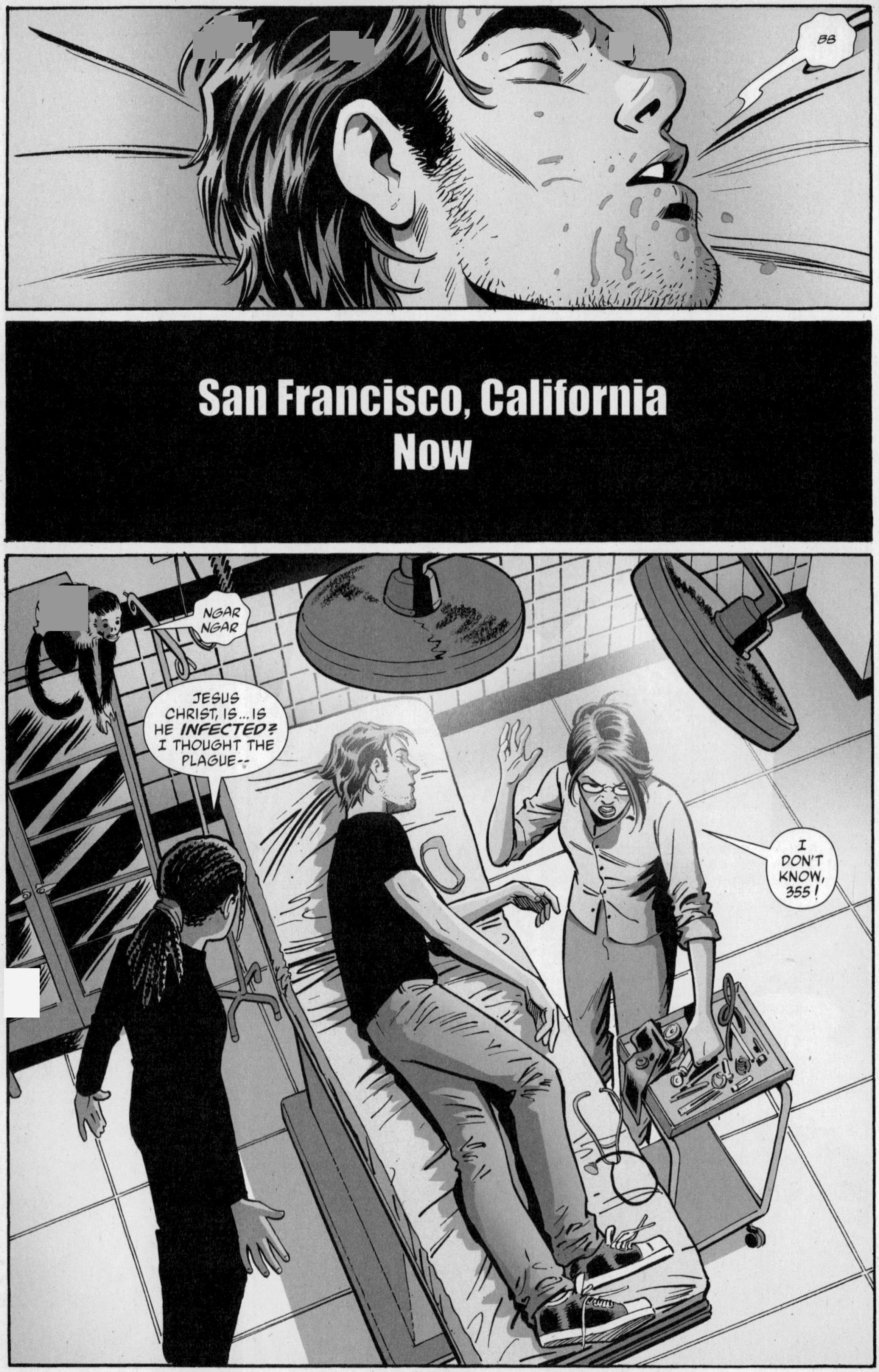
BB
San Francisco, California
Now
NGAR NGAR
JESUS CHRIST, IS... IS HE *INFECTED*? I THOUGHT THE PLAGUE--
I DON'T KNOW, 355!

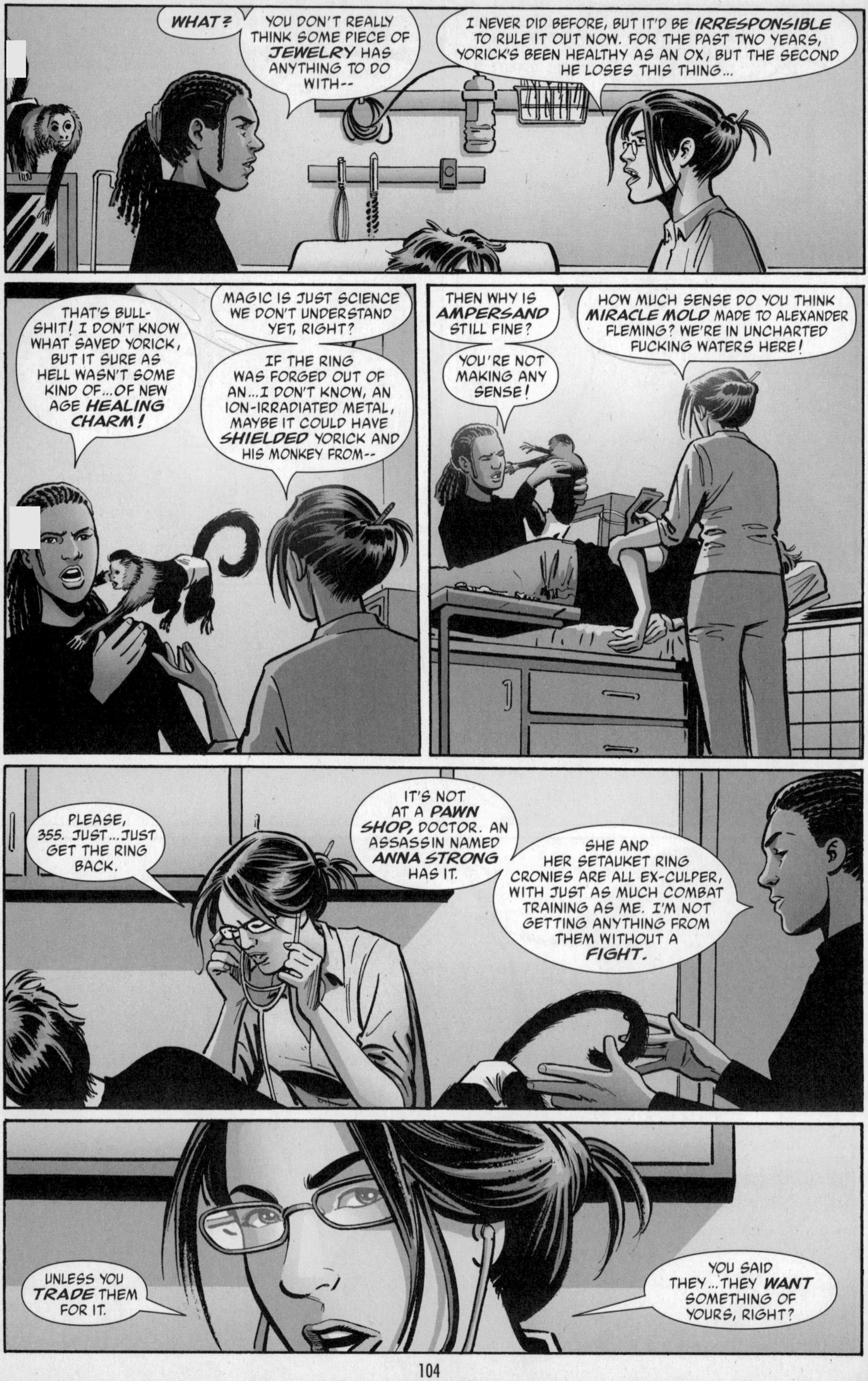

WHAT?
YOU DON'T REALLY THINK SOME PIECE OF JEWELRY HAS ANYTHING TO DO WITH--
I NEVER DID BEFORE, BUT IT'D BE IRRESPONSIBLE TO RULE IT OUT NOW. FOR THE PAST TWO YEARS, YORICK'S BEEN HEALTHY AS AN OX, BUT THE SECOND HE LOSES THIS THING...
THAT'S BULL-SHIT! I DON'T KNOW WHAT SAVED YORICK, BUT IT SURE AS HELL WASN'T SOME KIND OF...OF NEW AGE HEALING CHARM!
MAGIC IS JUST SCIENCE WE DON'T UNDERSTAND YET, RIGHT?
IF THE RING WAS FORGED OUT OF AN...I DON'T KNOW, AN ION-IRRADIATED METAL, MAYBE IT COULD HAVE SHIELDED YORICK AND HIS MONKEY FROM--
THEN WHY IS AMPERSAND STILL FINE?
YOU'RE NOT MAKING ANY SENSE!
HOW MUCH SENSE DO YOU THINK MIRACLE MOLD MADE TO ALEXANDER FLEMING? WE'RE IN UNCHARTED FUCKING WATERS HERE!
PLEASE, 355. JUST...JUST GET THE RING BACK.
IT'S NOT AT A PAWN SHOP, DOCTOR. AN ASSASSIN NAMED ANNA STRONG HAS IT.
SHE AND HER SETAUKET RING CRONIES ARE ALL EX-CULPER, WITH JUST AS MUCH COMBAT TRAINING AS ME. I'M NOT GETTING ANYTHING FROM THEM WITHOUT A FIGHT.
UNLESS YOU TRADE THEM FOR IT.
YOU SAID THEY...THEY WANT SOMETHING OF YOURS, RIGHT?

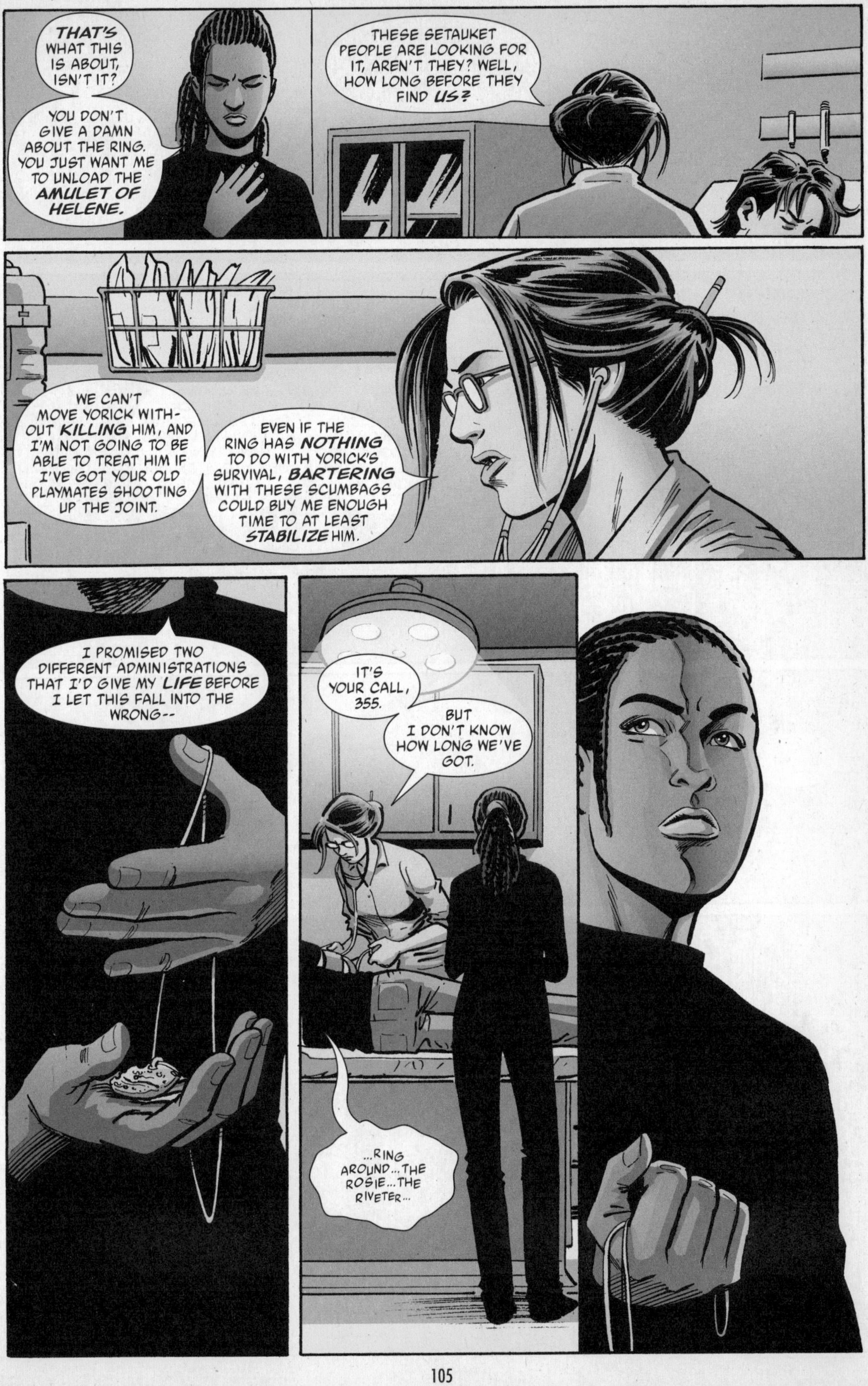
THAT'S WHAT THIS IS ABOUT, ISN'T IT?
YOU DON'T GIVE A DAMN ABOUT THE RING. YOU JUST WANT ME TO UNLOAD THE AMULET OF HELENE.
THESE SETAUKET PEOPLE ARE LOOKING FOR IT, AREN'T THEY? WELL, HOW LONG BEFORE THEY FIND US?
WE CAN'T MOVE YORICK WITHOUT KILLING HIM, AND I'M NOT GOING TO BE ABLE TO TREAT HIM IF I'VE GOT YOUR OLD PLAYMATES SHOOTING UP THE JOINT.
EVEN IF THE RING HAS NOTHING TO DO WITH YORICK'S SURVIVAL, BARTERING WITH THESE SCUMBAGS COULD BUY ME ENOUGH TIME TO AT LEAST STABILIZE HIM.
I PROMISED TWO DIFFERENT ADMINISTRATIONS THAT I'D GIVE MY LIFE BEFORE I LET THIS FALL INTO THE WRONG--
IT'S YOUR CALL, 355.
BUT I DON'T KNOW HOW LONG WE'VE GOT.
...RING AROUND...THE ROSIE...THE RIVETER...

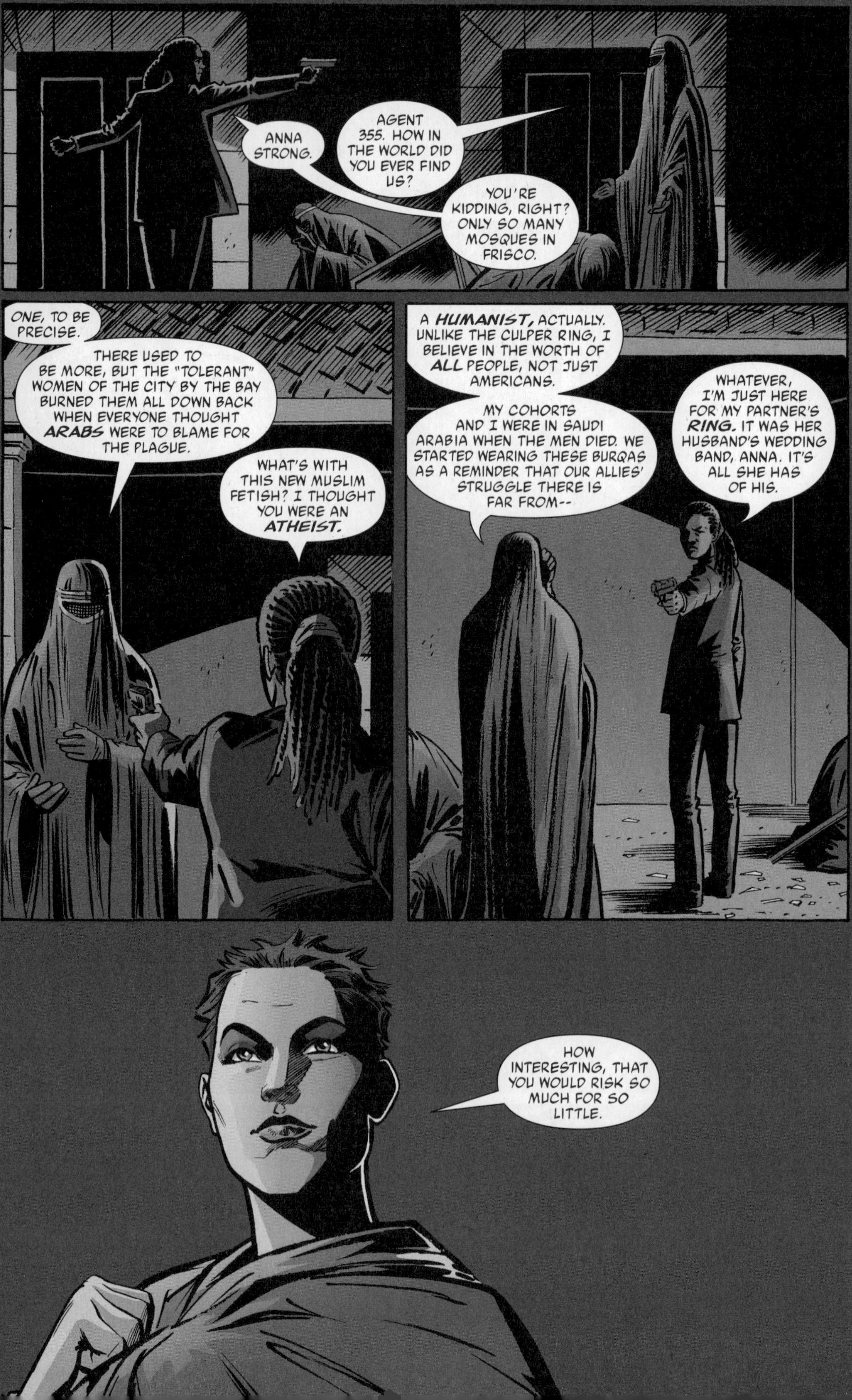
ANNA STRONG.
AGENT 355. HOW IN THE WORLD DID YOU EVER FIND US?
YOU'RE KIDDING, RIGHT? ONLY SO MANY MOSQUES IN FRISCO.
ONE, TO BE PRECISE.
THERE USED TO BE MORE, BUT THE "TOLERANT" WOMEN OF THE CITY BY THE BAY BURNED THEM ALL DOWN BACK WHEN EVERYONE THOUGHT ARABS WERE TO BLAME FOR THE PLAGUE.
WHAT'S WITH THIS NEW MUSLIM FETISH? I THOUGHT YOU WERE AN ATHEIST.
A HUMANIST, ACTUALLY. UNLIKE THE CULPER RING, I BELIEVE IN THE WORTH OF ALL PEOPLE, NOT JUST AMERICANS.
MY COHORTS AND I WERE IN SAUDI ARABIA WHEN THE MEN DIED. WE STARTED WEARING THESE BURQAS AS A REMINDER THAT OUR ALLIES' STRUGGLE THERE IS FAR FROM--
WHATEVER, I'M JUST HERE FOR MY PARTNER'S RING. IT WAS HER HUSBAND'S WEDDING BAND, ANNA. IT'S ALL SHE HAS OF HIS.
HOW INTERESTING, THAT YOU WOULD RISK SO MUCH FOR SO LITTLE.

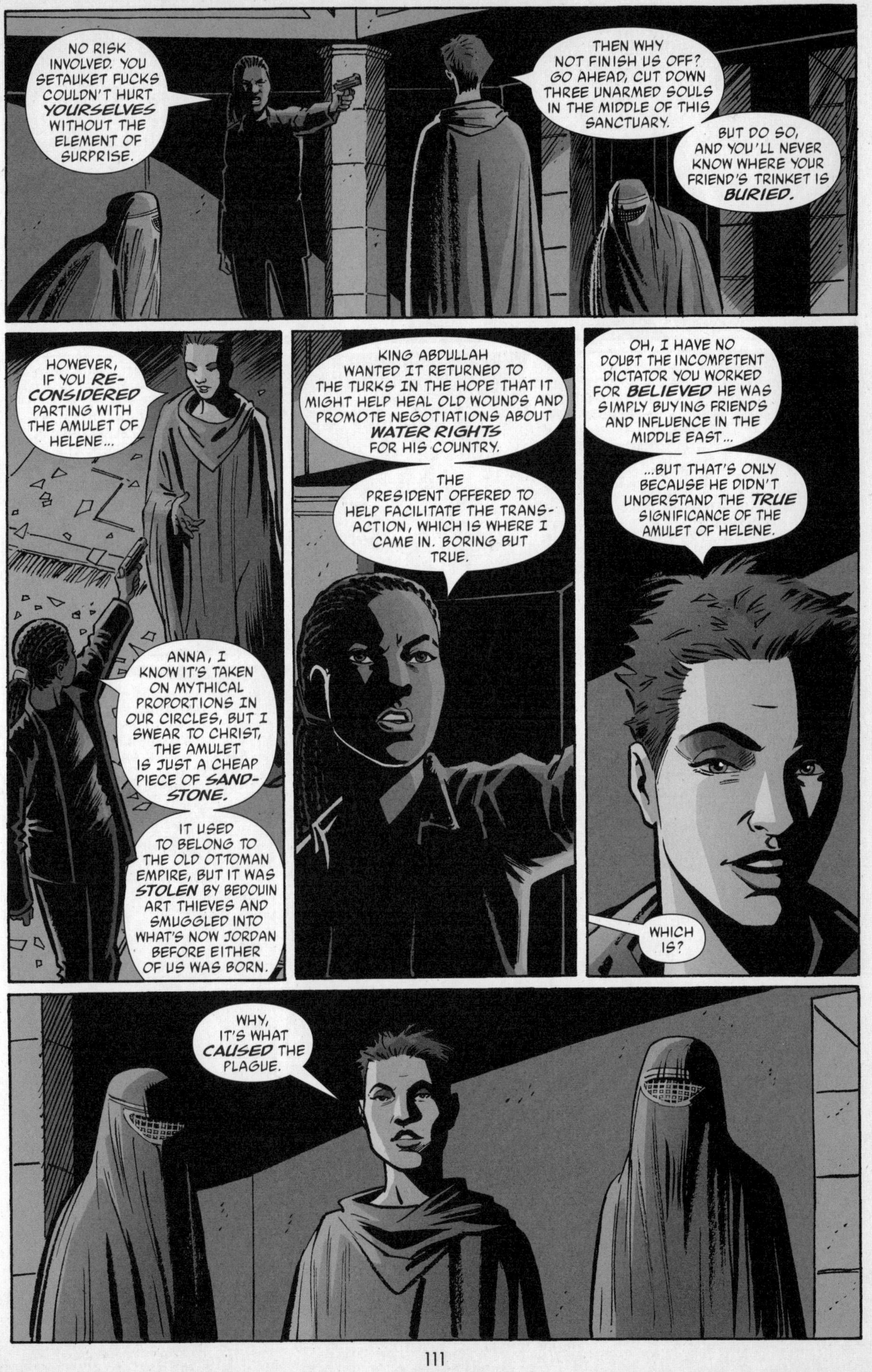
NO RISK INVOLVED. YOU SETAUKET FUCKS COULDN'T HURT *YOURSELVES* WITHOUT THE ELEMENT OF SURPRISE.
THEN WHY NOT FINISH US OFF? GO AHEAD, CUT DOWN THREE UNARMED SOULS IN THE MIDDLE OF THIS SANCTUARY.
BUT DO SO, AND YOU'LL NEVER KNOW WHERE YOUR FRIEND'S TRINKET IS *BURIED.*
HOWEVER, IF YOU *RECONSIDERED* PARTING WITH THE AMULET OF HELENE...
ANNA, I KNOW IT'S TAKEN ON MYTHICAL PROPORTIONS IN OUR CIRCLES, BUT I SWEAR TO CHRIST, THE AMULET IS JUST A CHEAP PIECE OF *SANDSTONE.*
IT USED TO BELONG TO THE OLD OTTOMAN EMPIRE, BUT IT WAS *STOLEN* BY BEDOUIN ART THIEVES AND SMUGGLED INTO WHAT'S NOW JORDAN BEFORE EITHER OF US WAS BORN.
KING ABDULLAH WANTED IT RETURNED TO THE TURKS IN THE HOPE THAT IT MIGHT HELP HEAL OLD WOUNDS AND PROMOTE NEGOTIATIONS ABOUT *WATER RIGHTS* FOR HIS COUNTRY.
THE PRESIDENT OFFERED TO HELP FACILITATE THE TRANSACTION, WHICH IS WHERE I CAME IN. BORING BUT TRUE.
OH, I HAVE NO DOUBT THE INCOMPETENT DICTATOR YOU WORKED FOR *BELIEVED* HE WAS SIMPLY BUYING FRIENDS AND INFLUENCE IN THE MIDDLE EAST...
...BUT THAT'S ONLY BECAUSE HE DIDN'T UNDERSTAND THE *TRUE* SIGNIFICANCE OF THE AMULET OF HELENE.
WHICH IS?
WHY, IT'S WHAT *CAUSED* THE PLAGUE.

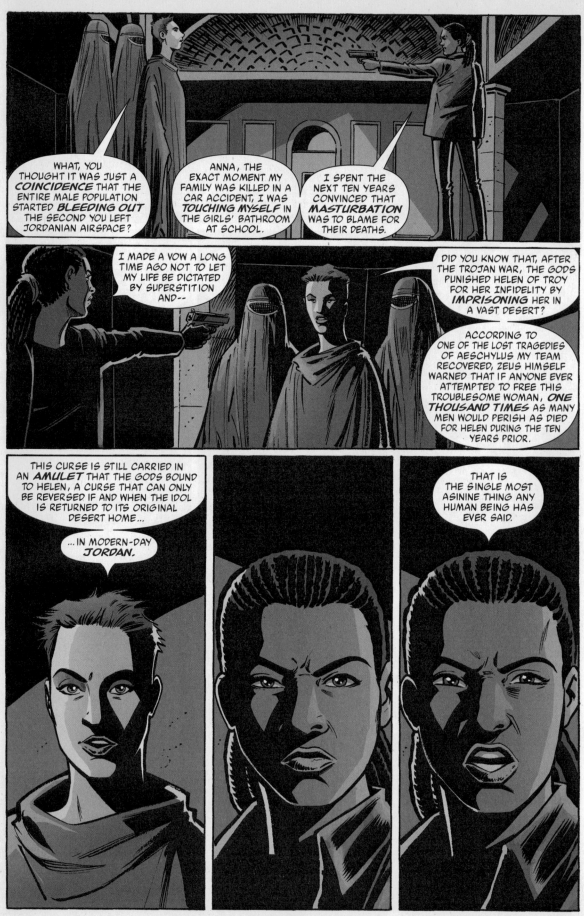

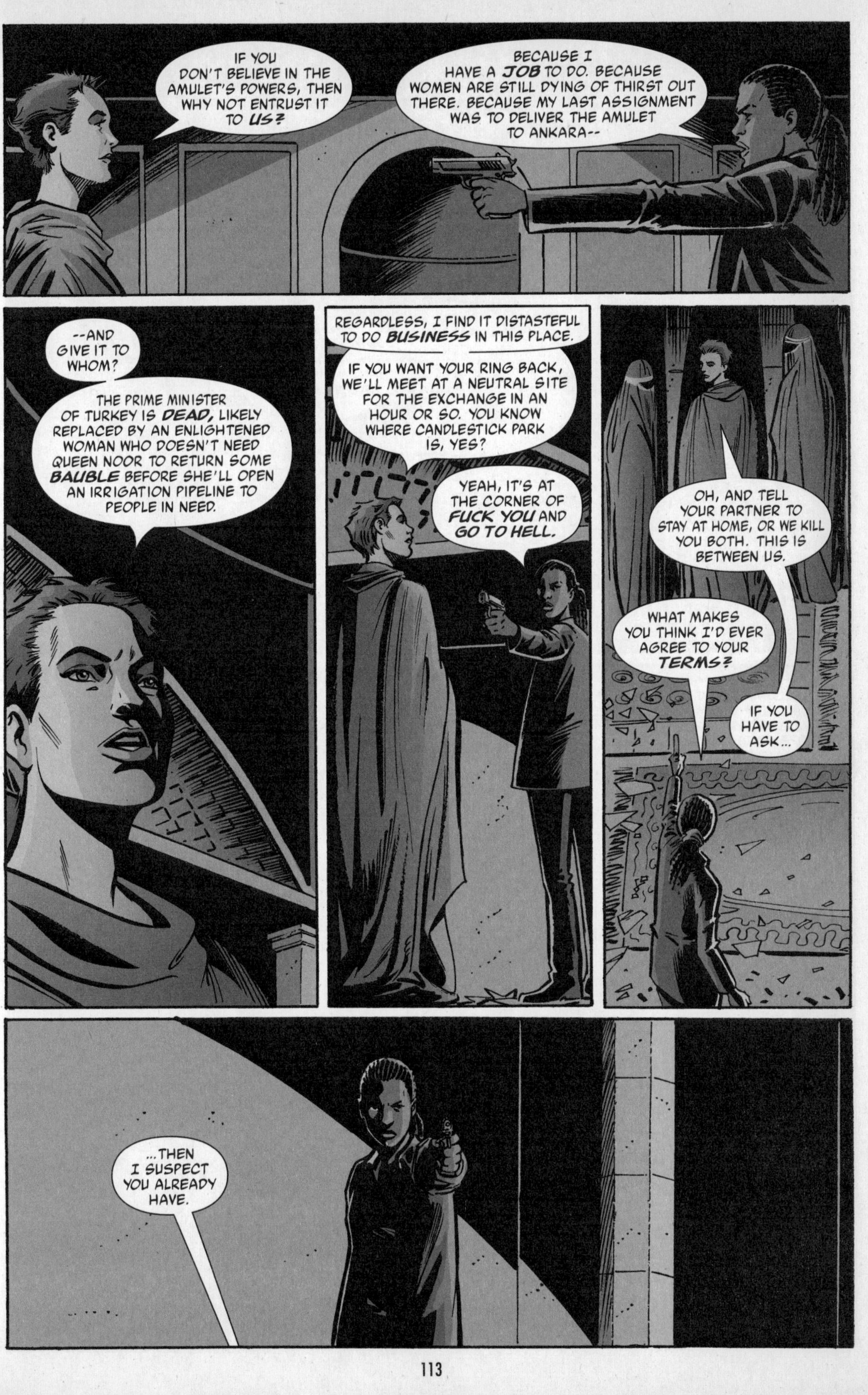
IF YOU DON'T BELIEVE IN THE AMULET'S POWERS, THEN WHY NOT ENTRUST IT TO US?
BECAUSE I HAVE A JOB TO DO. BECAUSE WOMEN ARE STILL DYING OF THIRST OUT THERE. BECAUSE MY LAST ASSIGNMENT WAS TO DELIVER THE AMULET TO ANKARA--
--AND GIVE IT TO WHOM?
THE PRIME MINISTER OF TURKEY IS DEAD, LIKELY REPLACED BY AN ENLIGHTENED WOMAN WHO DOESN'T NEED QUEEN NOOR TO RETURN SOME BAUBLE BEFORE SHE'LL OPEN AN IRRIGATION PIPELINE TO PEOPLE IN NEED.
REGARDLESS, I FIND IT DISTASTEFUL TO DO BUSINESS IN THIS PLACE.
IF YOU WANT YOUR RING BACK, WE'LL MEET AT A NEUTRAL SITE FOR THE EXCHANGE IN AN HOUR OR SO. YOU KNOW WHERE CANDLESTICK PARK IS, YES?
YEAH, IT'S AT THE CORNER OF FUCK YOU AND GO TO HELL.
OH, AND TELL YOUR PARTNER TO STAY AT HOME, OR WE KILL YOU BOTH. THIS IS BETWEEN US.
WHAT MAKES YOU THINK I'D EVER AGREE TO YOUR TERMS?
IF YOU HAVE TO ASK...
...THEN I SUSPECT YOU ALREADY HAVE.

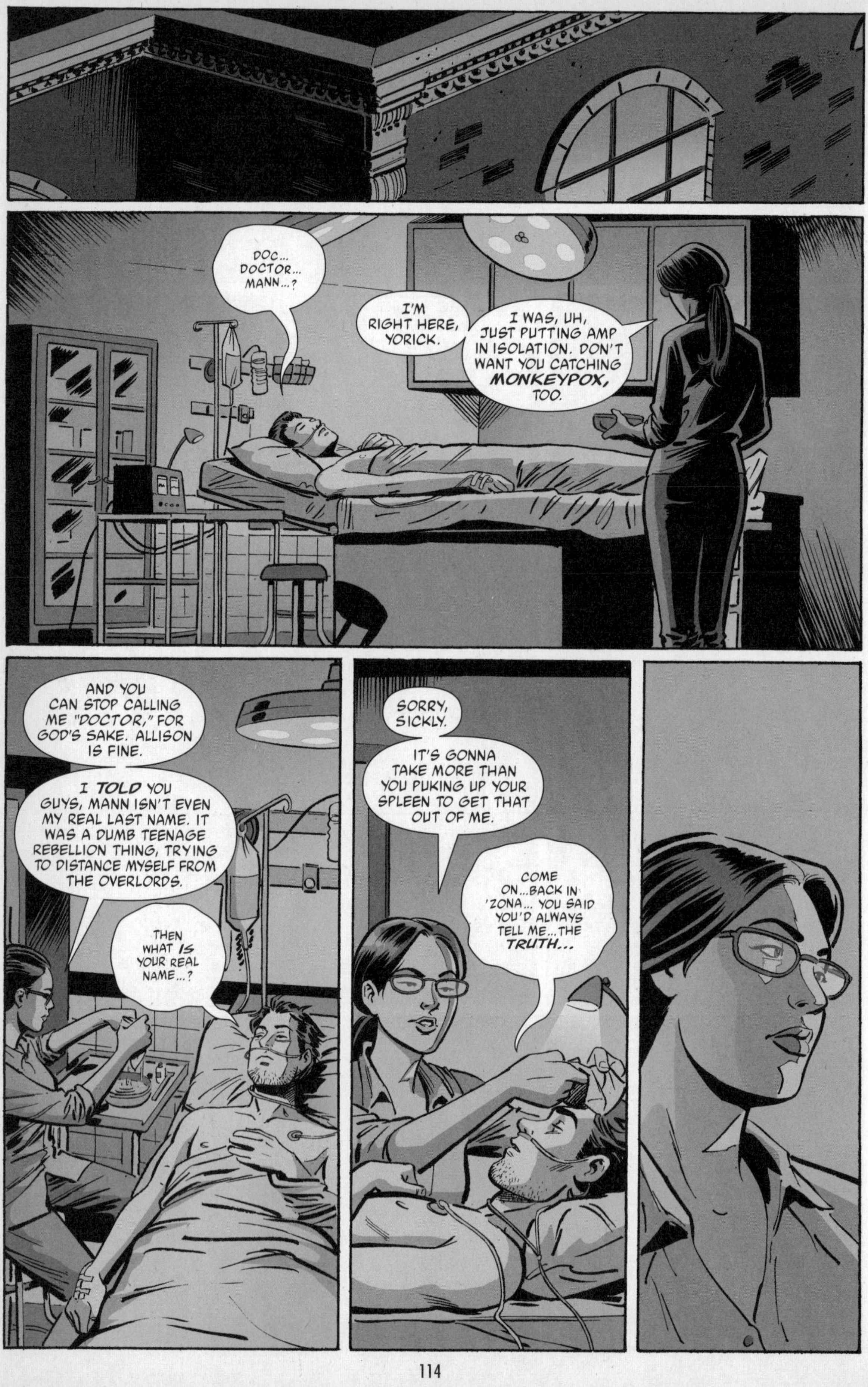
DOC... DOCTOR... MANN...?
I'M RIGHT HERE, YORICK.
I WAS, UH, JUST PUTTING AMP IN ISOLATION. DON'T WANT YOU CATCHING MONKEYPOX, TOO.
AND YOU CAN STOP CALLING ME "DOCTOR," FOR GOD'S SAKE. ALLISON IS FINE.
I TOLD YOU GUYS, MANN ISN'T EVEN MY REAL LAST NAME. IT WAS A DUMB TEENAGE REBELLION THING, TRYING TO DISTANCE MYSELF FROM THE OVERLORDS.
THEN WHAT IS YOUR REAL NAME...?
SORRY, SICKLY.
IT'S GONNA TAKE MORE THAN YOU PUKING UP YOUR SPLEEN TO GET THAT OUT OF ME.
COME ON...BACK IN 'ZONA... YOU SAID YOU'D ALWAYS TELL ME...THE TRUTH...

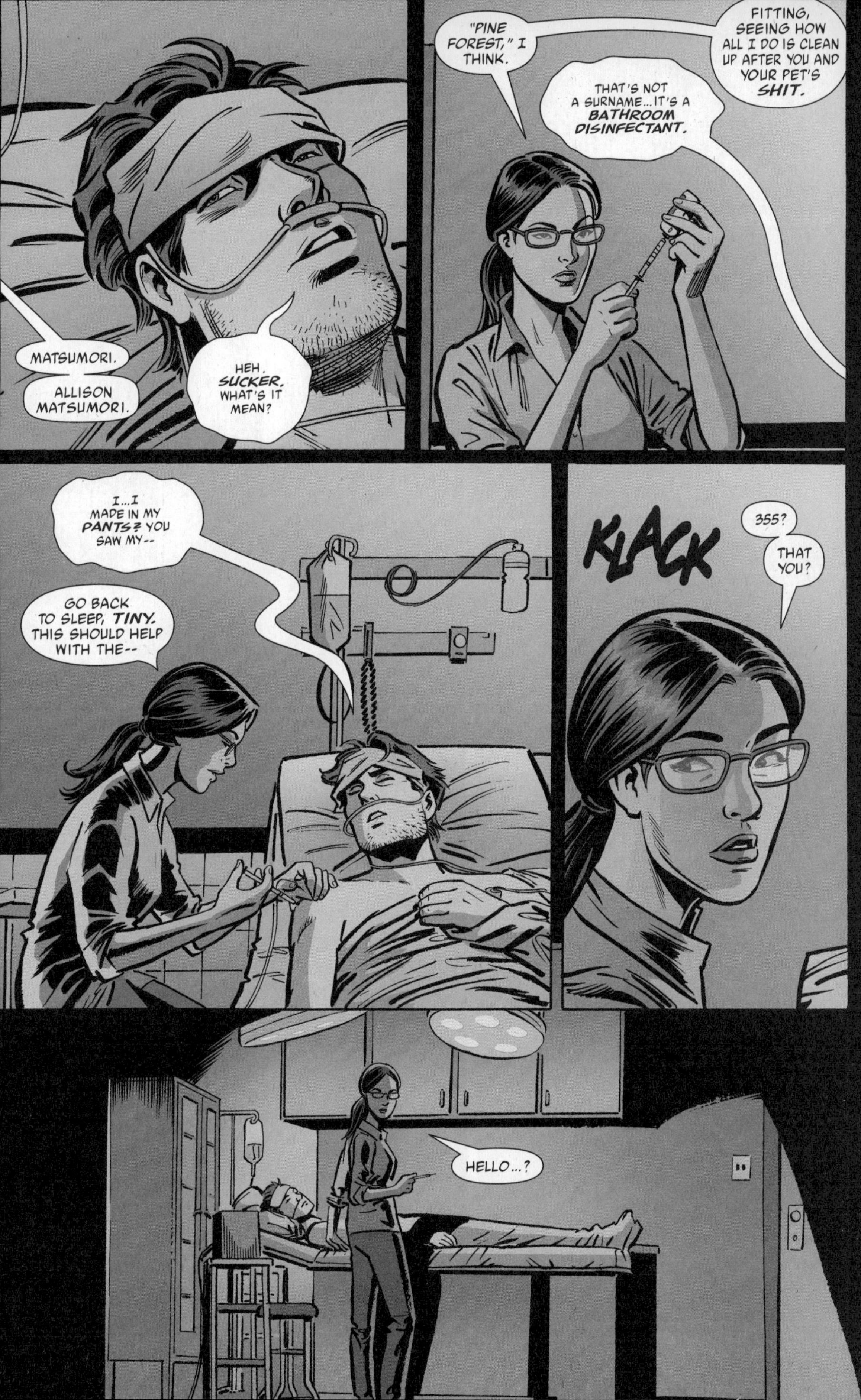
MATSUMORI.
ALLISON MATSUMORI.
HEH. SUCKER. WHAT'S IT MEAN?
"PINE FOREST," I THINK.
THAT'S NOT A SURNAME...IT'S A BATHROOM DISINFECTANT.
FITTING, SEEING HOW ALL I DO IS CLEAN UP AFTER YOU AND YOUR PET'S SHIT.
I...I MADE IN MY PANTS? YOU SAW MY--
GO BACK TO SLEEP, TINY. THIS SHOULD HELP WITH THE--
KLACK
355?
THAT YOU?
HELLO...?

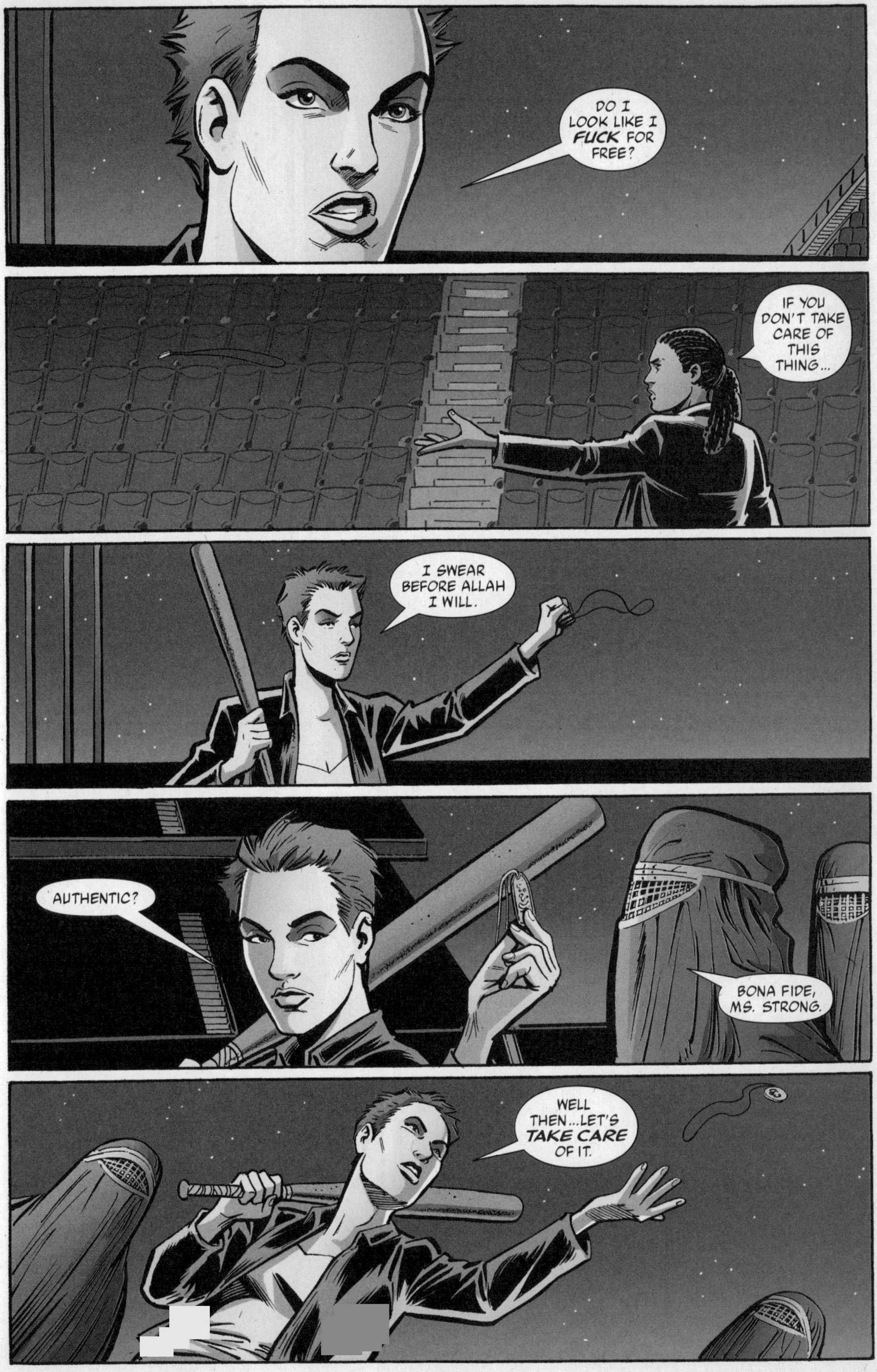
DO I LOOK LIKE I FUCK FOR FREE?
IF YOU DON'T TAKE CARE OF THIS THING...
I SWEAR BEFORE ALLAH I WILL.
AUTHENTIC?
BONA FIDE, MS. STRONG.
WELL THEN...LET'S TAKE CARE OF IT.

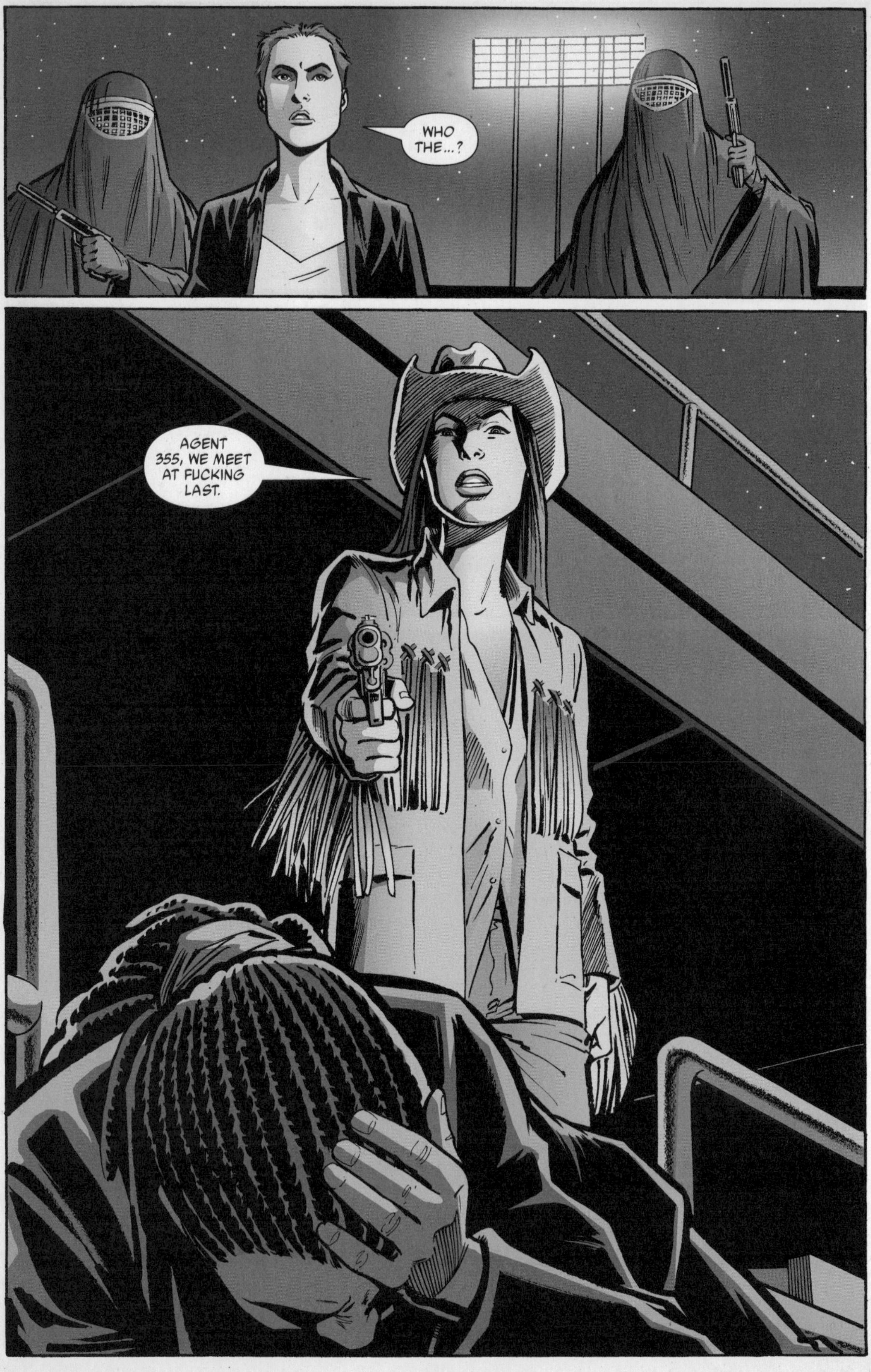
WHO THE...?
AGENT 355, WE MEET AT FUCKING LAST.

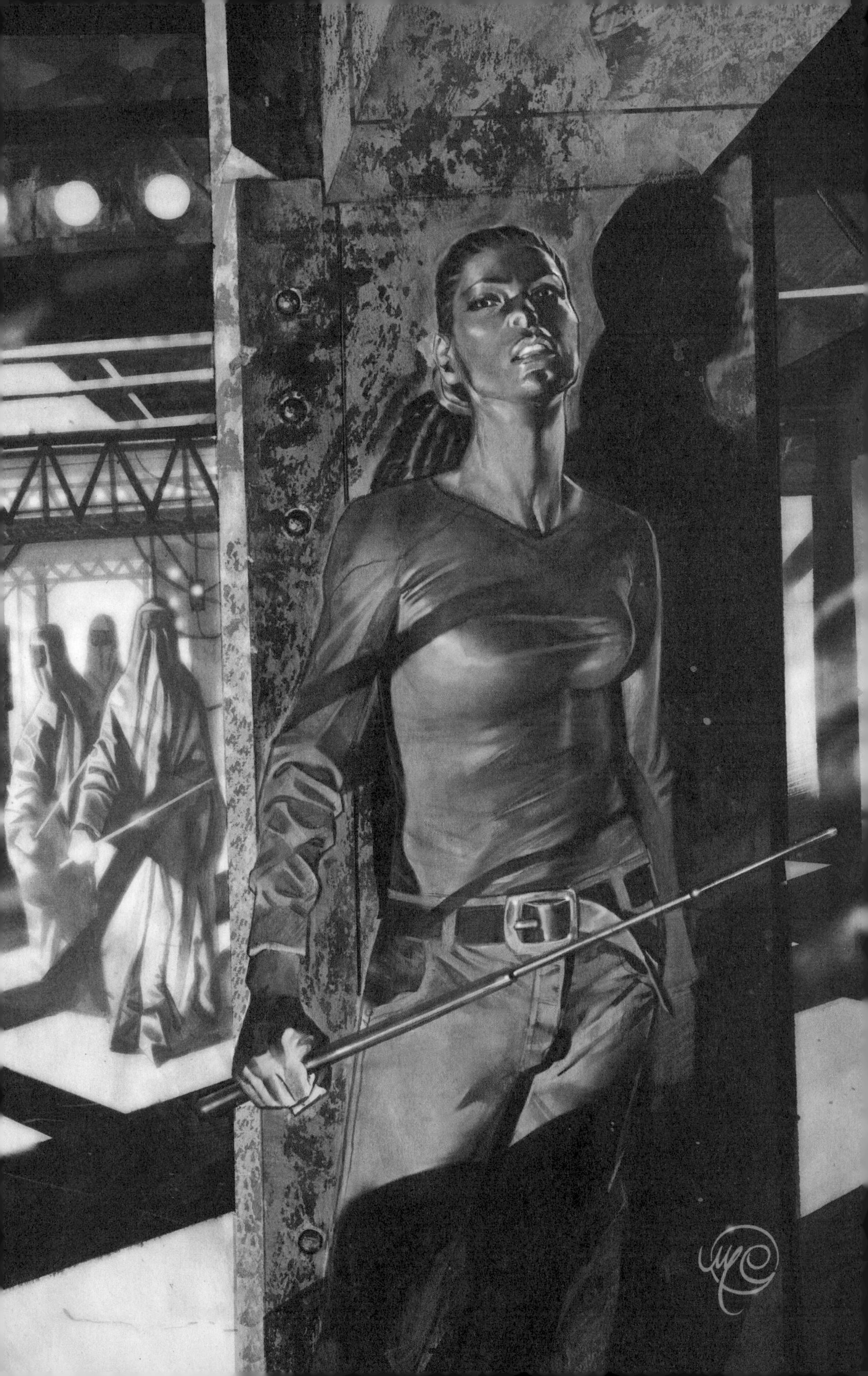

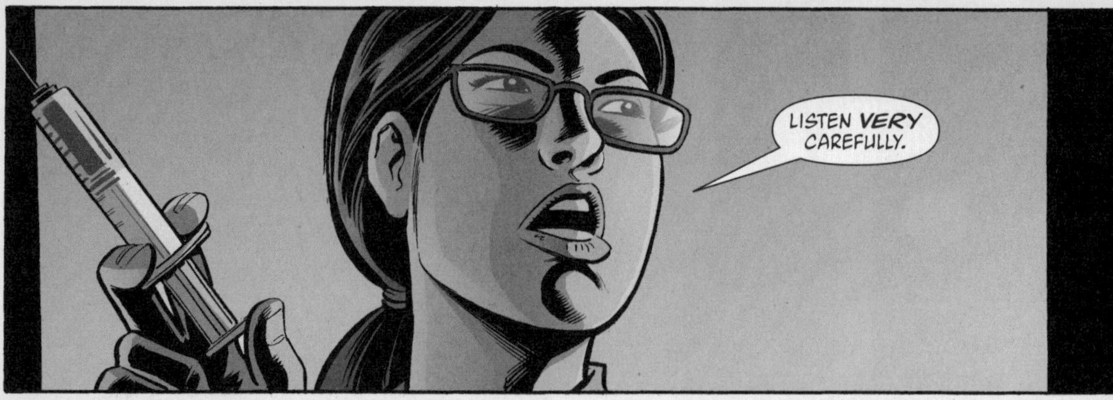
LISTEN VERY CAREFULLY.

San Francisco, California
Now

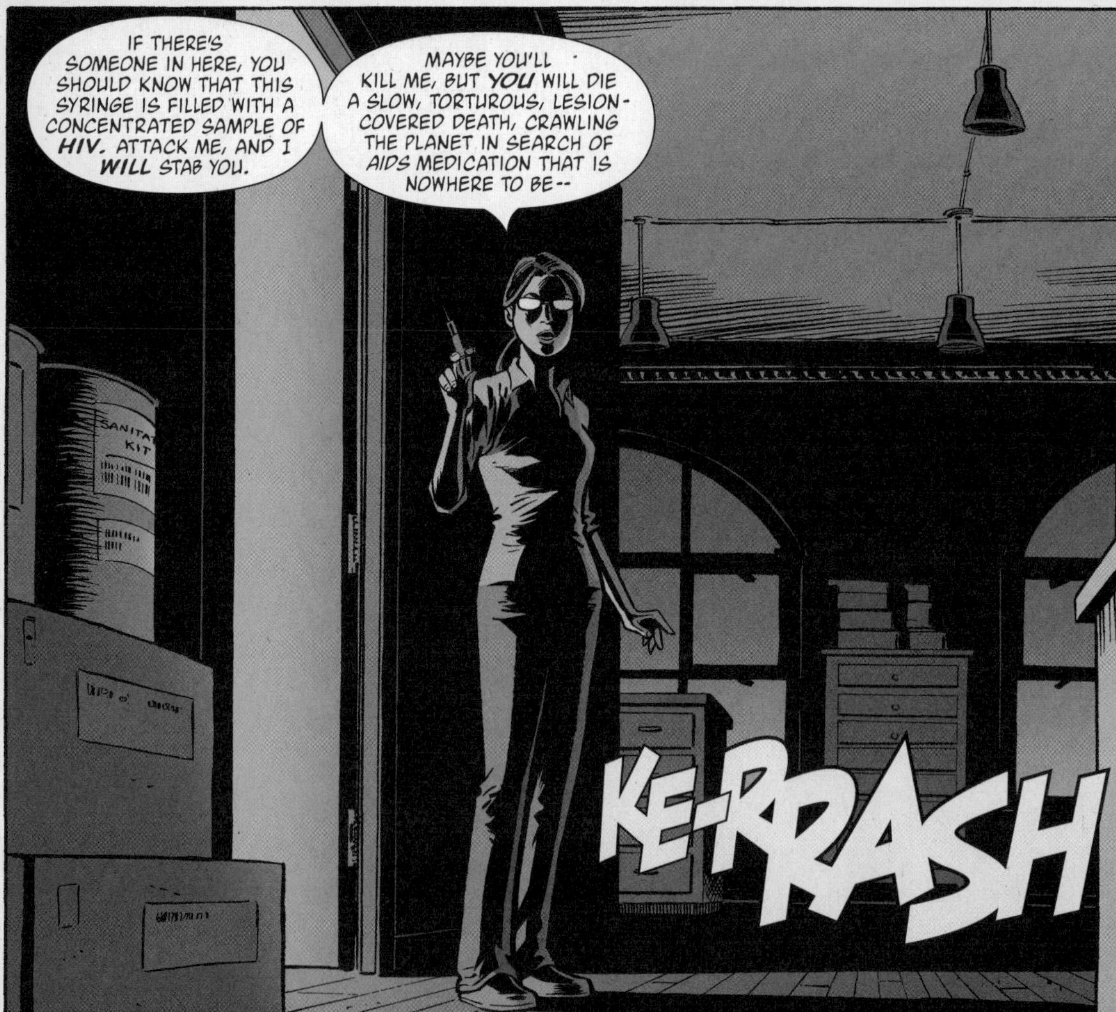
IF THERE'S SOMEONE IN HERE, YOU SHOULD KNOW THAT THIS SYRINGE IS FILLED WITH A CONCENTRATED SAMPLE OF HIV. ATTACK ME, AND I WILL STAB YOU.
MAYBE YOU'LL KILL ME, BUT YOU WILL DIE A SLOW, TORTUROUS, LESION-COVERED DEATH, CRAWLING THE PLANET IN SEARCH OF AIDS MEDICATION THAT IS NOWHERE TO BE--
KE-RRASH

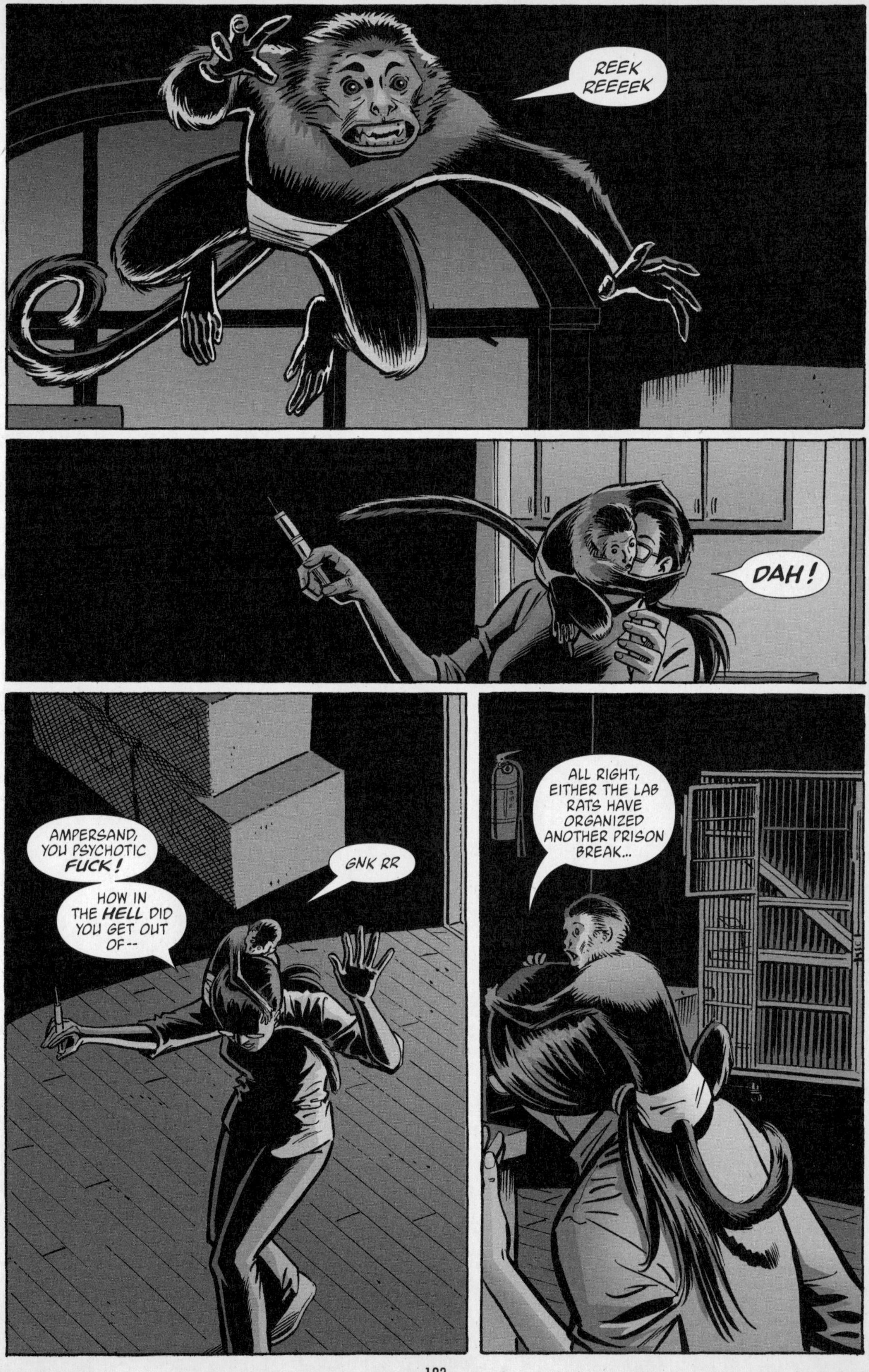
REEK REEEEK
DAH!
AMPERSAND, YOU PSYCHOTIC FUCK!
HOW IN THE HELL DID YOU GET OUT OF--
GNK RR
ALL RIGHT, EITHER THE LAB RATS HAVE ORGANIZED ANOTHER PRISON BREAK...

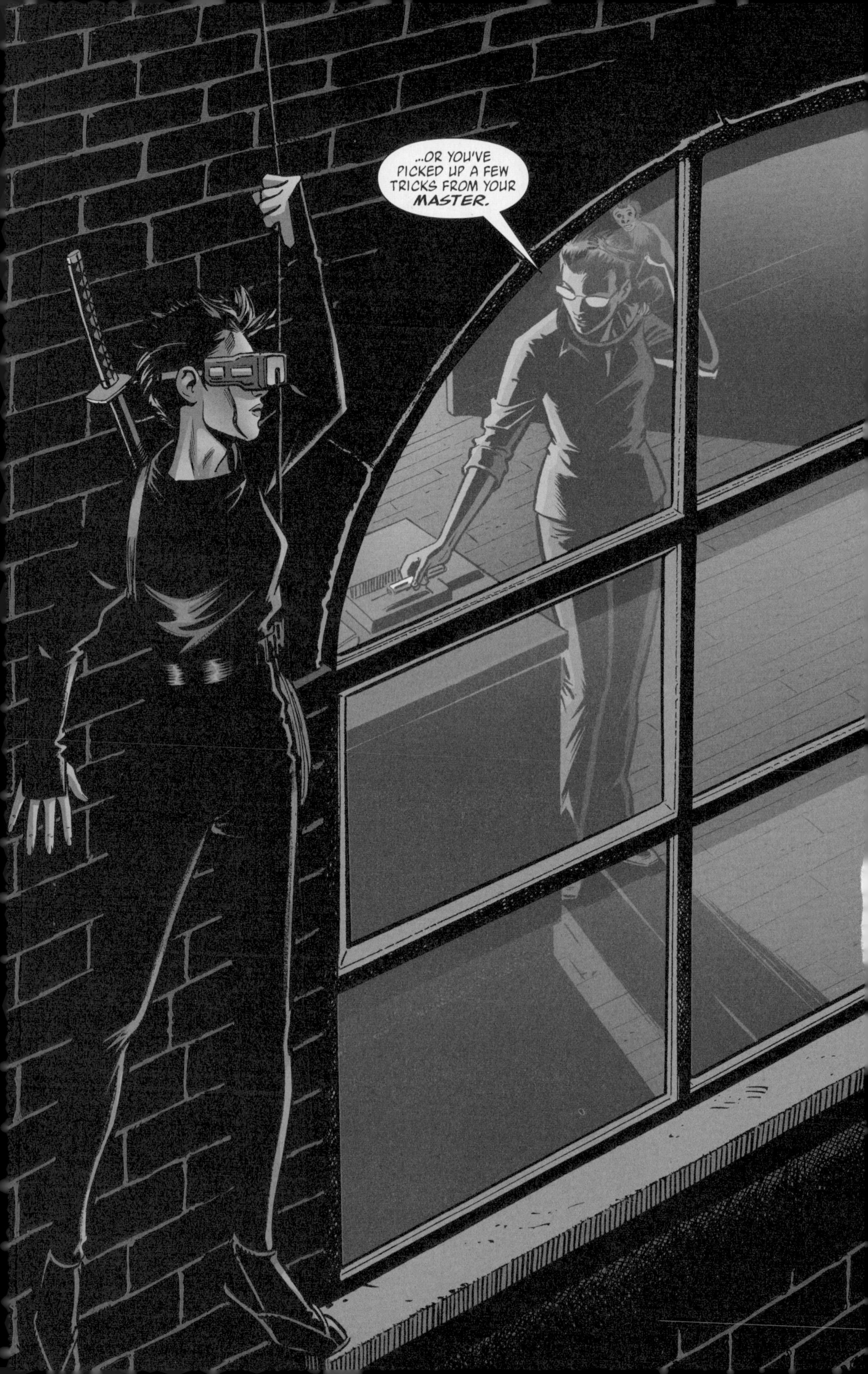
...OR YOU'VE PICKED UP A FEW TRICKS FROM YOUR MASTER.

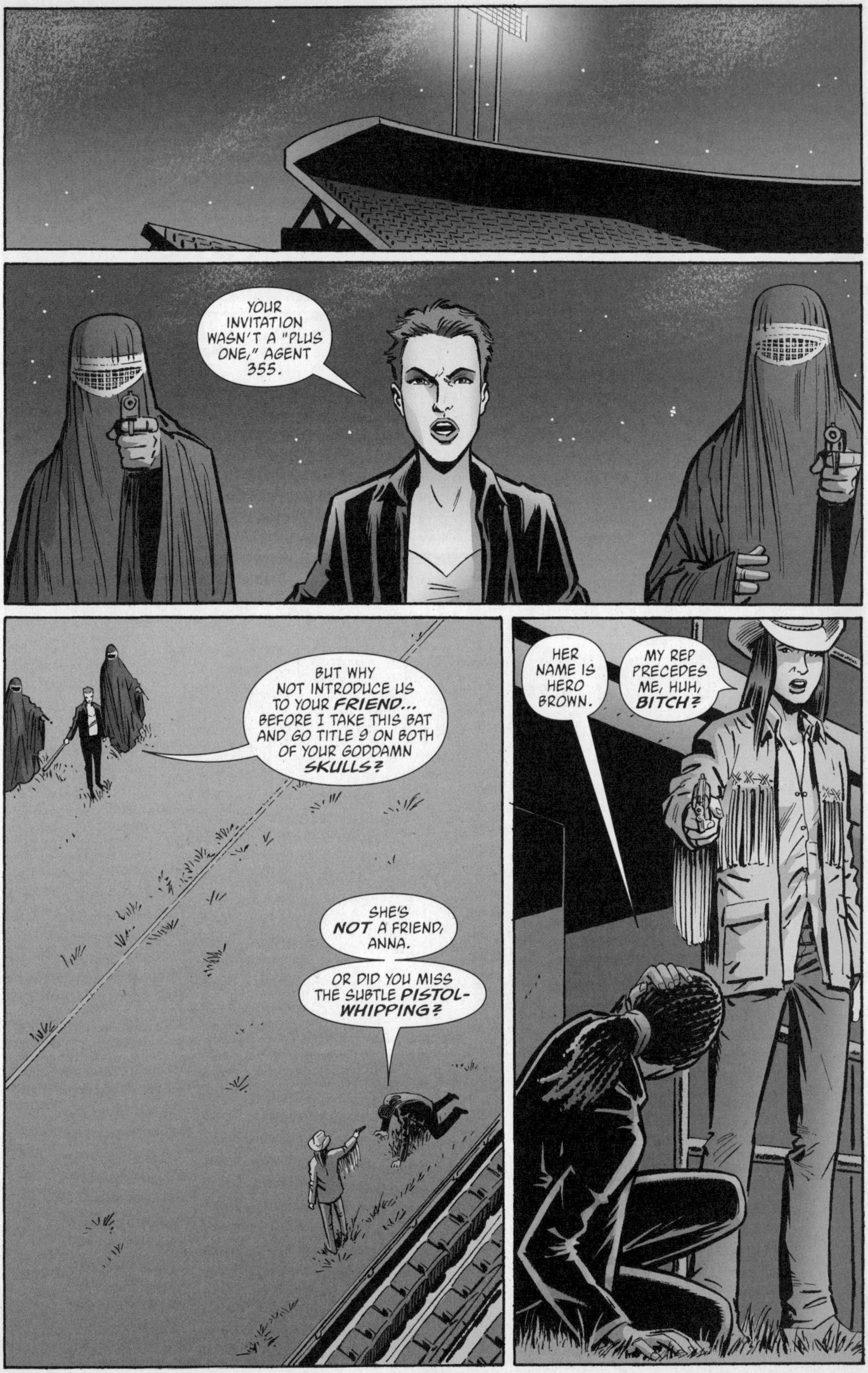
YOUR INVITATION WASN'T A "PLUS ONE," AGENT 355.
BUT WHY NOT INTRODUCE US TO YOUR FRIEND... BEFORE I TAKE THIS BAT AND GO TITLE 9 ON BOTH OF YOUR GODDAMN SKULLS?
SHE'S NOT A FRIEND, ANNA.
OR DID YOU MISS THE SUBTLE PISTOL-WHIPPING?
HER NAME IS HERO BROWN.
MY REP PRECEDES ME, HUH, BITCH?

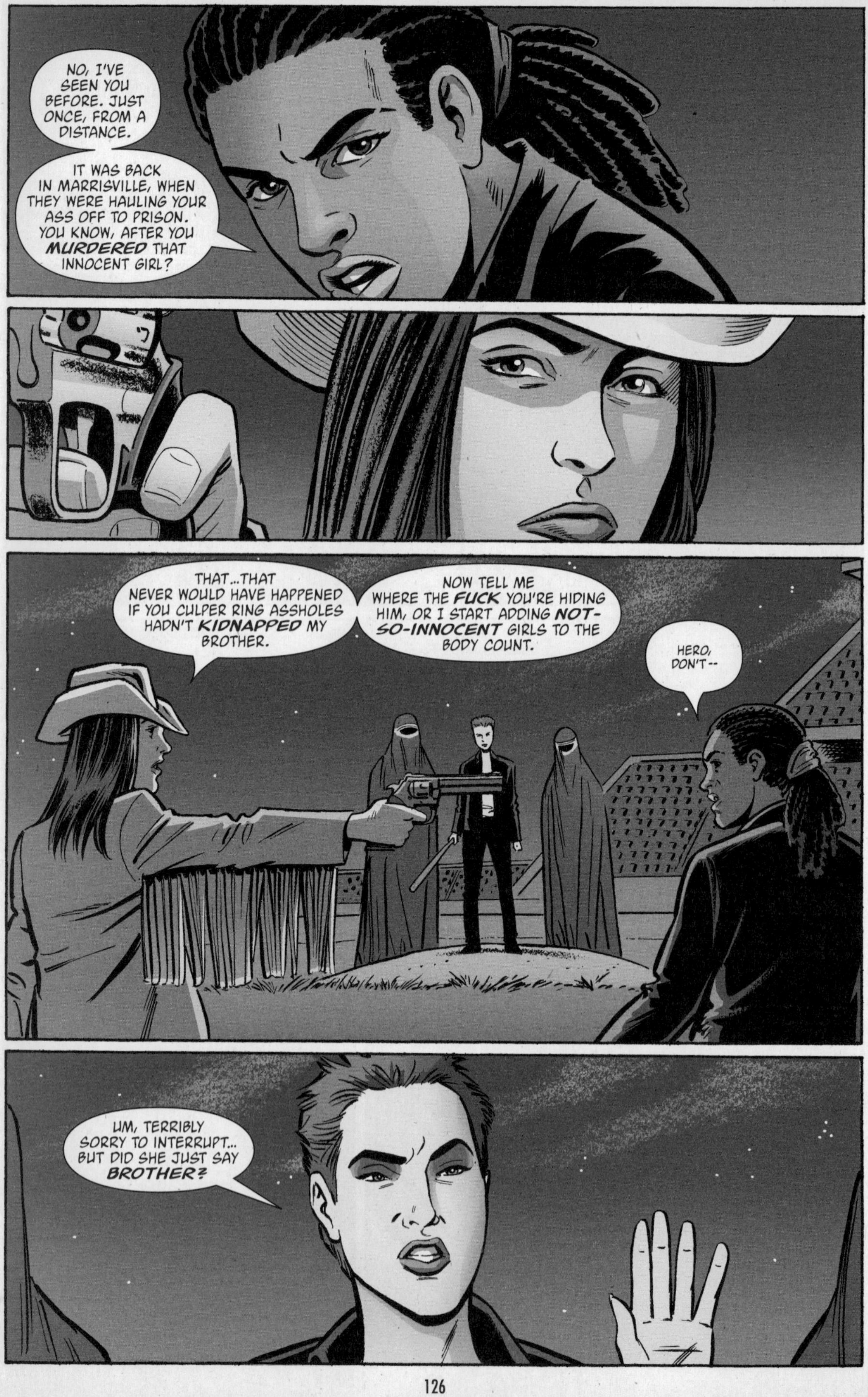
NO, I'VE SEEN YOU BEFORE. JUST ONCE, FROM A DISTANCE.
IT WAS BACK IN MARRISVILLE, WHEN THEY WERE HAULING YOUR ASS OFF TO PRISON. YOU KNOW, AFTER YOU MURDERED THAT INNOCENT GIRL?
THAT...THAT NEVER WOULD HAVE HAPPENED IF YOU CULPER RING ASSHOLES HADN'T KIDNAPPED MY BROTHER.
NOW TELL ME WHERE THE FUCK YOU'RE HIDING HIM, OR I START ADDING NOT-SO-INNOCENT GIRLS TO THE BODY COUNT.
HERO, DON'T--
UM, TERRIBLY SORRY TO INTERRUPT... BUT DID SHE JUST SAY BROTHER?

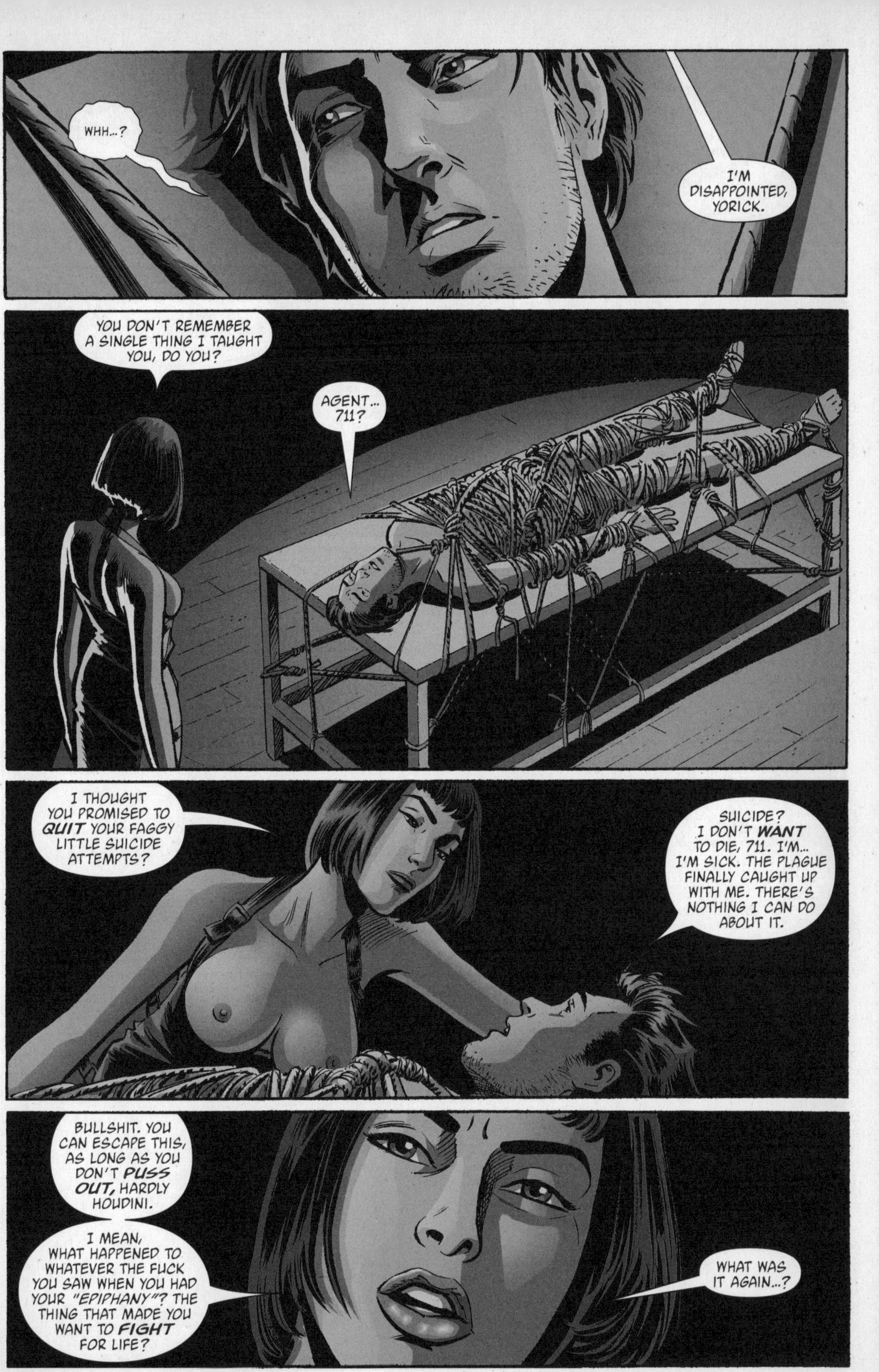
WHH...?
I'M DISAPPOINTED, YORICK.
YOU DON'T REMEMBER A SINGLE THING I TAUGHT YOU, DO YOU?
AGENT... 711?
I THOUGHT YOU PROMISED TO QUIT YOUR FAGGY LITTLE SUICIDE ATTEMPTS?
SUICIDE? I DON'T WANT TO DIE, 711. I'M... I'M SICK. THE PLAGUE FINALLY CAUGHT UP WITH ME. THERE'S NOTHING I CAN DO ABOUT IT.
BULLSHIT. YOU CAN ESCAPE THIS, AS LONG AS YOU DON'T PUSS OUT, HARDLY HOUDINI.
I MEAN, WHAT HAPPENED TO WHATEVER THE FUCK YOU SAW WHEN YOU HAD YOUR "EPIPHANY"? THE THING THAT MADE YOU WANT TO FIGHT FOR LIFE?
WHAT WAS IT AGAIN...?

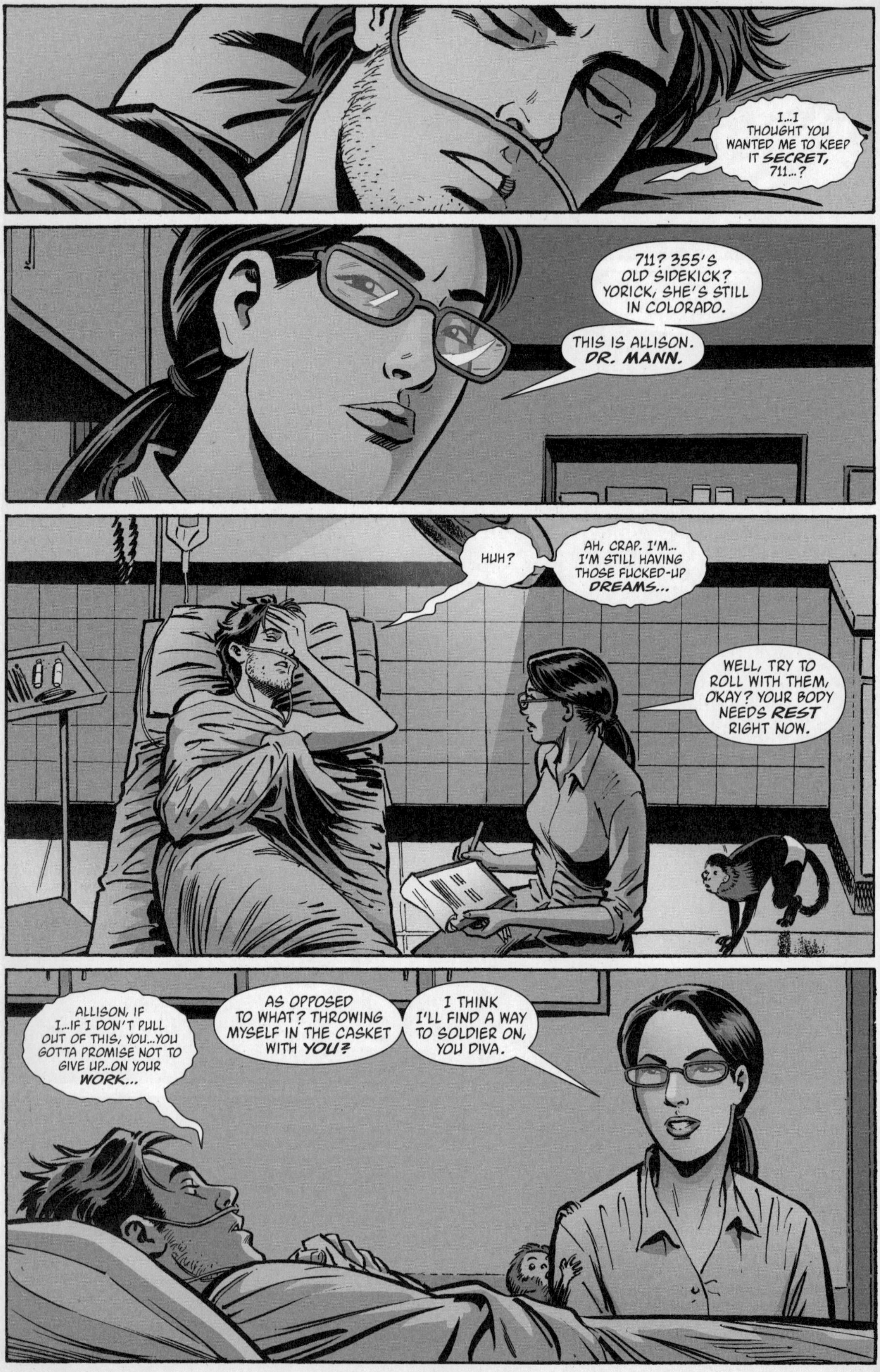
I...I THOUGHT YOU WANTED ME TO KEEP IT SECRET, 711...?
711? 355'S OLD SIDEKICK? YORICK, SHE'S STILL IN COLORADO.
THIS IS ALLISON. DR. MANN.
HUH?
AH, CRAP. I'M... I'M STILL HAVING THOSE FUCKED-UP DREAMS...
WELL, TRY TO ROLL WITH THEM, OKAY? YOUR BODY NEEDS REST RIGHT NOW.
ALLISON, IF I...IF I DON'T PULL OUT OF THIS, YOU...YOU GOTTA PROMISE NOT TO GIVE UP...ON YOUR WORK...
AS OPPOSED TO WHAT? THROWING MYSELF IN THE CASKET WITH YOU?
I THINK I'LL FIND A WAY TO SOLDIER ON, YOU DIVA.

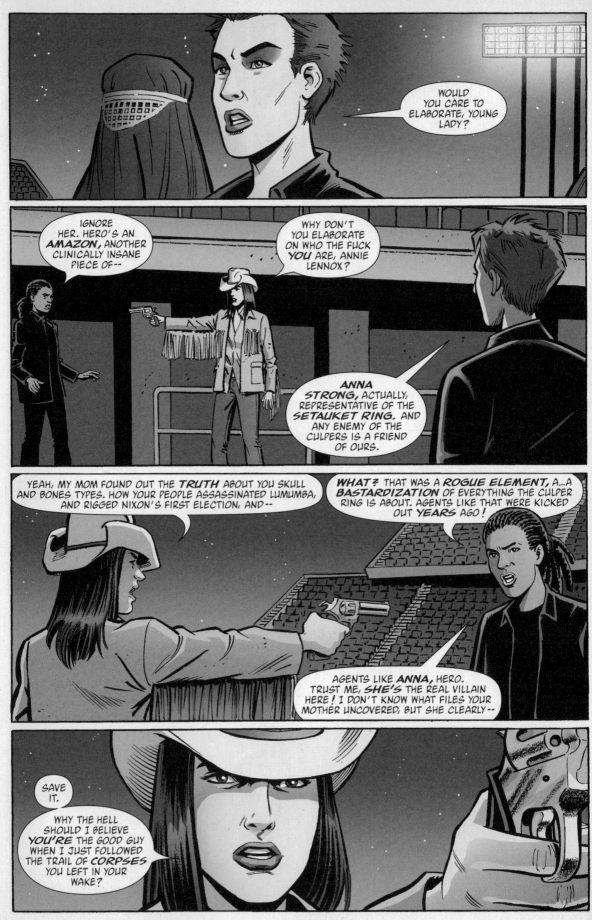

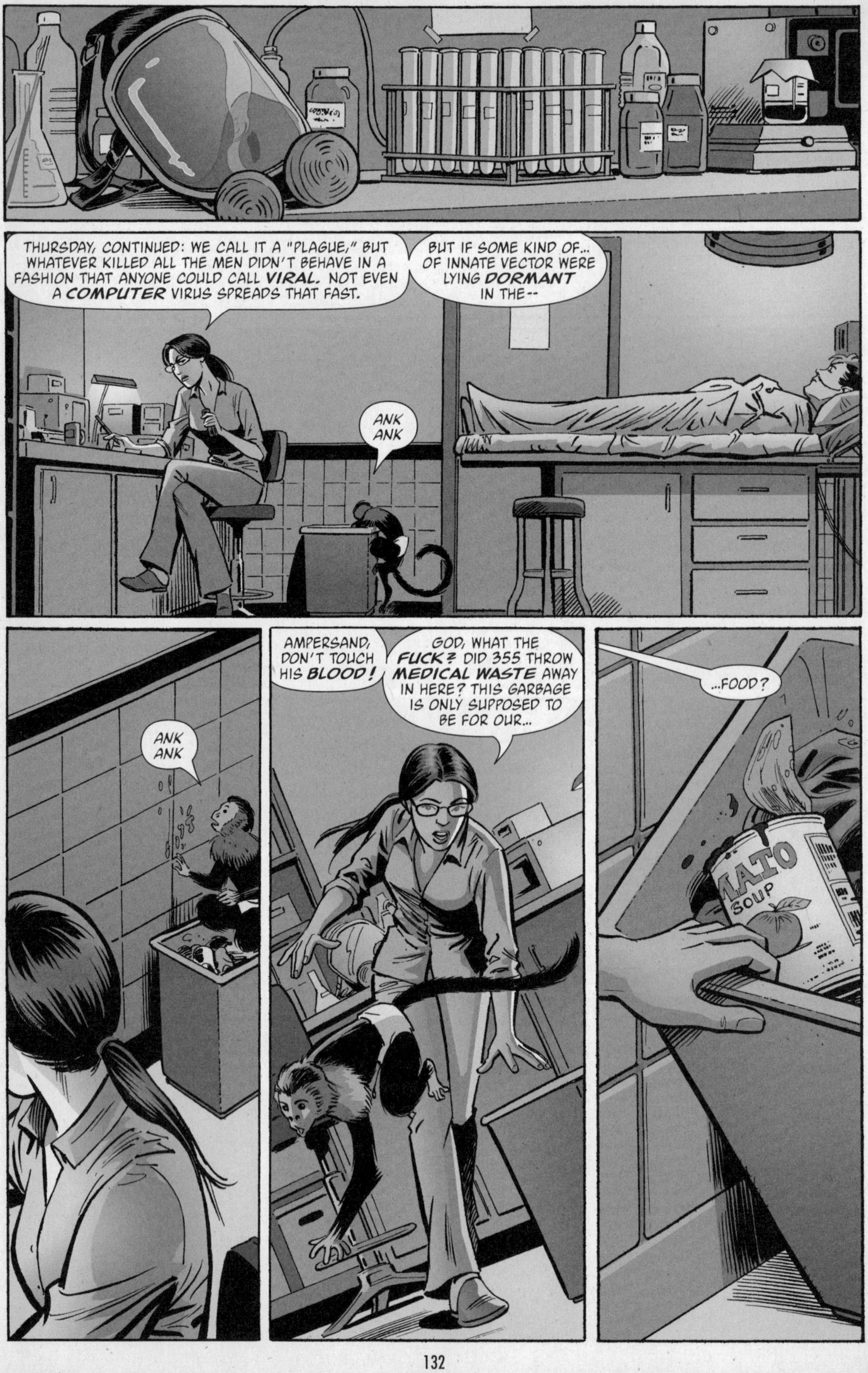
THURSDAY, CONTINUED: WE CALL IT A "PLAGUE," BUT WHATEVER KILLED ALL THE MEN DIDN'T BEHAVE IN A FASHION THAT ANYONE COULD CALL **VIRAL**. NOT EVEN A **COMPUTER** VIRUS SPREADS THAT FAST.
BUT IF SOME KIND OF... OF INNATE VECTOR WERE LYING **DORMANT** IN THE--
ANK ANK
ANK ANK
AMPERSAND, DON'T TOUCH HIS **BLOOD!**
GOD, WHAT THE **FUCK?** DID 355 THROW **MEDICAL WASTE** AWAY IN HERE? THIS GARBAGE IS ONLY SUPPOSED TO BE FOR OUR...
...FOOD?
MATO SOUP

134

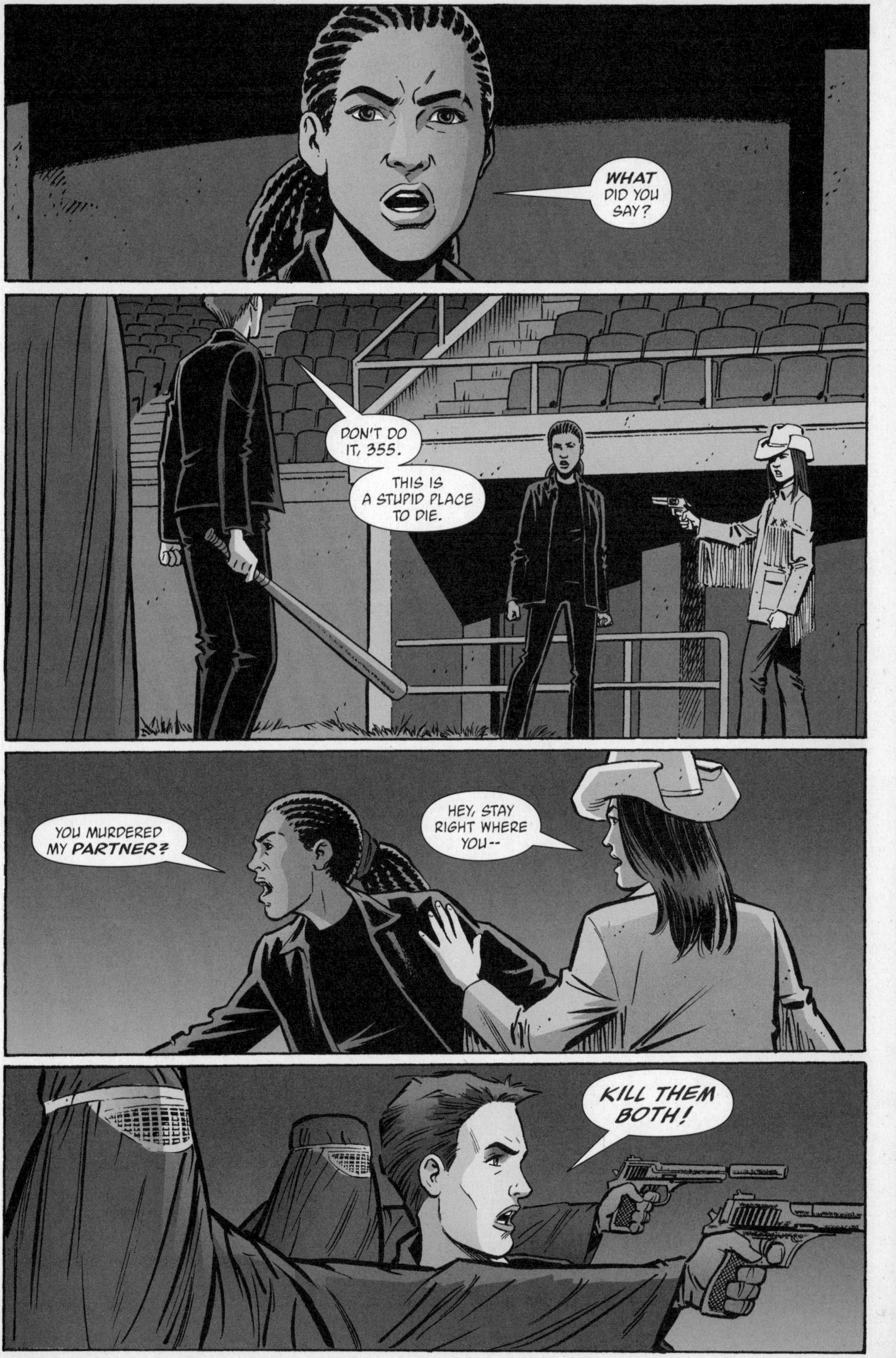
WHAT DID YOU SAY?
DON'T DO IT, 355.
THIS IS A STUPID PLACE TO DIE.
YOU MURDERED MY PARTNER?
HEY, STAY RIGHT WHERE YOU--
KILL THEM BOTH!

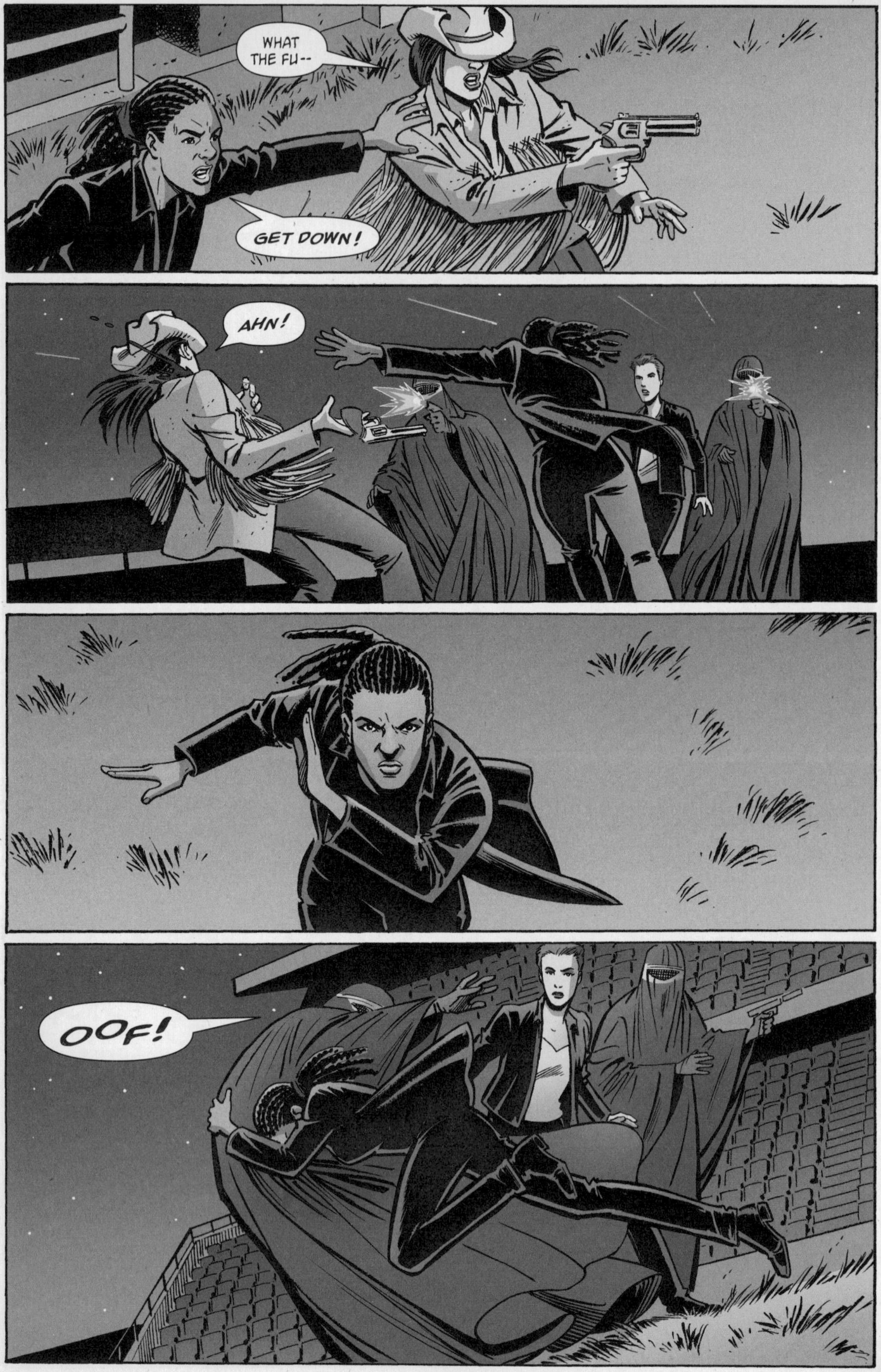

WHAT THE FU--
GET DOWN!
AHN!
OOF!

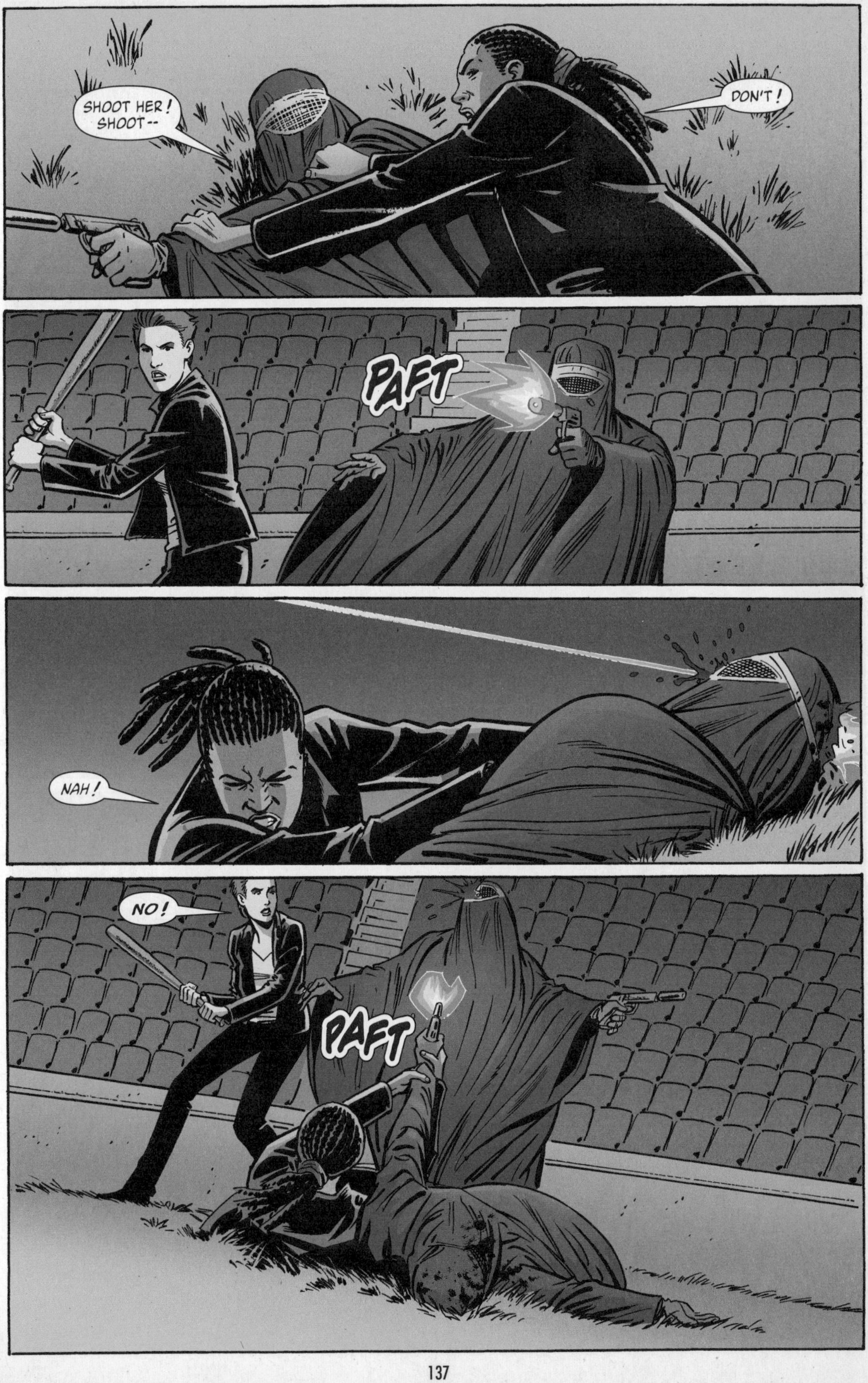
SHOOT HER! SHOOT--
DON'T!
PAFT
NAH!
NO!
PAFT

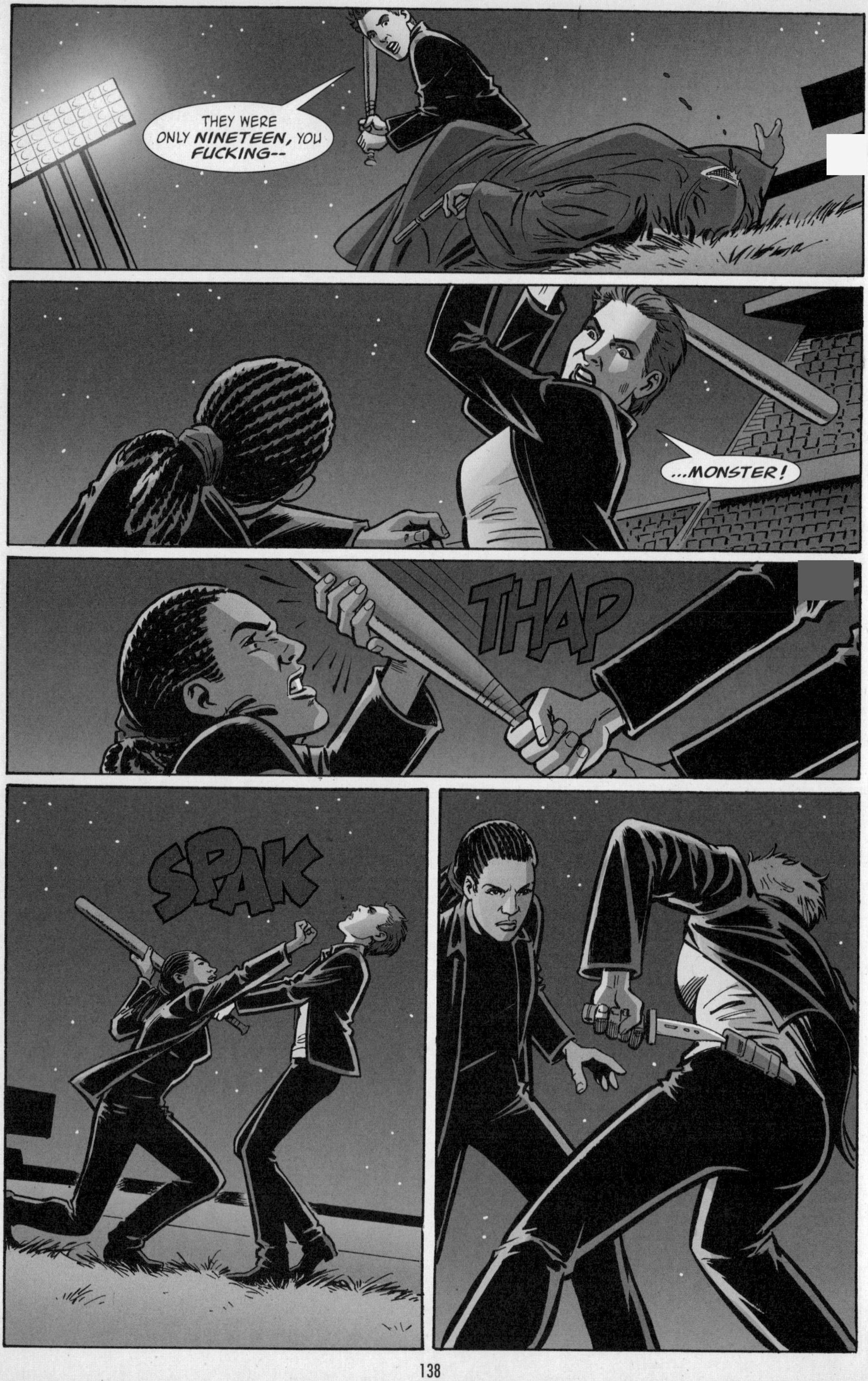
THEY WERE ONLY NINETEEN, YOU FUCKING--
...MONSTER!
THAP
SPAK

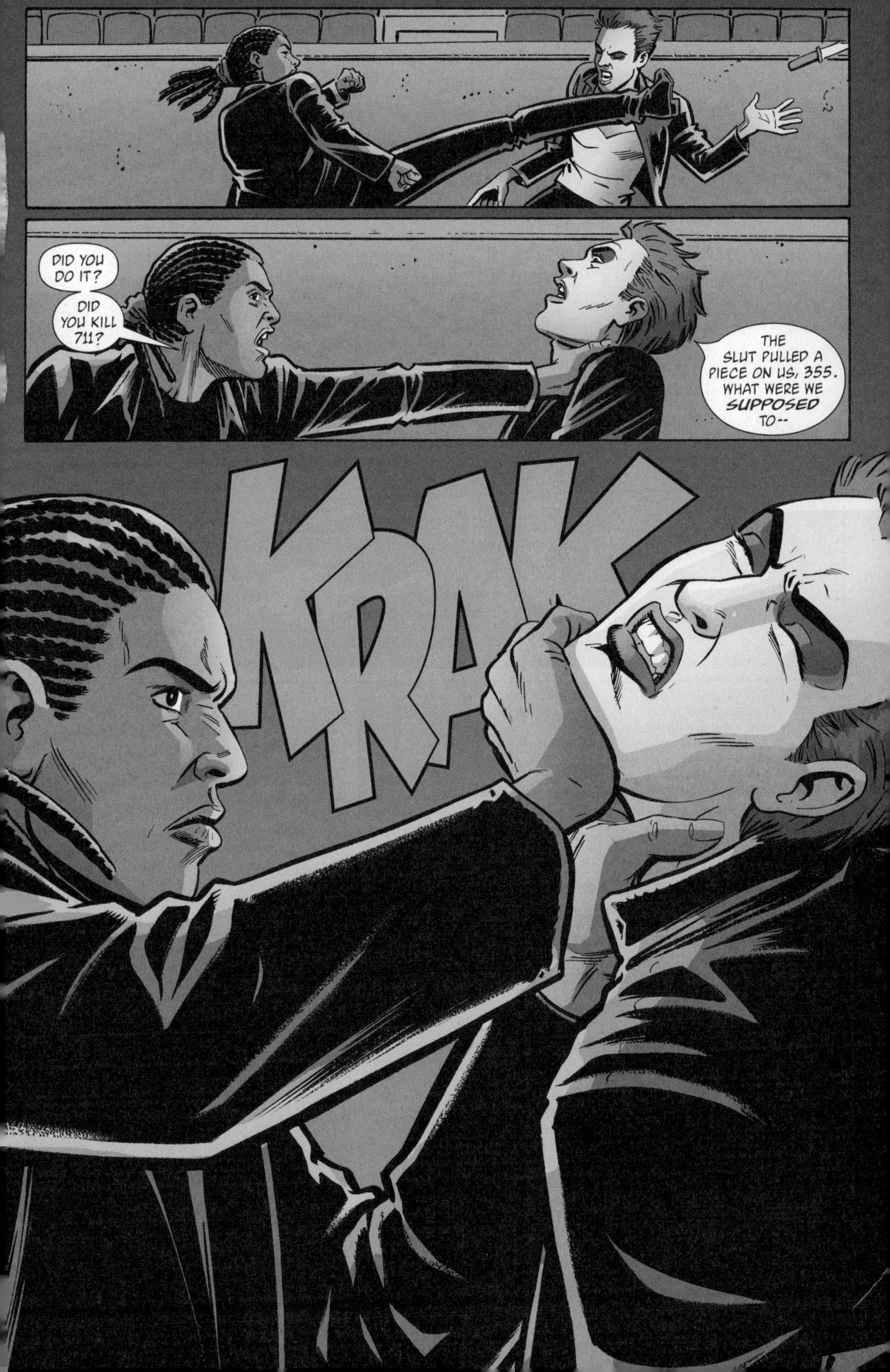
DID YOU DO IT?
DID YOU KILL 711?
THE SLUT PULLED A PIECE ON US, 355. WHAT WERE WE SUPPOSED TO--
KRAK

140

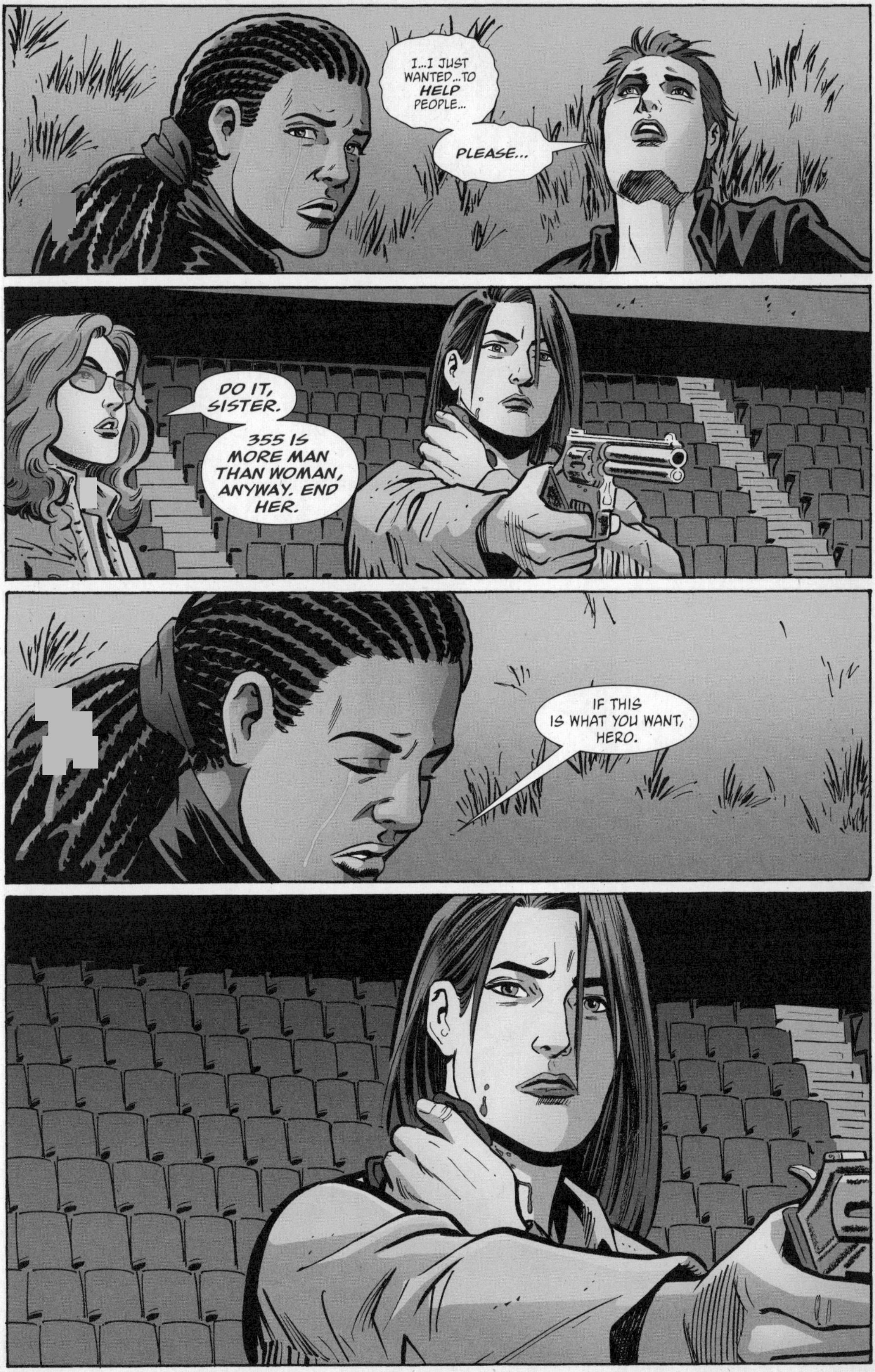
I...I JUST WANTED...TO HELP PEOPLE...
PLEASE...
DO IT, SISTER.
355 IS MORE MAN THAN WOMAN, ANYWAY. END HER.
IF THIS IS WHAT YOU WANT, HERO.

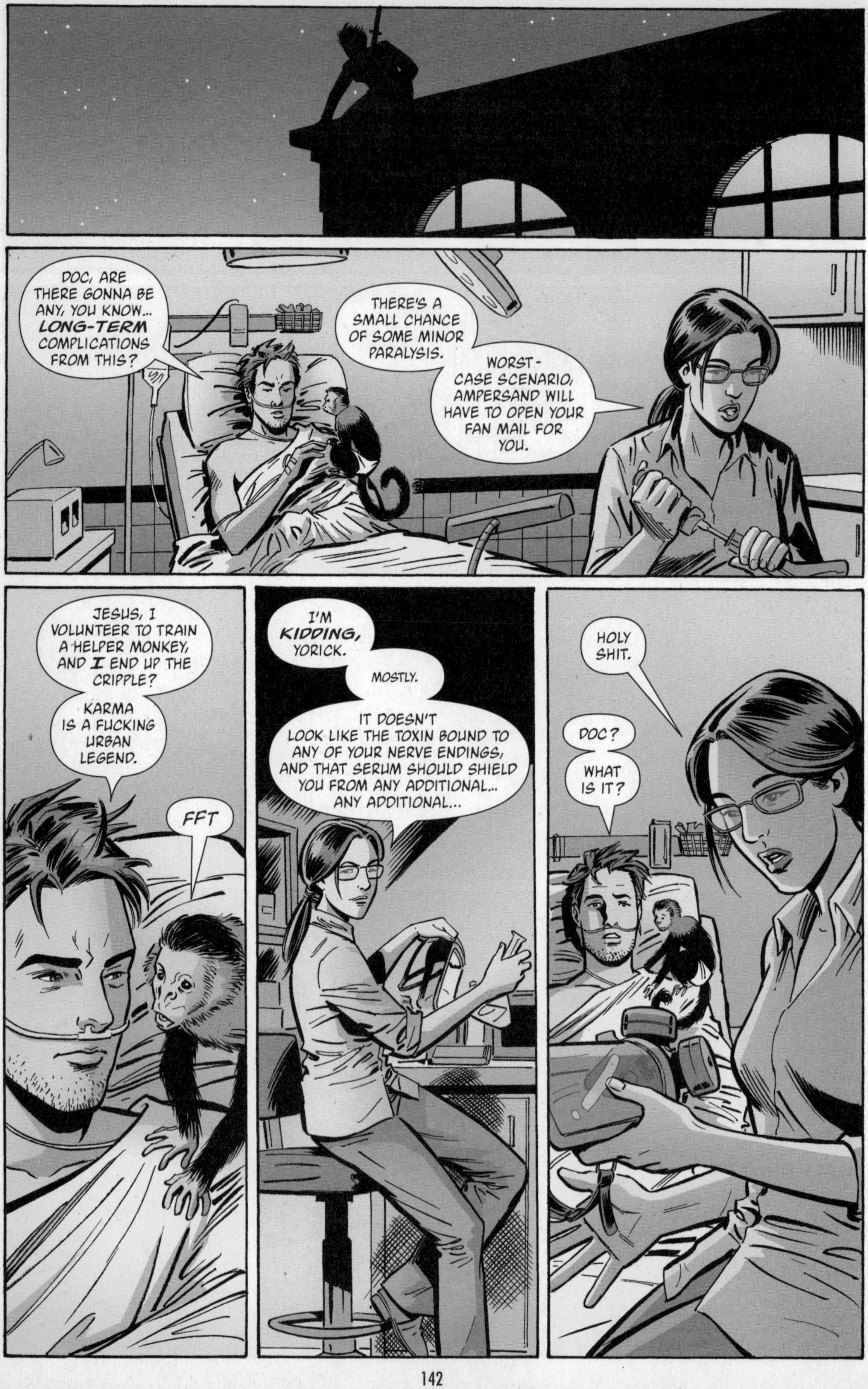
DOC, ARE THERE GONNA BE ANY, YOU KNOW... LONG-TERM COMPLICATIONS FROM THIS?
THERE'S A SMALL CHANCE OF SOME MINOR PARALYSIS.
WORST-CASE SCENARIO, AMPERSAND WILL HAVE TO OPEN YOUR FAN MAIL FOR YOU.
JESUS, I VOLUNTEER TO TRAIN A HELPER MONKEY, AND I END UP THE CRIPPLE?
KARMA IS A FUCKING URBAN LEGEND.
FFT
I'M KIDDING, YORICK.
MOSTLY.
IT DOESN'T LOOK LIKE THE TOXIN BOUND TO ANY OF YOUR NERVE ENDINGS, AND THAT SERUM SHOULD SHIELD YOU FROM ANY ADDITIONAL... ANY ADDITIONAL...
HOLY SHIT.
DOC?
WHAT IS IT?

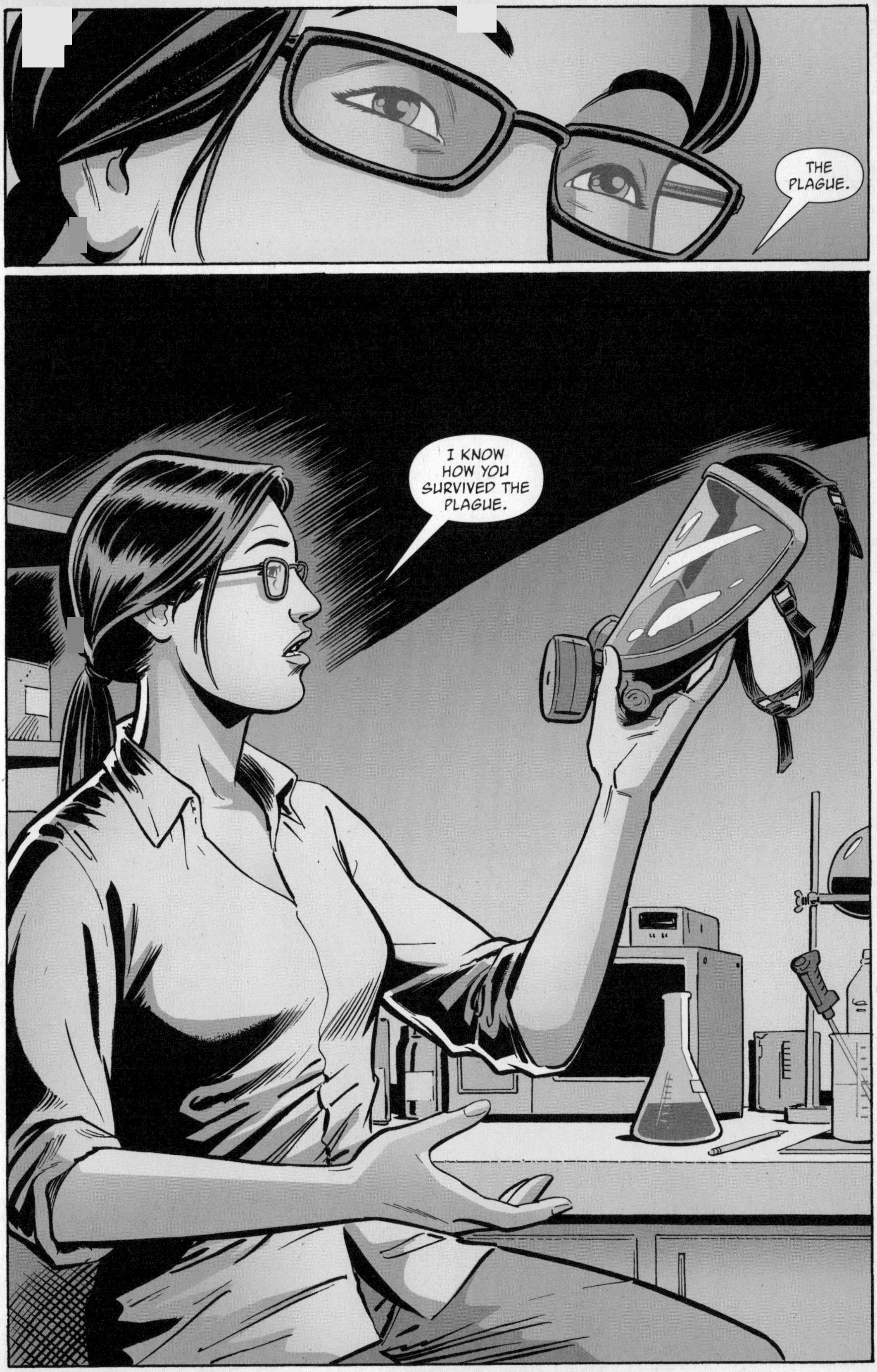
THE PLAGUE.
I KNOW HOW YOU SURVIVED THE PLAGUE.

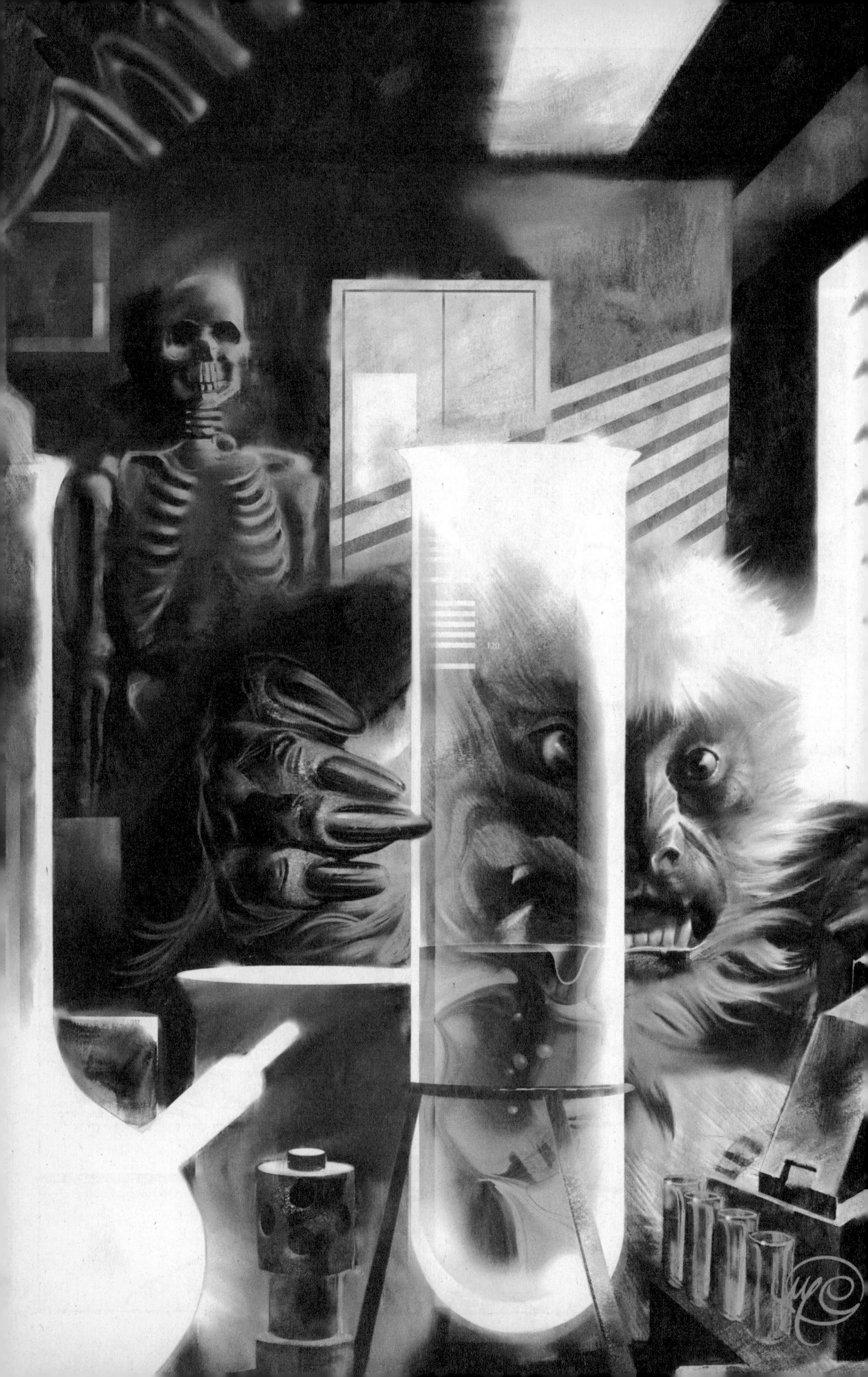
120

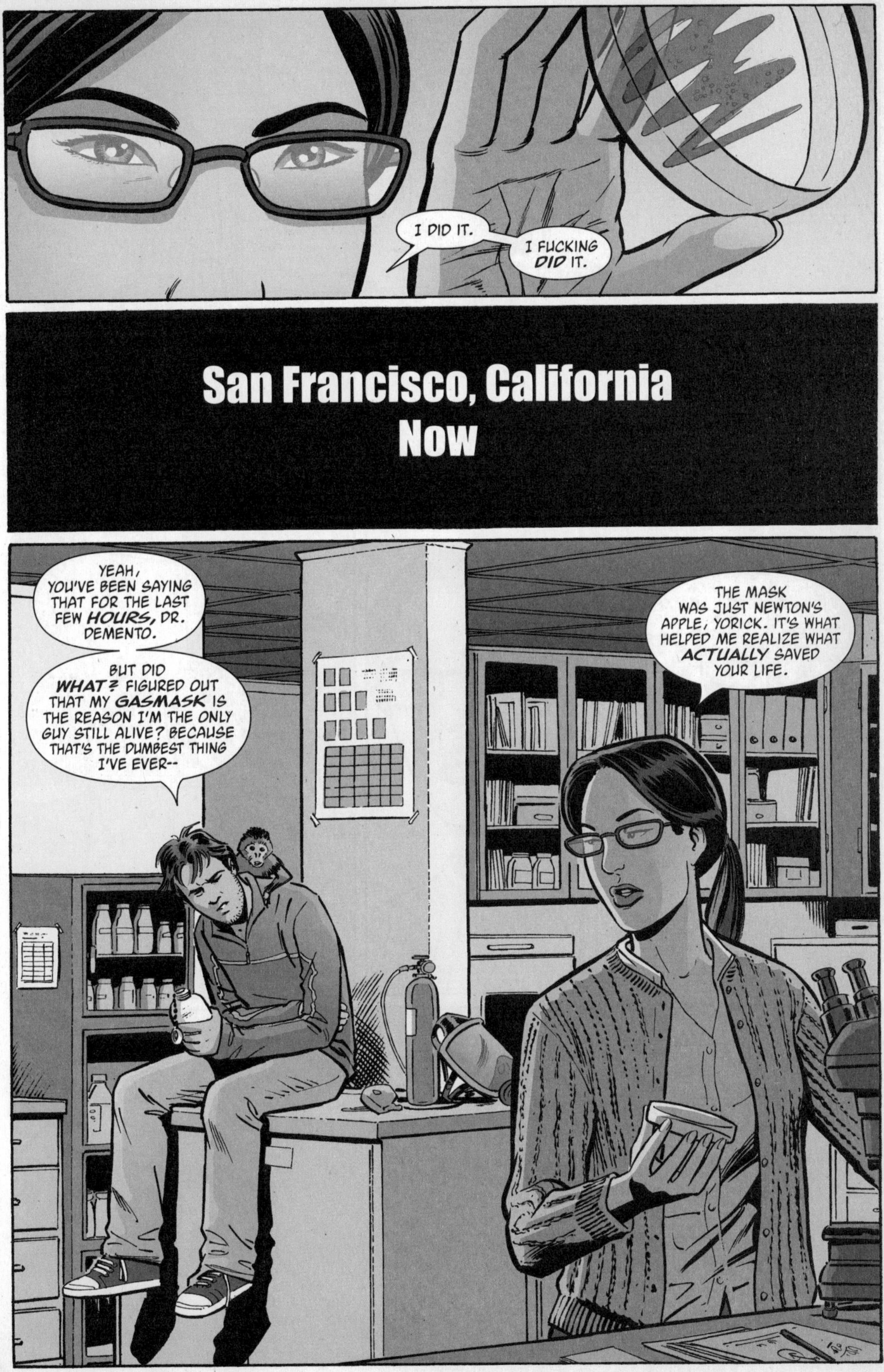
I DID IT.
I FUCKING DID IT.
San Francisco, California
Now
YEAH, YOU'VE BEEN SAYING THAT FOR THE LAST FEW HOURS, DR. DEMENTO.
BUT DID WHAT? FIGURED OUT THAT MY GASMASK IS THE REASON I'M THE ONLY GUY STILL ALIVE? BECAUSE THAT'S THE DUMBEST THING I'VE EVER--
THE MASK WAS JUST NEWTON'S APPLE, YORICK. IT'S WHAT HELPED ME REALIZE WHAT ACTUALLY SAVED YOUR LIFE.

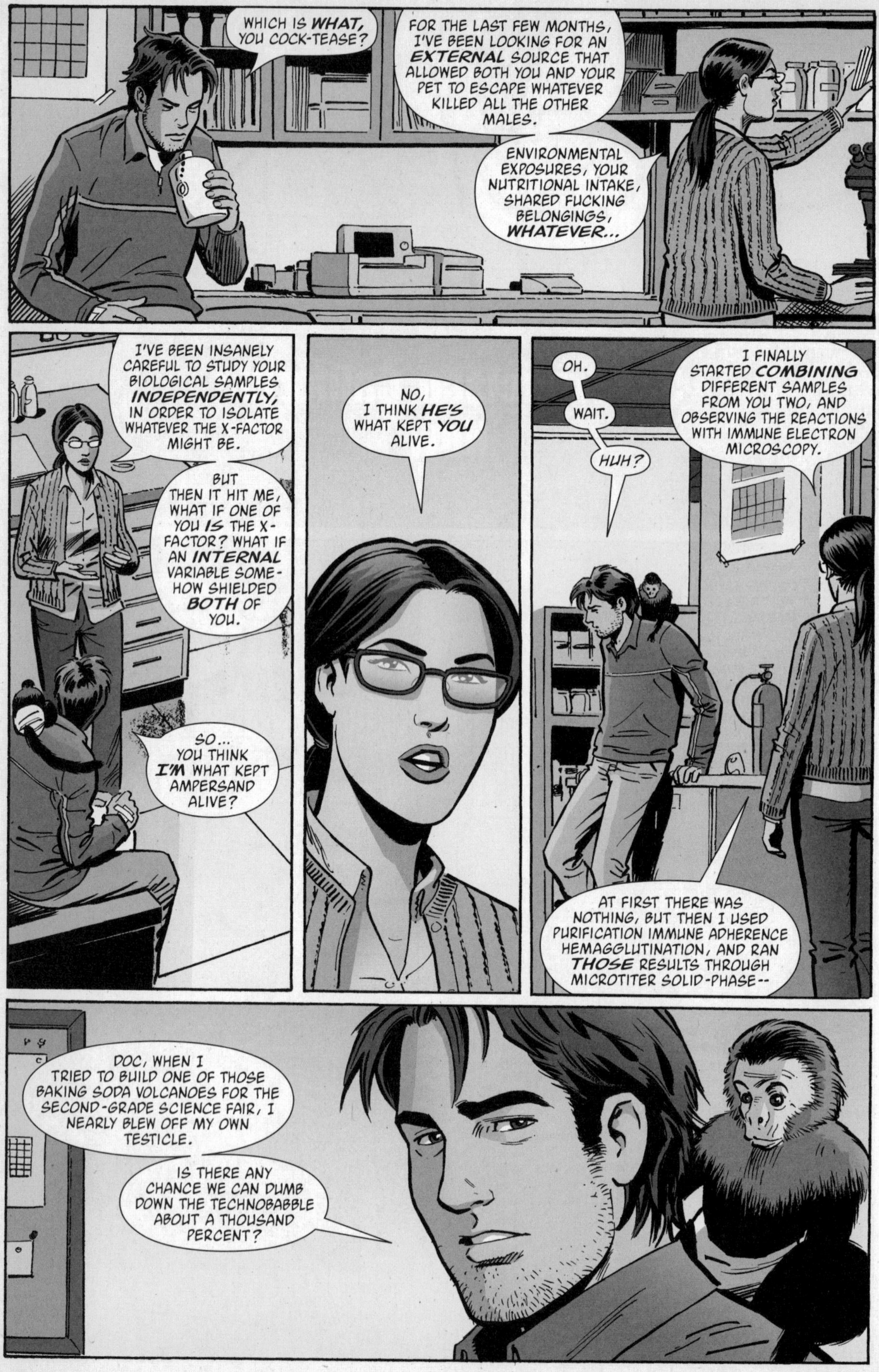
WHICH IS **WHAT,** YOU COCK-TEASE?
FOR THE LAST FEW MONTHS, I'VE BEEN LOOKING FOR AN **EXTERNAL** SOURCE THAT ALLOWED BOTH YOU AND YOUR PET TO ESCAPE WHATEVER KILLED ALL THE OTHER MALES.
ENVIRONMENTAL EXPOSURES, YOUR NUTRITIONAL INTAKE, SHARED FUCKING BELONGINGS, **WHATEVER...**
I'VE BEEN INSANELY CAREFUL TO STUDY YOUR BIOLOGICAL SAMPLES **INDEPENDENTLY,** IN ORDER TO ISOLATE WHATEVER THE X-FACTOR MIGHT BE.
BUT THEN IT HIT ME, WHAT IF ONE OF YOU **IS** THE X-FACTOR? WHAT IF AN **INTERNAL** VARIABLE SOME-HOW SHIELDED **BOTH** OF YOU.
SO... YOU THINK **I'M** WHAT KEPT AMPERSAND ALIVE?
NO, I THINK **HE'S** WHAT KEPT **YOU** ALIVE.
OH.
WAIT.
HUH?
I FINALLY STARTED **COMBINING** DIFFERENT SAMPLES FROM YOU TWO, AND OBSERVING THE REACTIONS WITH IMMUNE ELECTRON MICROSCOPY.
AT FIRST THERE WAS NOTHING, BUT THEN I USED PURIFICATION IMMUNE ADHERENCE HEMAGGLUTINATION, AND RAN **THOSE** RESULTS THROUGH MICROTITER SOLID-PHASE--
DOC, WHEN I TRIED TO BUILD ONE OF THOSE BAKING SODA VOLCANOES FOR THE SECOND-GRADE SCIENCE FAIR, I NEARLY BLEW OFF MY OWN TESTICLE.
IS THERE ANY CHANCE WE CAN DUMB DOWN THE TECHNOBABBLE ABOUT A THOUSAND PERCENT?

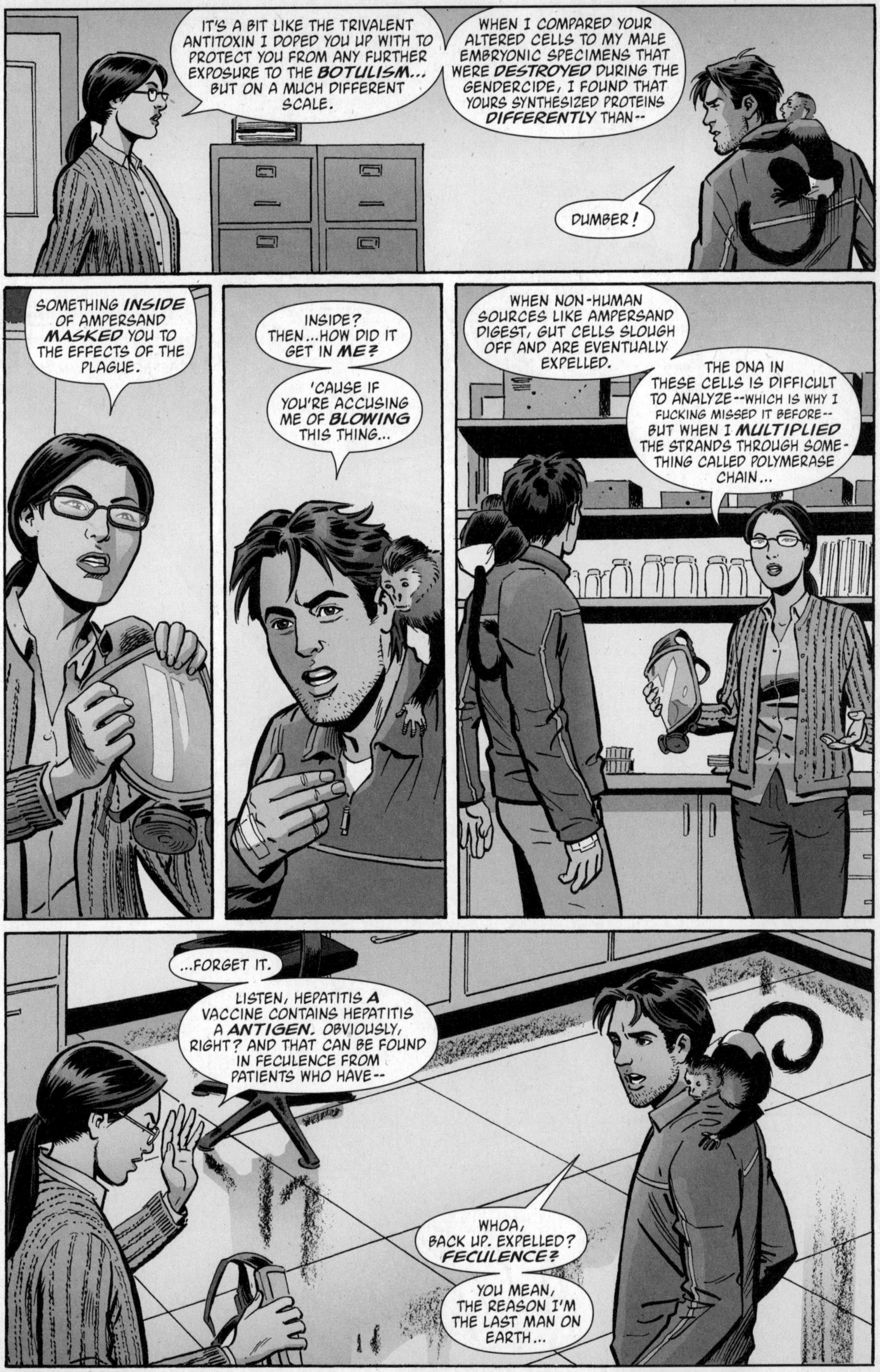
IT'S A BIT LIKE THE TRIVALENT ANTITOXIN I DOPED YOU UP WITH TO PROTECT YOU FROM ANY FURTHER EXPOSURE TO THE BOTULISM... BUT ON A MUCH DIFFERENT SCALE.
WHEN I COMPARED YOUR ALTERED CELLS TO MY MALE EMBRYONIC SPECIMENS THAT WERE DESTROYED DURING THE GENDERCIDE, I FOUND THAT YOURS SYNTHESIZED PROTEINS DIFFERENTLY THAN--
DUMBER!
SOMETHING INSIDE OF AMPERSAND MASKED YOU TO THE EFFECTS OF THE PLAGUE.
INSIDE? THEN...HOW DID IT GET IN ME?
'CAUSE IF YOU'RE ACCUSING ME OF BLOWING THIS THING...
WHEN NON-HUMAN SOURCES LIKE AMPERSAND DIGEST, GUT CELLS SLOUGH OFF AND ARE EVENTUALLY EXPELLED.
THE DNA IN THESE CELLS IS DIFFICULT TO ANALYZE--WHICH IS WHY I FUCKING MISSED IT BEFORE--BUT WHEN I MULTIPLIED THE STRANDS THROUGH SOMETHING CALLED POLYMERASE CHAIN...
...FORGET IT.
LISTEN, HEPATITIS A VACCINE CONTAINS HEPATITIS A ANTIGEN. OBVIOUSLY, RIGHT? AND THAT CAN BE FOUND IN FECULENCE FROM PATIENTS WHO HAVE--
WHOA, BACK UP. EXPELLED? FECULENCE?
YOU MEAN, THE REASON I'M THE LAST MAN ON EARTH...

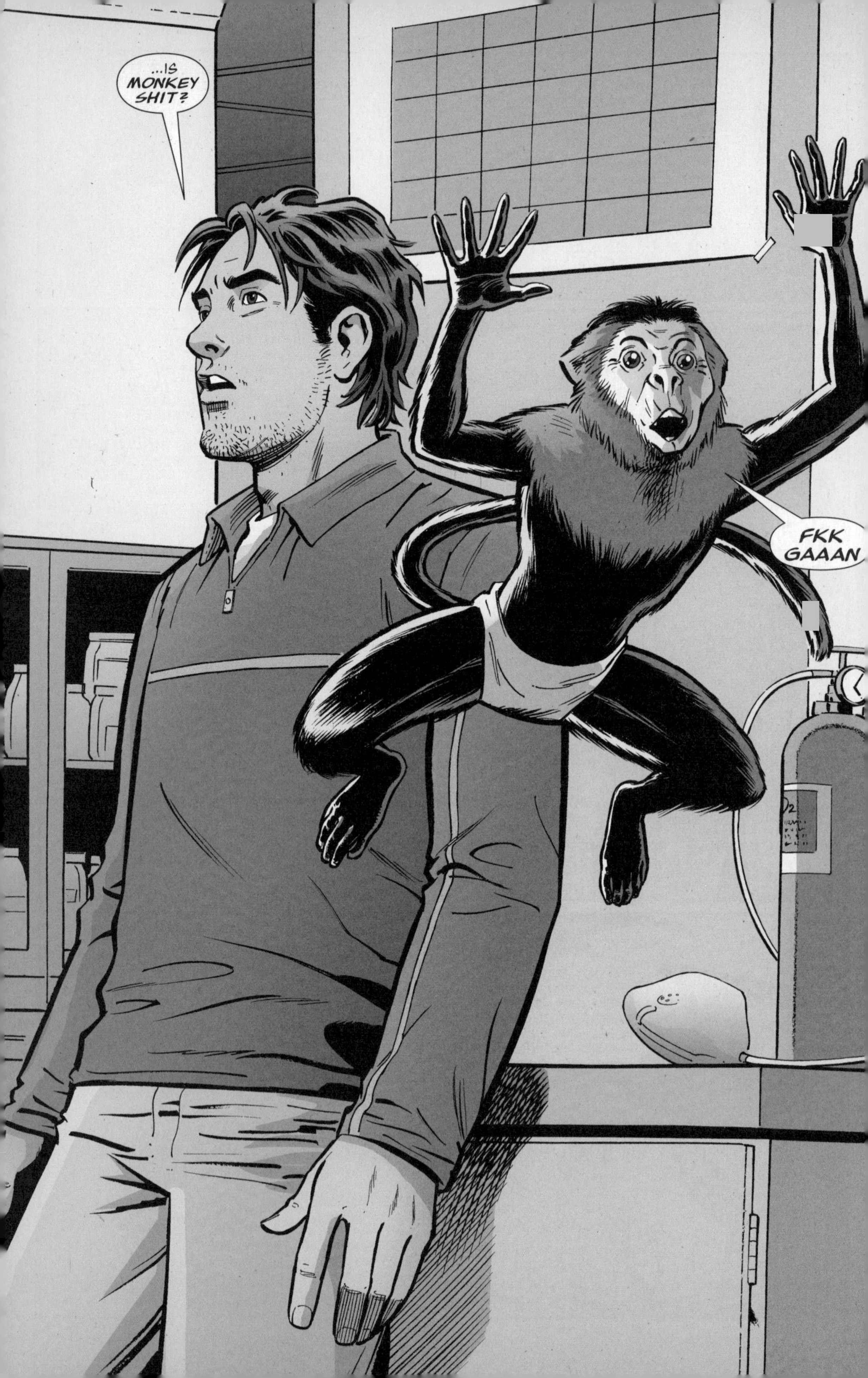
...IS MONKEY SHIT?
FKK GAAAN

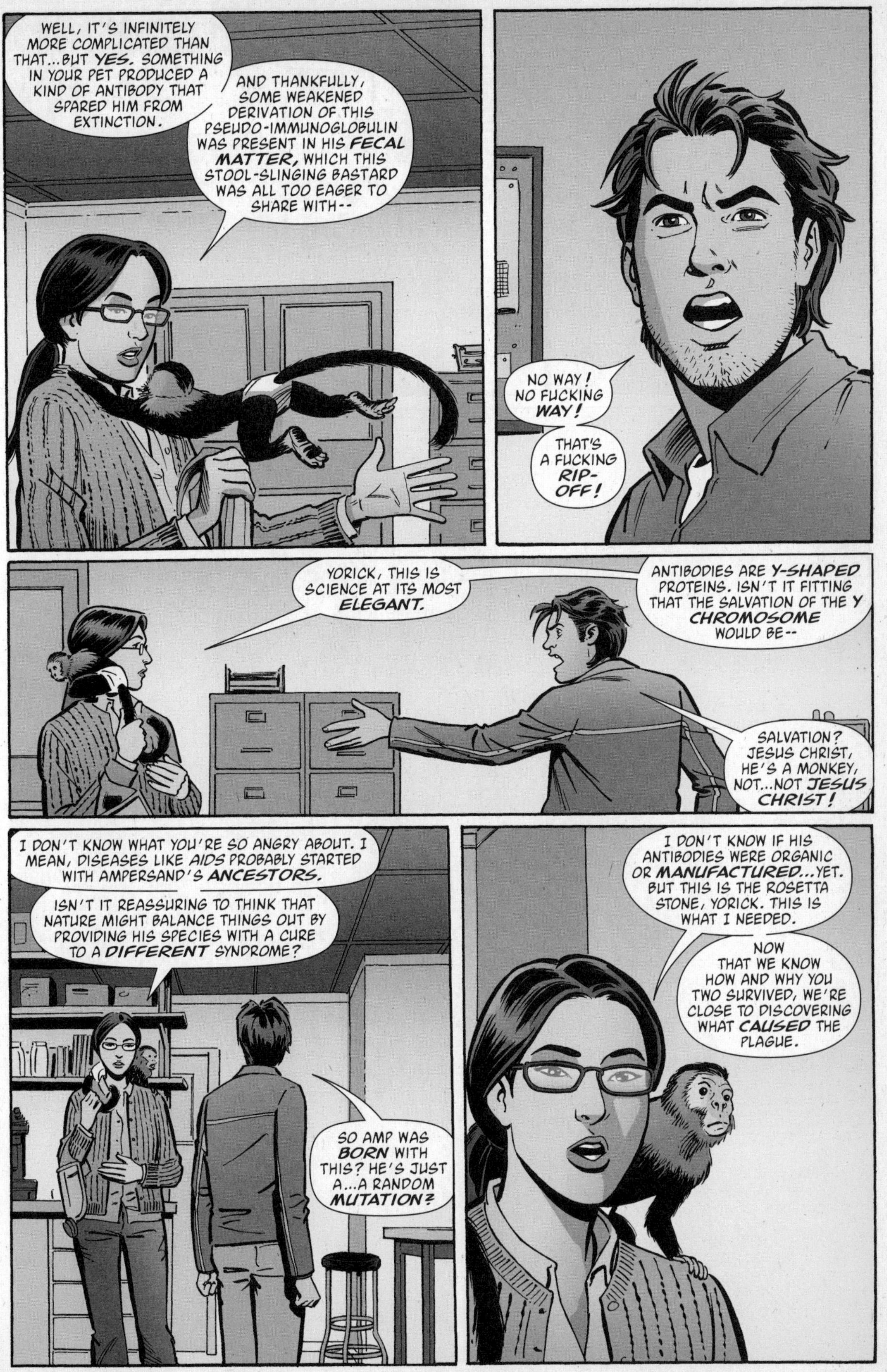

WELL, IT'S INFINITELY MORE COMPLICATED THAN THAT...BUT YES. SOMETHING IN YOUR PET PRODUCED A KIND OF ANTIBODY THAT SPARED HIM FROM EXTINCTION.
AND THANKFULLY, SOME WEAKENED DERIVATION OF THIS PSEUDO-IMMUNOGLOBULIN WAS PRESENT IN HIS FECAL MATTER, WHICH THIS STOOL-SLINGING BASTARD WAS ALL TOO EAGER TO SHARE WITH--
NO WAY! NO FUCKING WAY!
THAT'S A FUCKING RIP-OFF!
YORICK, THIS IS SCIENCE AT ITS MOST ELEGANT.
ANTIBODIES ARE Y-SHAPED PROTEINS. ISN'T IT FITTING THAT THE SALVATION OF THE Y CHROMOSOME WOULD BE--
SALVATION? JESUS CHRIST, HE'S A MONKEY, NOT...NOT JESUS CHRIST!
I DON'T KNOW WHAT YOU'RE SO ANGRY ABOUT. I MEAN, DISEASES LIKE AIDS PROBABLY STARTED WITH AMPERSAND'S ANCESTORS.
ISN'T IT REASSURING TO THINK THAT NATURE MIGHT BALANCE THINGS OUT BY PROVIDING HIS SPECIES WITH A CURE TO A DIFFERENT SYNDROME?
SO AMP WAS BORN WITH THIS? HE'S JUST A...A RANDOM MUTATION?
I DON'T KNOW IF HIS ANTIBODIES WERE ORGANIC OR MANUFACTURED...YET. BUT THIS IS THE ROSETTA STONE, YORICK. THIS IS WHAT I NEEDED.
NOW THAT WE KNOW HOW AND WHY YOU TWO SURVIVED, WE'RE CLOSE TO DISCOVERING WHAT CAUSED THE PLAGUE.

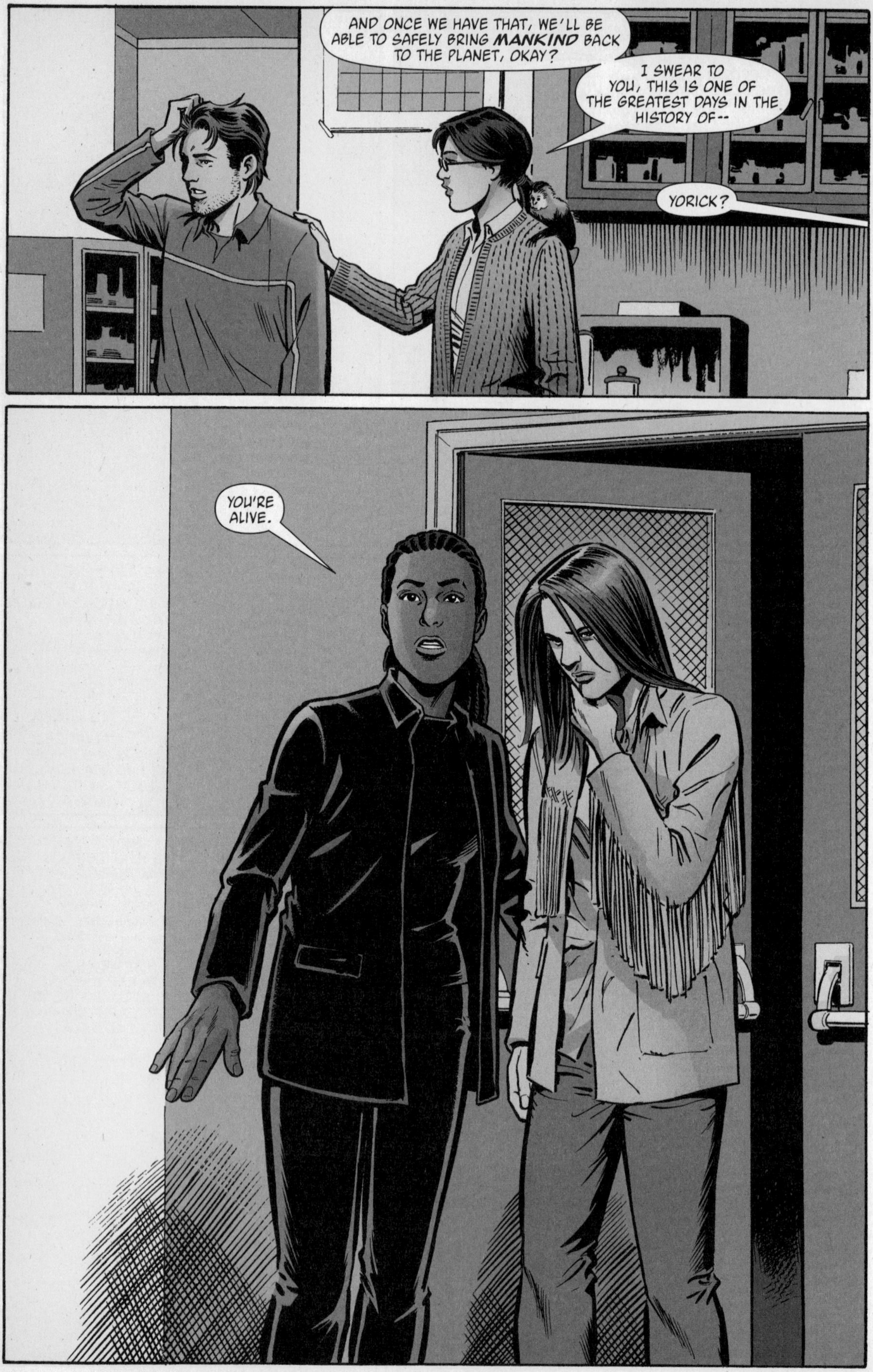
AND ONCE WE HAVE THAT, WE'LL BE ABLE TO SAFELY BRING MANKIND BACK TO THE PLANET, OKAY?
I SWEAR TO YOU, THIS IS ONE OF THE GREATEST DAYS IN THE HISTORY OF--
YORICK?
YOU'RE ALIVE.

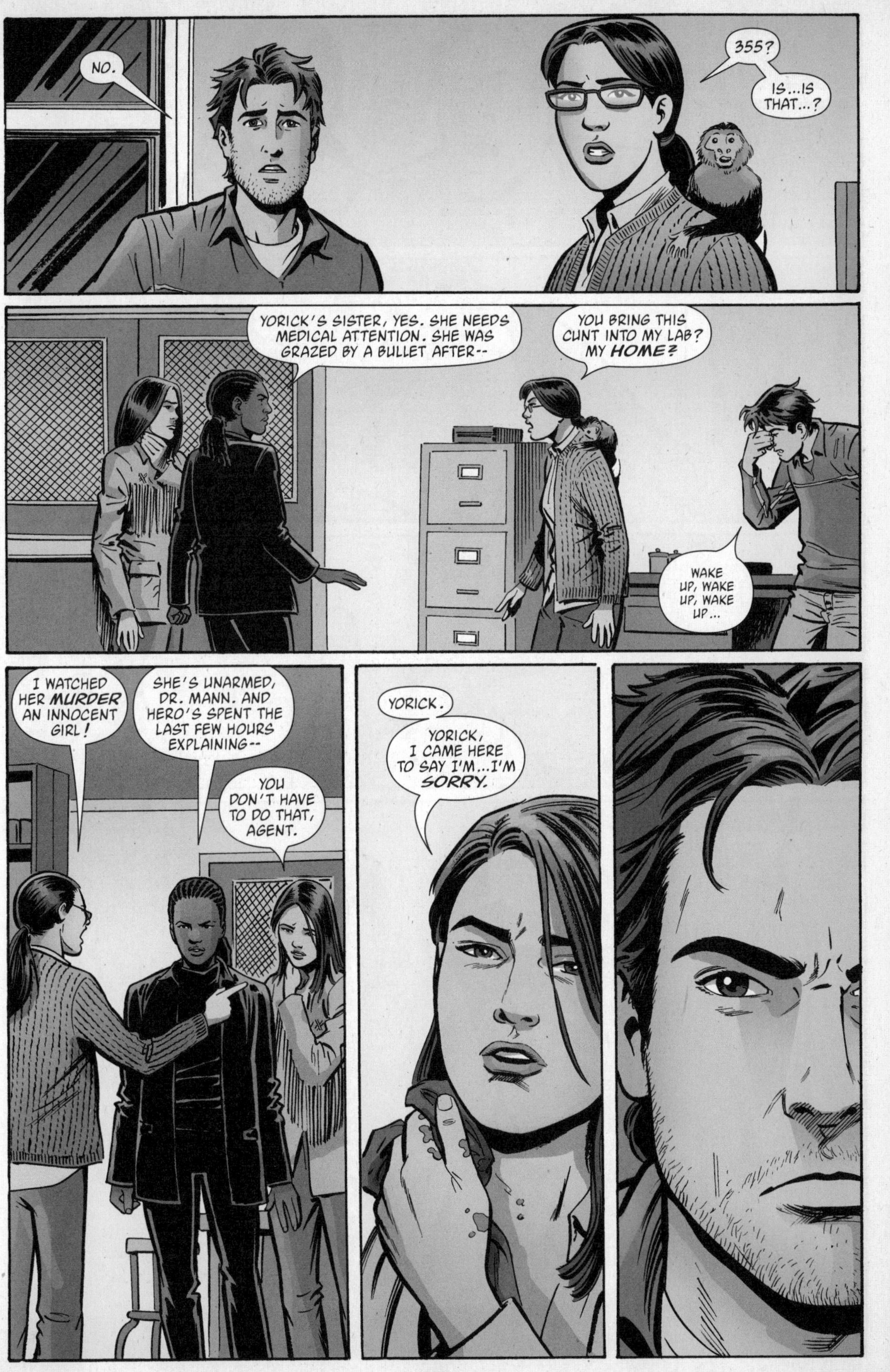
NO.
355?
IS...IS THAT...?
YORICK'S SISTER, YES. SHE NEEDS MEDICAL ATTENTION. SHE WAS GRAZED BY A BULLET AFTER--
YOU BRING THIS CUNT INTO MY LAB? MY HOME?
WAKE UP, WAKE UP, WAKE UP...
I WATCHED HER MURDER AN INNOCENT GIRL!
SHE'S UNARMED, DR. MANN. AND HERO'S SPENT THE LAST FEW HOURS EXPLAINING--
YOU DON'T HAVE TO DO THAT, AGENT.
YORICK.
YORICK, I CAME HERE TO SAY I'M...I'M SORRY.

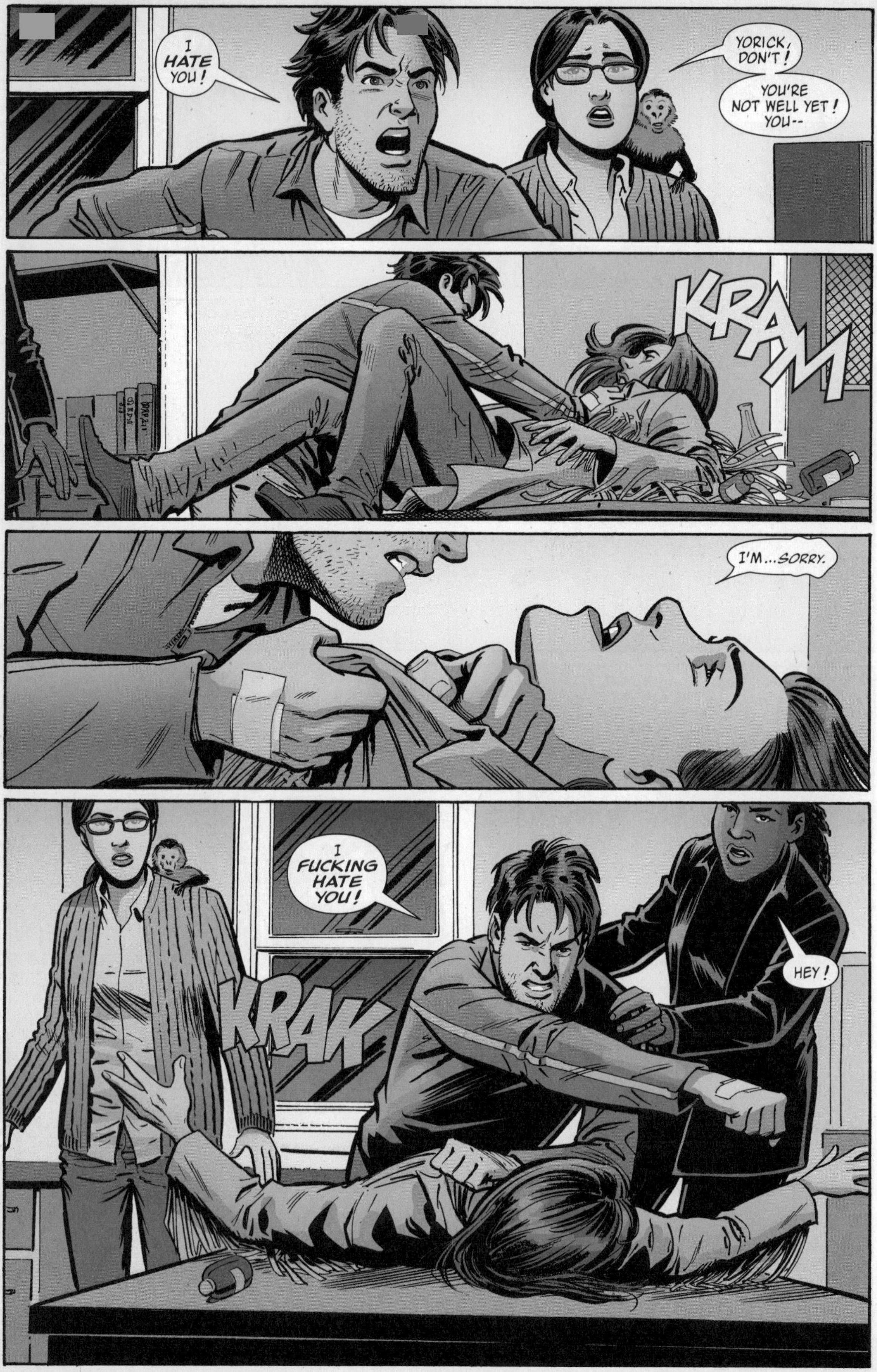
I HATE YOU!
YORICK, DON'T!
YOU'RE NOT WELL YET! YOU--
KRAM
I'M...SORRY.
I FUCKING HATE YOU!
KRAK
HEY!

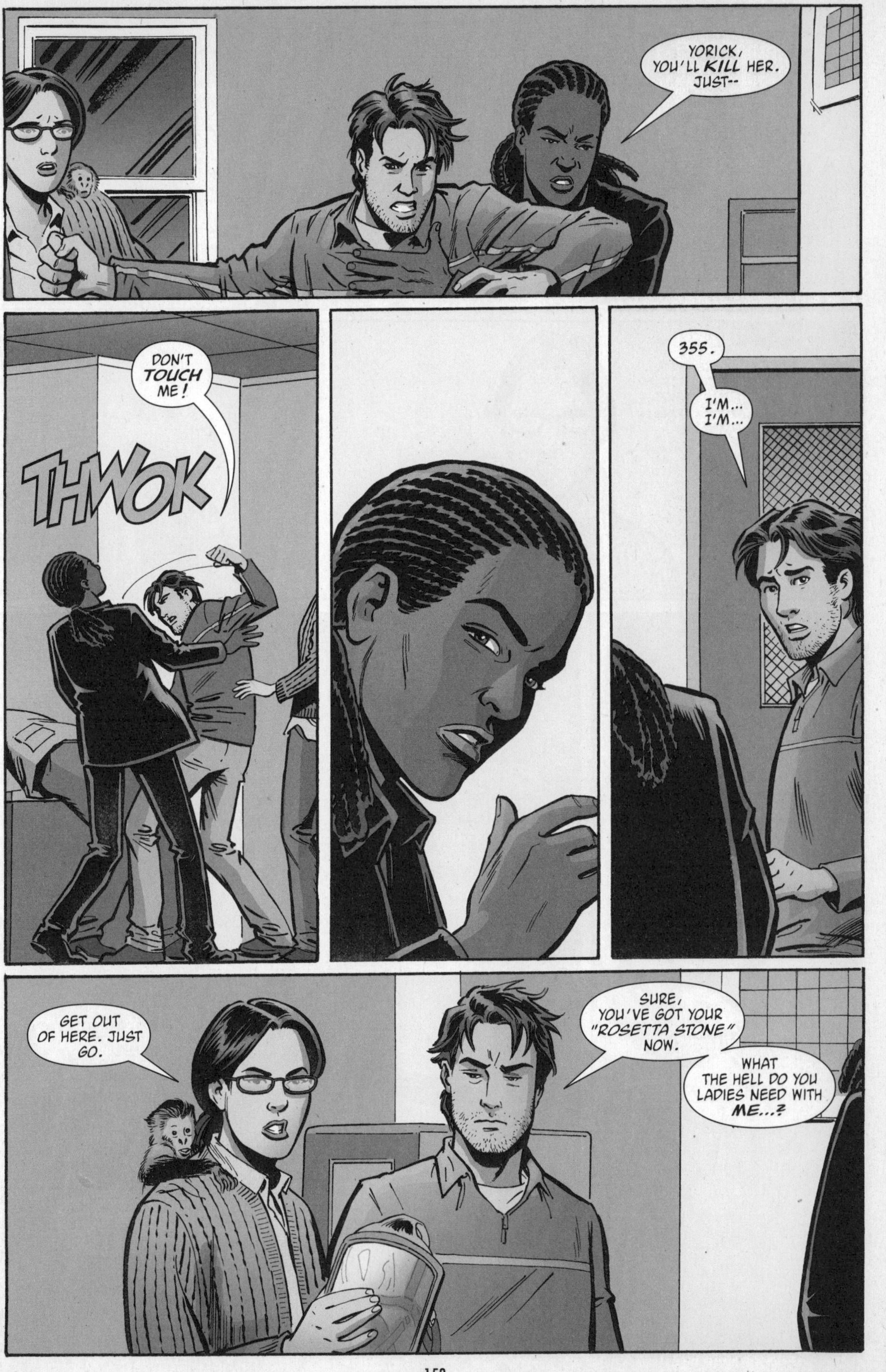
YORICK, YOU'LL KILL HER. JUST--
DON'T TOUCH ME!
THWOK
355.
I'M... I'M...
GET OUT OF HERE. JUST GO.
SURE, YOU'VE GOT YOUR "ROSETTA STONE" NOW.
WHAT THE HELL DO YOU LADIES NEED WITH ME...?

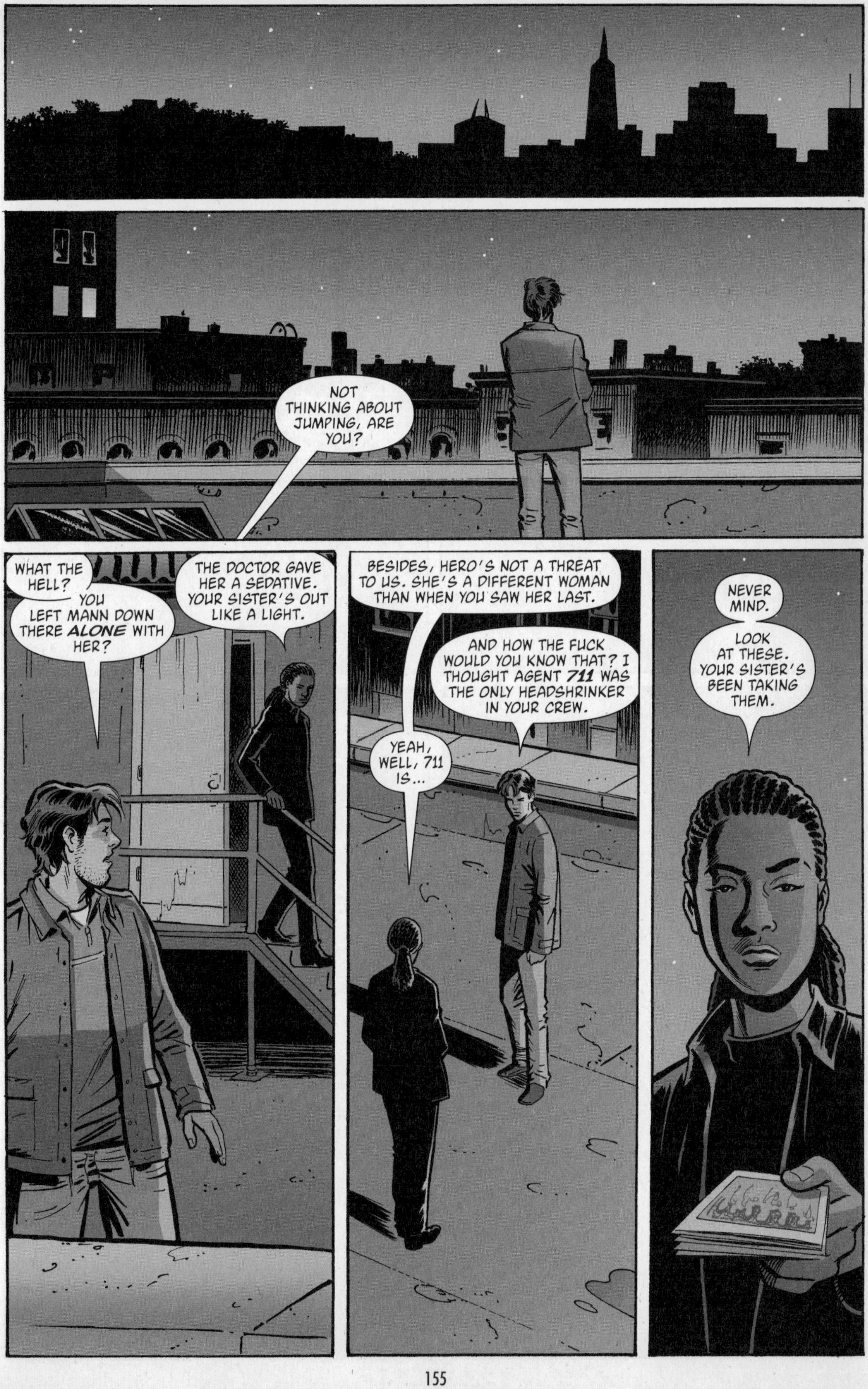
NOT THINKING ABOUT JUMPING, ARE YOU?
WHAT THE HELL?
YOU LEFT MANN DOWN THERE ALONE WITH HER?
THE DOCTOR GAVE HER A SEDATIVE. YOUR SISTER'S OUT LIKE A LIGHT.
BESIDES, HERO'S NOT A THREAT TO US. SHE'S A DIFFERENT WOMAN THAN WHEN YOU SAW HER LAST.
AND HOW THE FUCK WOULD YOU KNOW THAT? I THOUGHT AGENT 711 WAS THE ONLY HEADSHRINKER IN YOUR CREW.
YEAH, WELL, 711 IS...
NEVER MIND.
LOOK AT THESE. YOUR SISTER'S BEEN TAKING THEM.

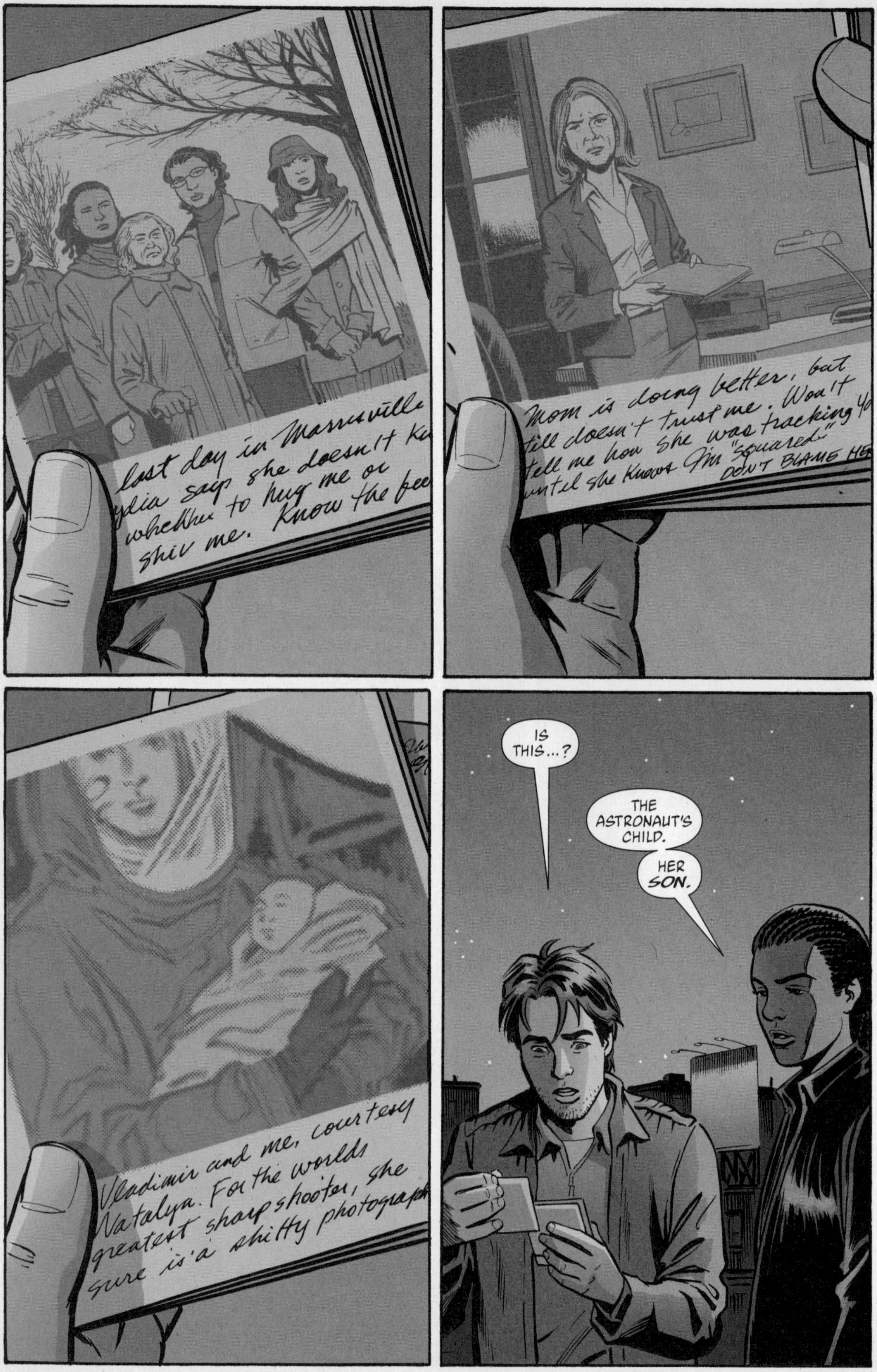
last day in Marrsvill
ylia says she doesn't k
whether to hug me or
shiv me. Know the fee
Mom is doing better, but
till doesn't trust me. Won't
tell me how she was tracking y
until she knows I'm "squared."
DON'T BLAME HE
Vladimir and me, courtesy
Natalya. For the worlds
greatest sharpshooter, she
sure is a shitty photograp
IS THIS...?
THE ASTRONAUT'S CHILD.
HER SON.

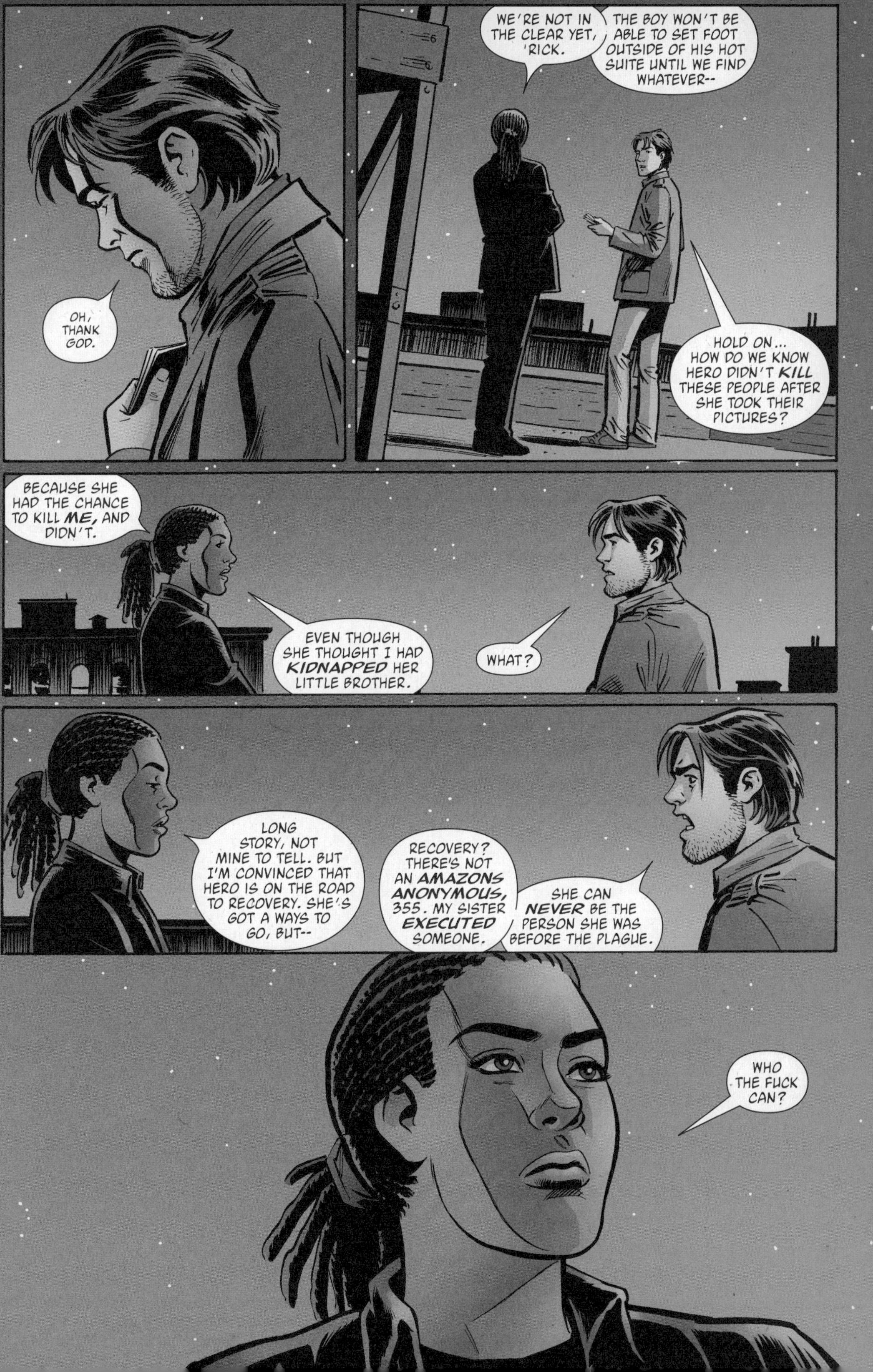
OH, THANK GOD.
WE'RE NOT IN THE CLEAR YET, 'RICK.
THE BOY WON'T BE ABLE TO SET FOOT OUTSIDE OF HIS HOT SUITE UNTIL WE FIND WHATEVER--
HOLD ON... HOW DO WE KNOW HERO DIDN'T KILL THESE PEOPLE AFTER SHE TOOK THEIR PICTURES?
BECAUSE SHE HAD THE CHANCE TO KILL ME, AND DIDN'T.
EVEN THOUGH SHE THOUGHT I HAD KIDNAPPED HER LITTLE BROTHER.
WHAT?
LONG STORY, NOT MINE TO TELL. BUT I'M CONVINCED THAT HERO IS ON THE ROAD TO RECOVERY. SHE'S GOT A WAYS TO GO, BUT--
RECOVERY? THERE'S NOT AN AMAZONS ANONYMOUS, 355. MY SISTER EXECUTED SOMEONE.
SHE CAN NEVER BE THE PERSON SHE WAS BEFORE THE PLAGUE.
WHO THE FUCK CAN?

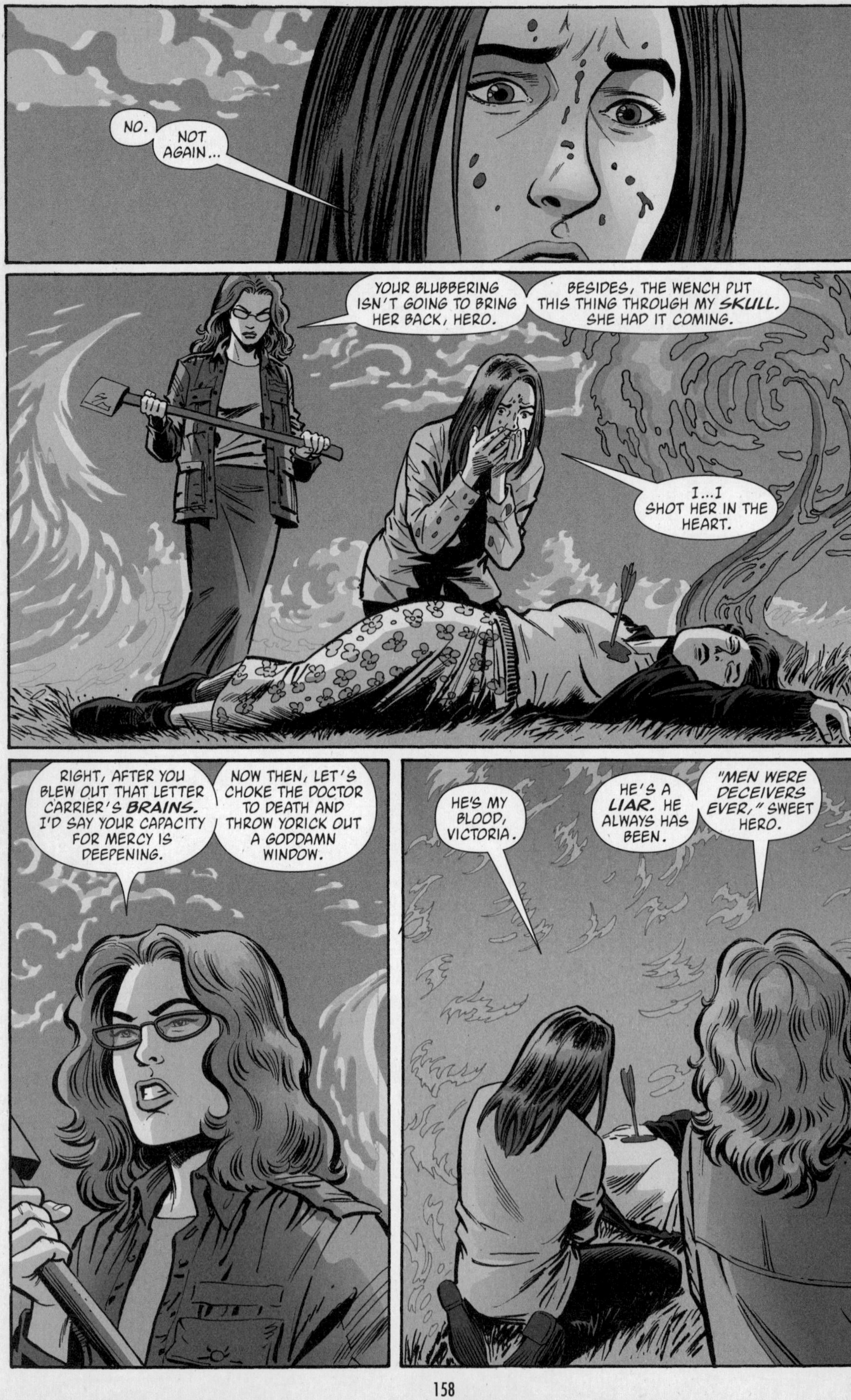
NO.
NOT AGAIN...
YOUR BLUBBERING ISN'T GOING TO BRING HER BACK, HERO.
BESIDES, THE WENCH PUT THIS THING THROUGH MY **SKULL.** SHE HAD IT COMING.
I...I SHOT HER IN THE HEART.
RIGHT, AFTER YOU BLEW OUT THAT LETTER CARRIER'S **BRAINS.** I'D SAY YOUR CAPACITY FOR MERCY IS DEEPENING.
NOW THEN, LET'S CHOKE THE DOCTOR TO DEATH AND THROW YORICK OUT A GODDAMN WINDOW.
HE'S MY BLOOD, VICTORIA.
HE'S A **LIAR.** HE ALWAYS HAS BEEN.
"MEN WERE DECEIVERS EVER," SWEET HERO.

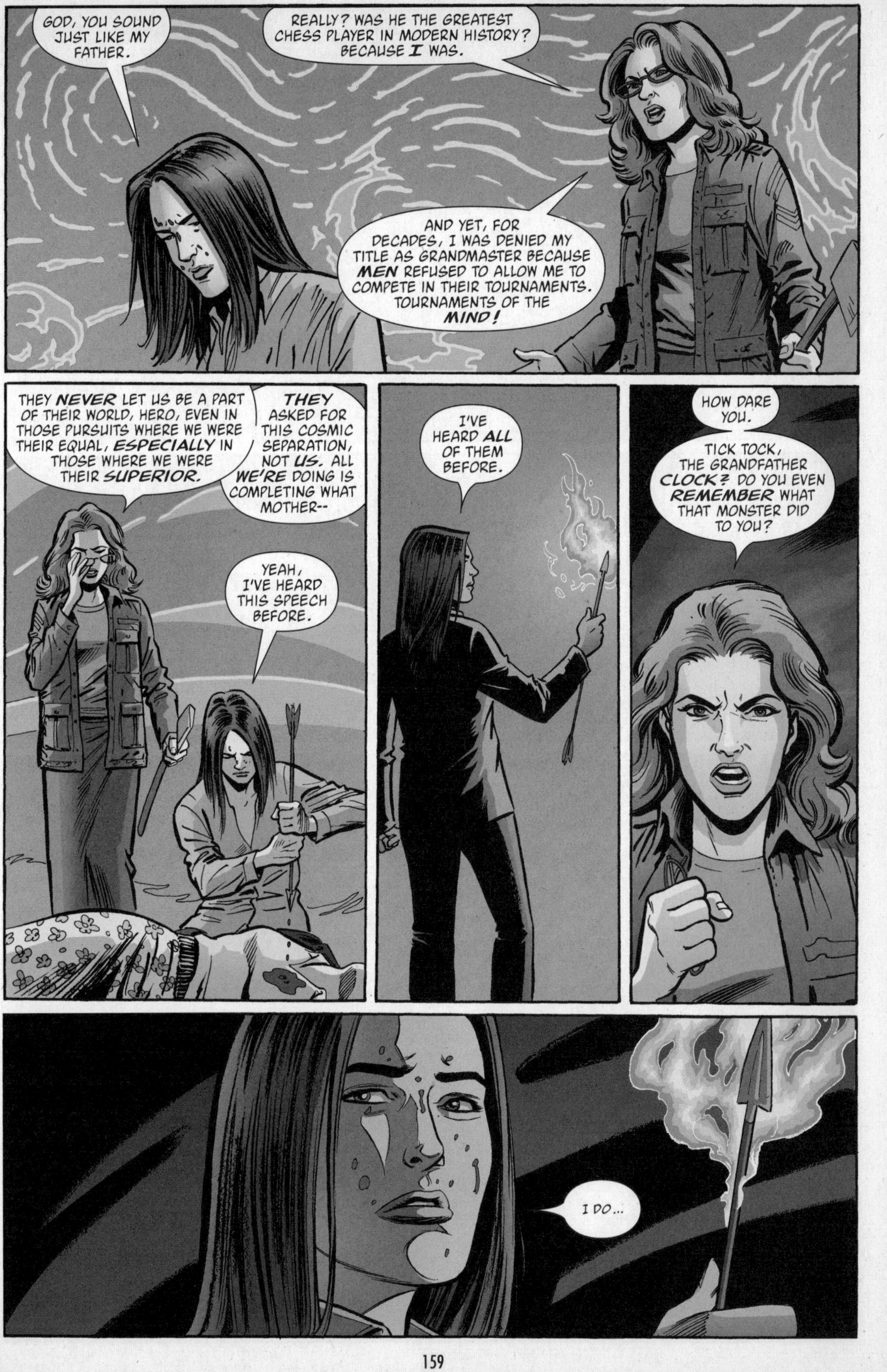
GOD, YOU SOUND JUST LIKE MY FATHER.
REALLY? WAS HE THE GREATEST CHESS PLAYER IN MODERN HISTORY? BECAUSE *I* WAS.
AND YET, FOR DECADES, I WAS DENIED MY TITLE AS GRANDMASTER BECAUSE *MEN* REFUSED TO ALLOW ME TO COMPETE IN THEIR TOURNAMENTS. TOURNAMENTS OF THE *MIND!*
THEY *NEVER* LET US BE A PART OF THEIR WORLD, HERO, EVEN IN THOSE PURSUITS WHERE WE WERE THEIR EQUAL, *ESPECIALLY* IN THOSE WHERE WE WERE THEIR *SUPERIOR.*
THEY ASKED FOR THIS COSMIC SEPARATION, NOT *US.* ALL *WE'RE* DOING IS COMPLETING WHAT MOTHER--
YEAH, I'VE HEARD THIS SPEECH BEFORE.
I'VE HEARD *ALL* OF THEM BEFORE.
HOW DARE YOU.
TICK TOCK, THE GRANDFATHER *CLOCK?* DO YOU EVEN *REMEMBER* WHAT THAT MONSTER DID TO YOU?
I DO...

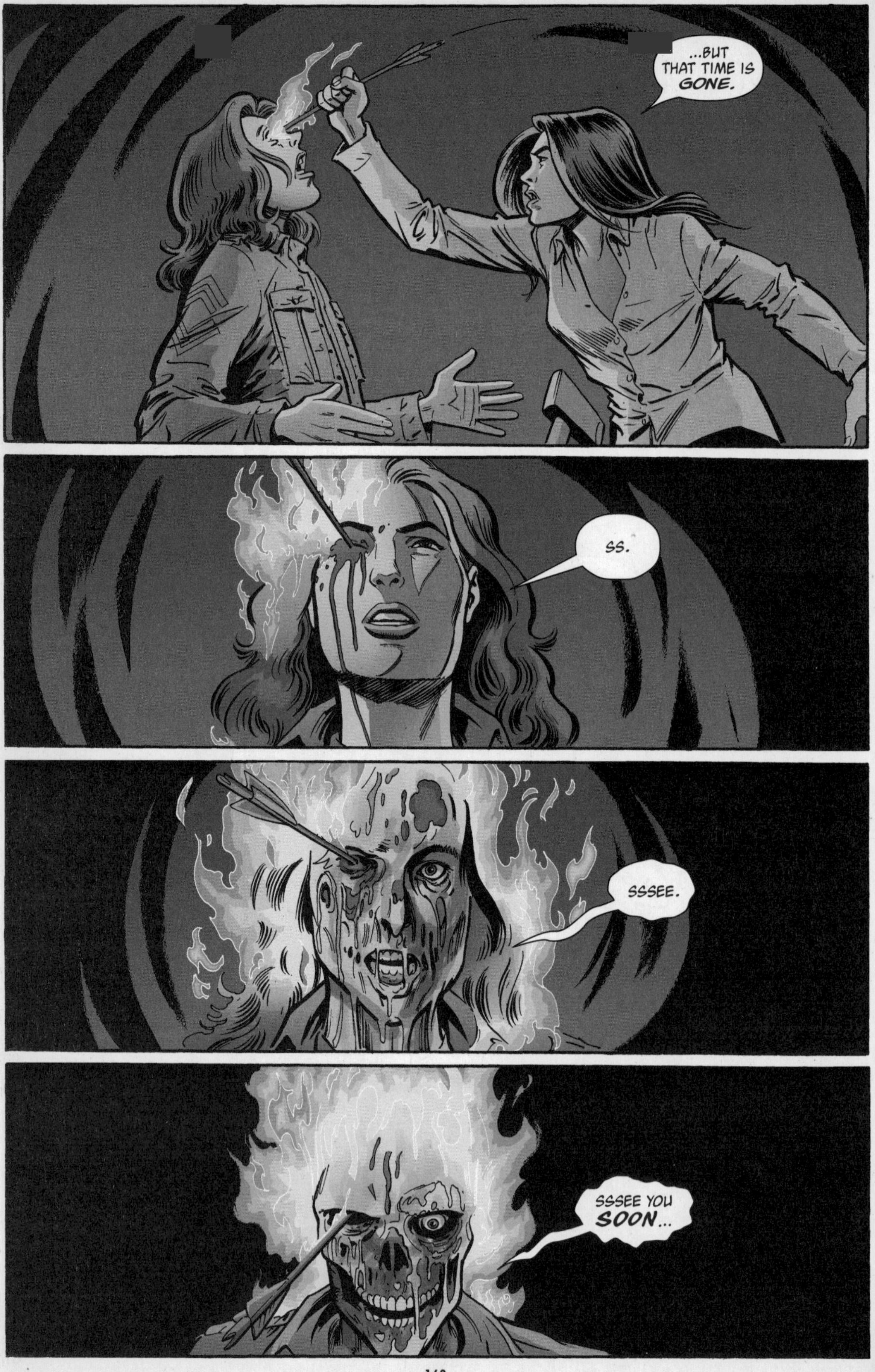
...BUT THAT TIME IS GONE.
SS.
SSSEE.
SSSEE YOU SOON...

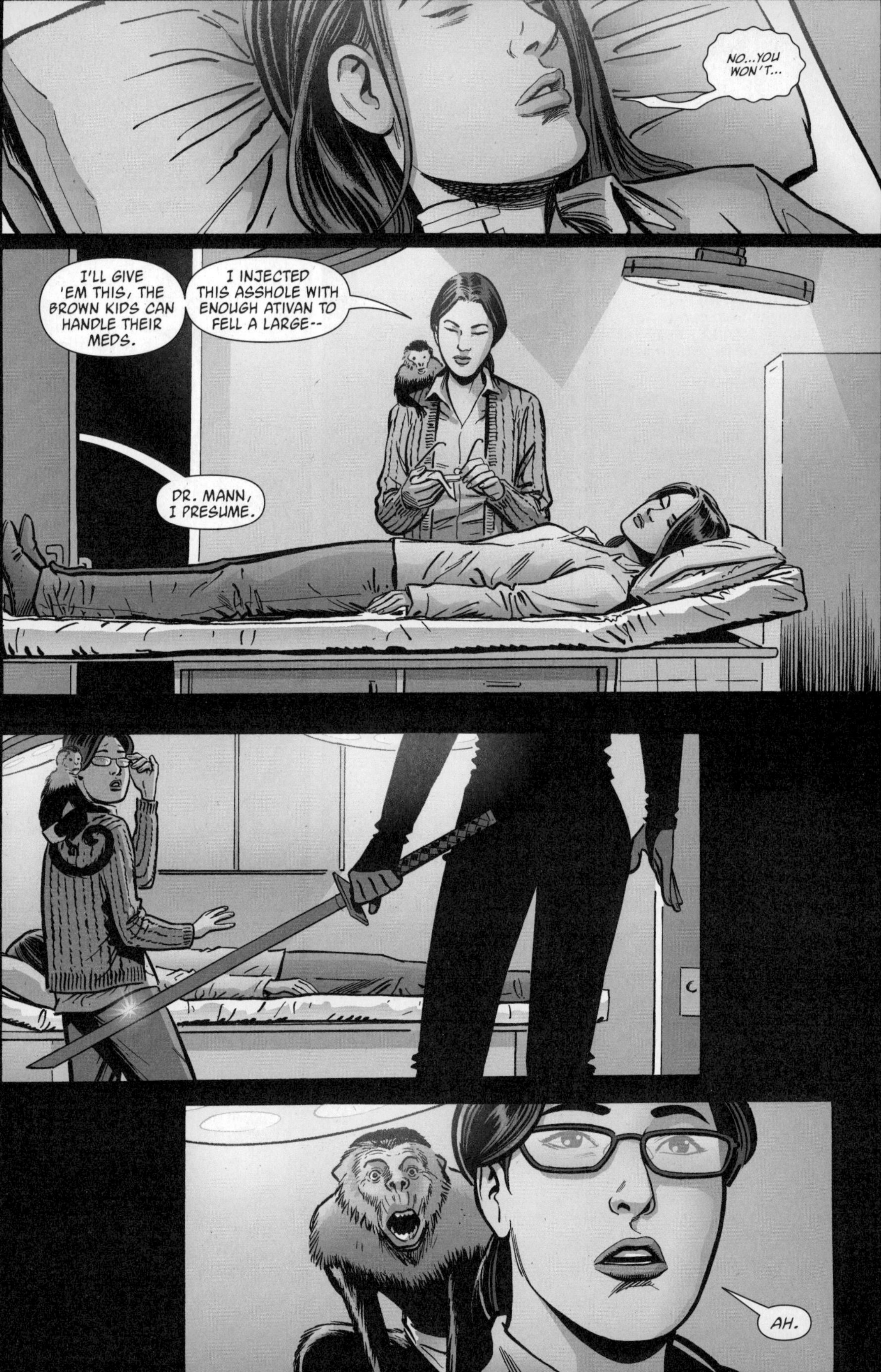
NO...YOU WON'T...
I'LL GIVE 'EM THIS, THE BROWN KIDS CAN HANDLE THEIR MEDS.
I INJECTED THIS ASSHOLE WITH ENOUGH ATIVAN TO FELL A LARGE--
DR. MANN, I PRESUME.
AH.

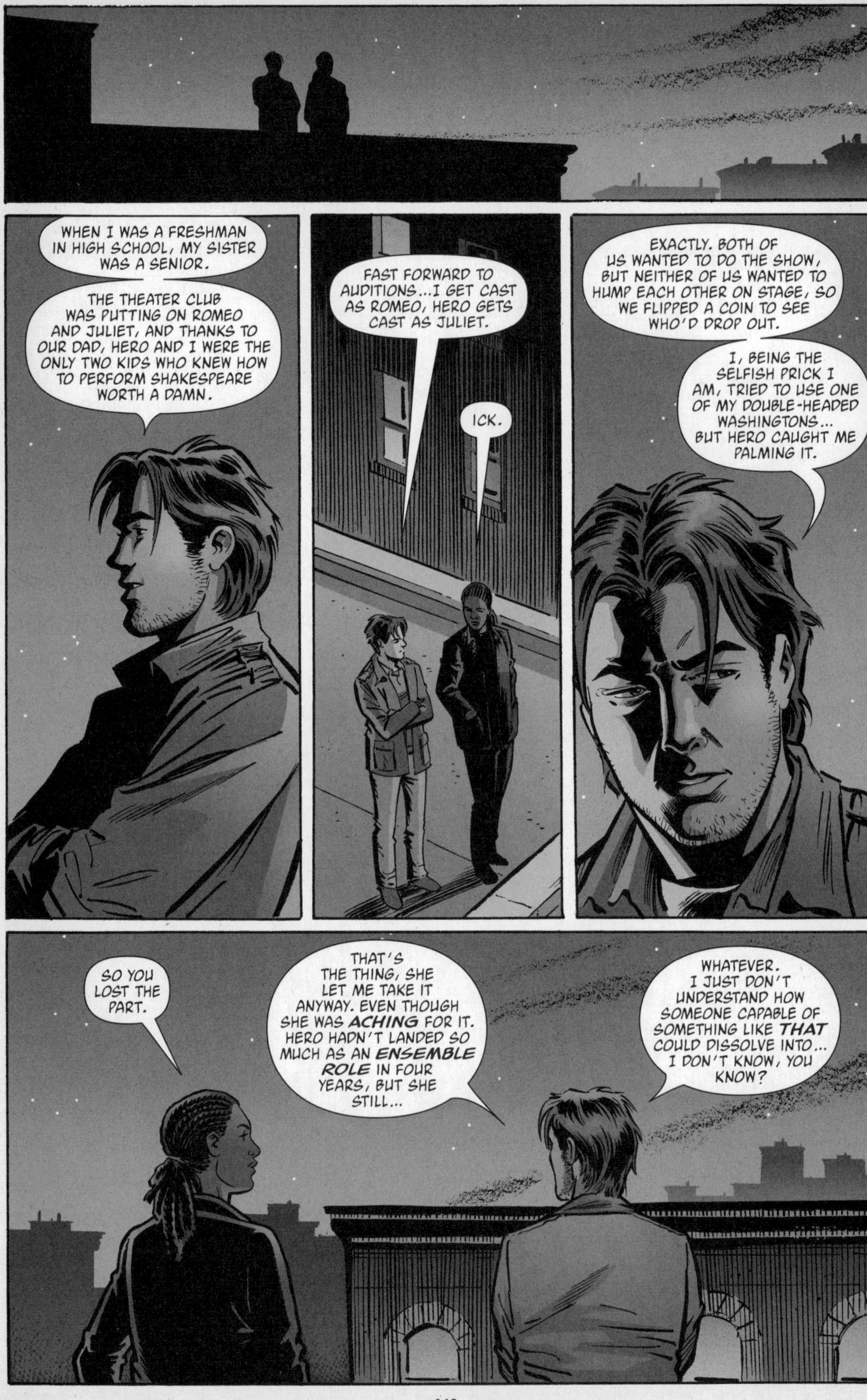
WHEN I WAS A FRESHMAN IN HIGH SCHOOL, MY SISTER WAS A SENIOR.
THE THEATER CLUB WAS PUTTING ON ROMEO AND JULIET, AND THANKS TO OUR DAD, HERO AND I WERE THE ONLY TWO KIDS WHO KNEW HOW TO PERFORM SHAKESPEARE WORTH A DAMN.
FAST FORWARD TO AUDITIONS...I GET CAST AS ROMEO, HERO GETS CAST AS JULIET.
ICK.
EXACTLY. BOTH OF US WANTED TO DO THE SHOW, BUT NEITHER OF US WANTED TO HUMP EACH OTHER ON STAGE, SO WE FLIPPED A COIN TO SEE WHO'D DROP OUT.
I, BEING THE SELFISH PRICK I AM, TRIED TO USE ONE OF MY DOUBLE-HEADED WASHINGTONS... BUT HERO CAUGHT ME PALMING IT.
SO YOU LOST THE PART.
THAT'S THE THING, SHE LET ME TAKE IT ANYWAY. EVEN THOUGH SHE WAS ACHING FOR IT. HERO HADN'T LANDED SO MUCH AS AN ENSEMBLE ROLE IN FOUR YEARS, BUT SHE STILL...
WHATEVER. I JUST DON'T UNDERSTAND HOW SOMEONE CAPABLE OF SOMETHING LIKE THAT COULD DISSOLVE INTO... I DON'T KNOW, YOU KNOW?

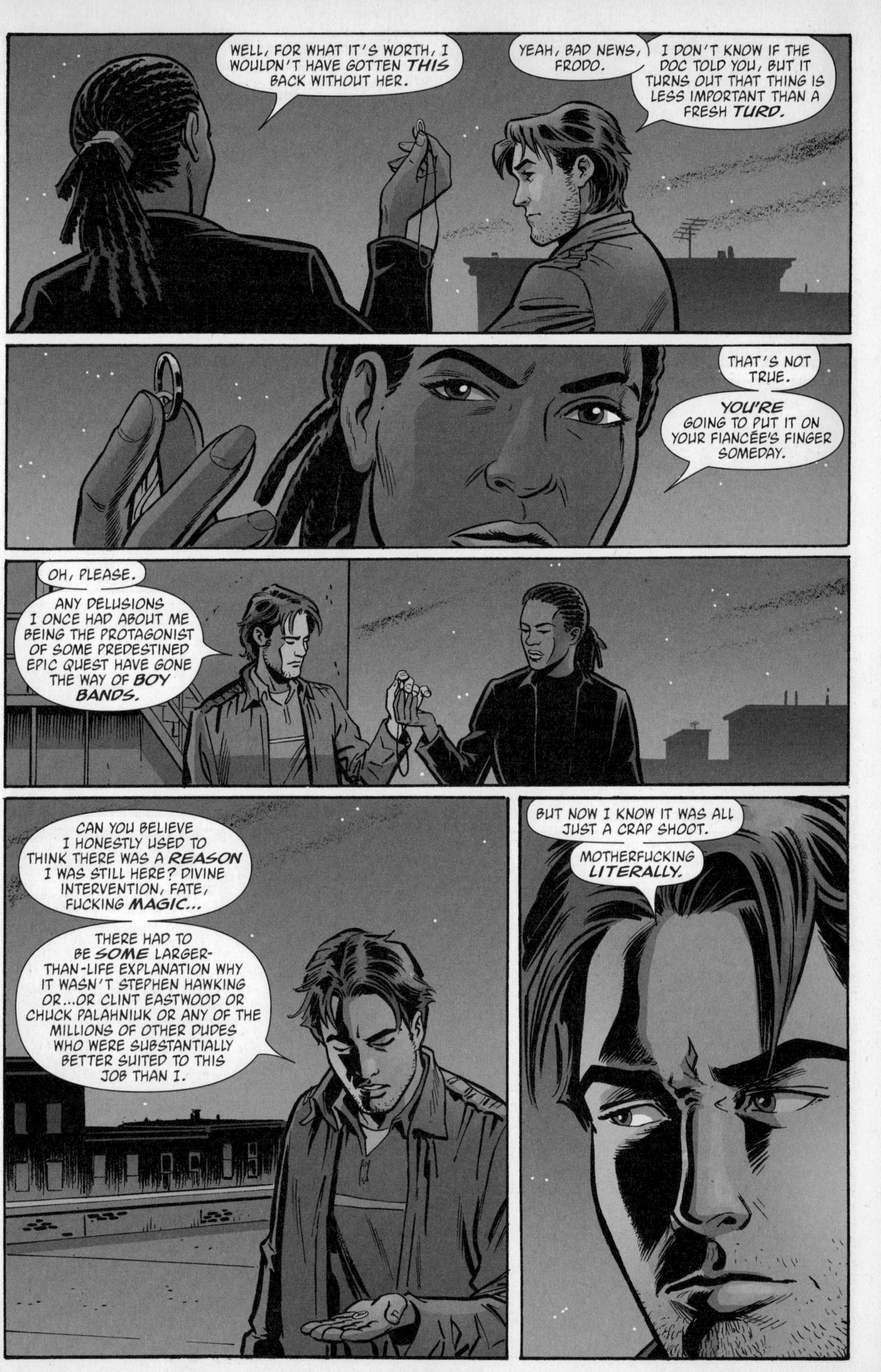
WELL, FOR WHAT IT'S WORTH, I WOULDN'T HAVE GOTTEN THIS BACK WITHOUT HER.
YEAH, BAD NEWS, FRODO.
I DON'T KNOW IF THE DOC TOLD YOU, BUT IT TURNS OUT THAT THING IS LESS IMPORTANT THAN A FRESH TURD.
THAT'S NOT TRUE.
YOU'RE GOING TO PUT IT ON YOUR FIANCÉE'S FINGER SOMEDAY.
OH, PLEASE.
ANY DELUSIONS I ONCE HAD ABOUT ME BEING THE PROTAGONIST OF SOME PREDESTINED EPIC QUEST HAVE GONE THE WAY OF BOY BANDS.
CAN YOU BELIEVE I HONESTLY USED TO THINK THERE WAS A REASON I WAS STILL HERE? DIVINE INTERVENTION, FATE, FUCKING MAGIC...
THERE HAD TO BE SOME LARGER-THAN-LIFE EXPLANATION WHY IT WASN'T STEPHEN HAWKING OR...OR CLINT EASTWOOD OR CHUCK PALAHNIUK OR ANY OF THE MILLIONS OF OTHER DUDES WHO WERE SUBSTANTIALLY BETTER SUITED TO THIS JOB THAN I.
BUT NOW I KNOW IT WAS ALL JUST A CRAP SHOOT.
MOTHERFUCKING LITERALLY.

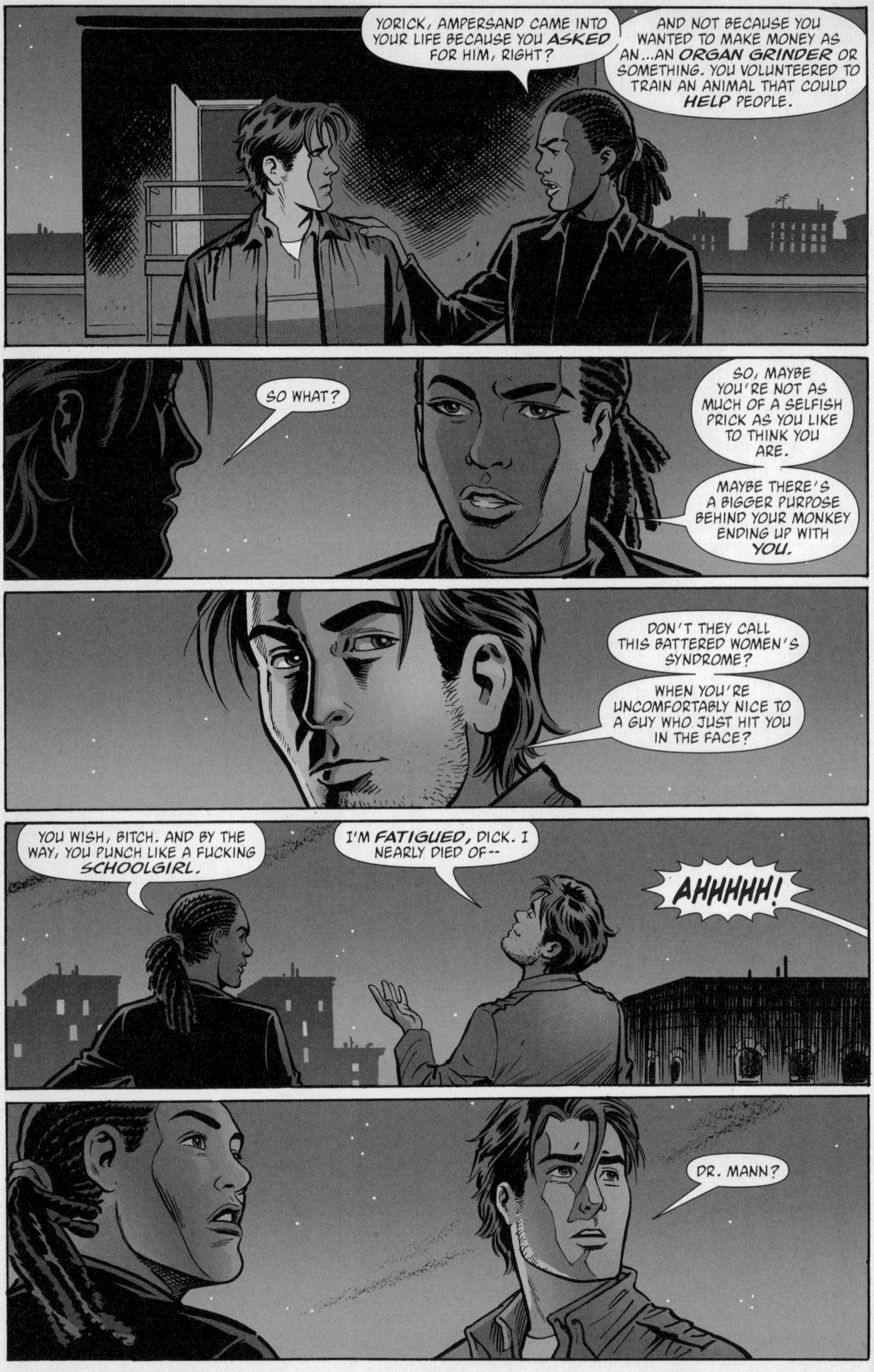
YORICK, AMPERSAND CAME INTO YOUR LIFE BECAUSE YOU ASKED FOR HIM, RIGHT?
AND NOT BECAUSE YOU WANTED TO MAKE MONEY AS AN...AN ORGAN GRINDER OR SOMETHING. YOU VOLUNTEERED TO TRAIN AN ANIMAL THAT COULD HELP PEOPLE.
SO WHAT?
SO, MAYBE YOU'RE NOT AS MUCH OF A SELFISH PRICK AS YOU LIKE TO THINK YOU ARE.
MAYBE THERE'S A BIGGER PURPOSE BEHIND YOUR MONKEY ENDING UP WITH YOU.
DON'T THEY CALL THIS BATTERED WOMEN'S SYNDROME?
WHEN YOU'RE UNCOMFORTABLY NICE TO A GUY WHO JUST HIT YOU IN THE FACE?
YOU WISH, BITCH. AND BY THE WAY, YOU PUNCH LIKE A FUCKING SCHOOLGIRL.
I'M FATIGUED, DICK. I NEARLY DIED OF--
AHHHHH!
DR. MANN?

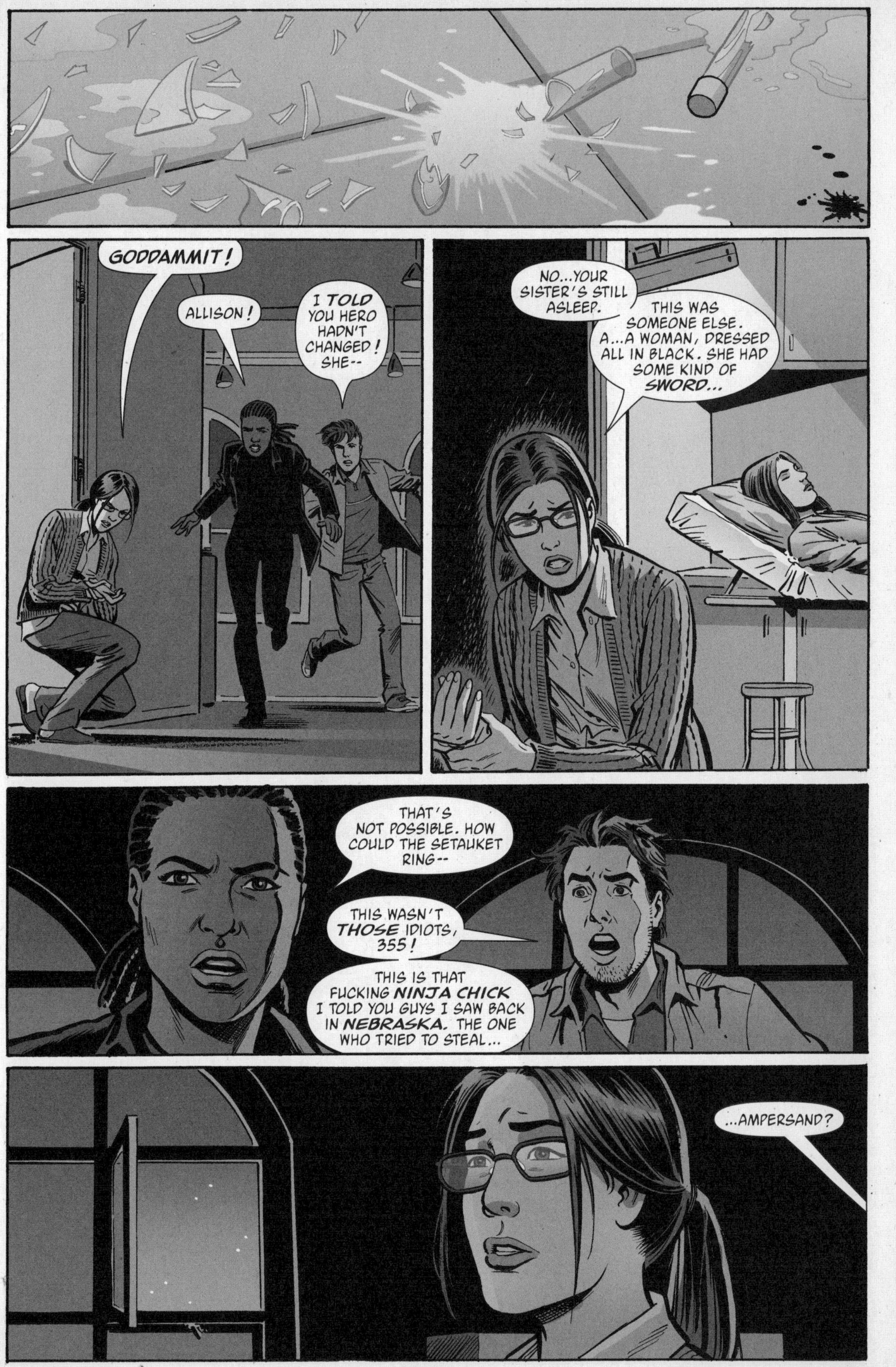
GODDAMMIT!
ALLISON!
I TOLD YOU HERO HADN'T CHANGED! SHE--
NO...YOUR SISTER'S STILL ASLEEP.
THIS WAS SOMEONE ELSE. A...A WOMAN, DRESSED ALL IN BLACK. SHE HAD SOME KIND OF SWORD...
THAT'S NOT POSSIBLE. HOW COULD THE SETAUKET RING--
THIS WASN'T THOSE IDIOTS, 355!
THIS IS THAT FUCKING NINJA CHICK I TOLD YOU GUYS I SAW BACK IN NEBRASKA. THE ONE WHO TRIED TO STEAL...
...AMPERSAND?

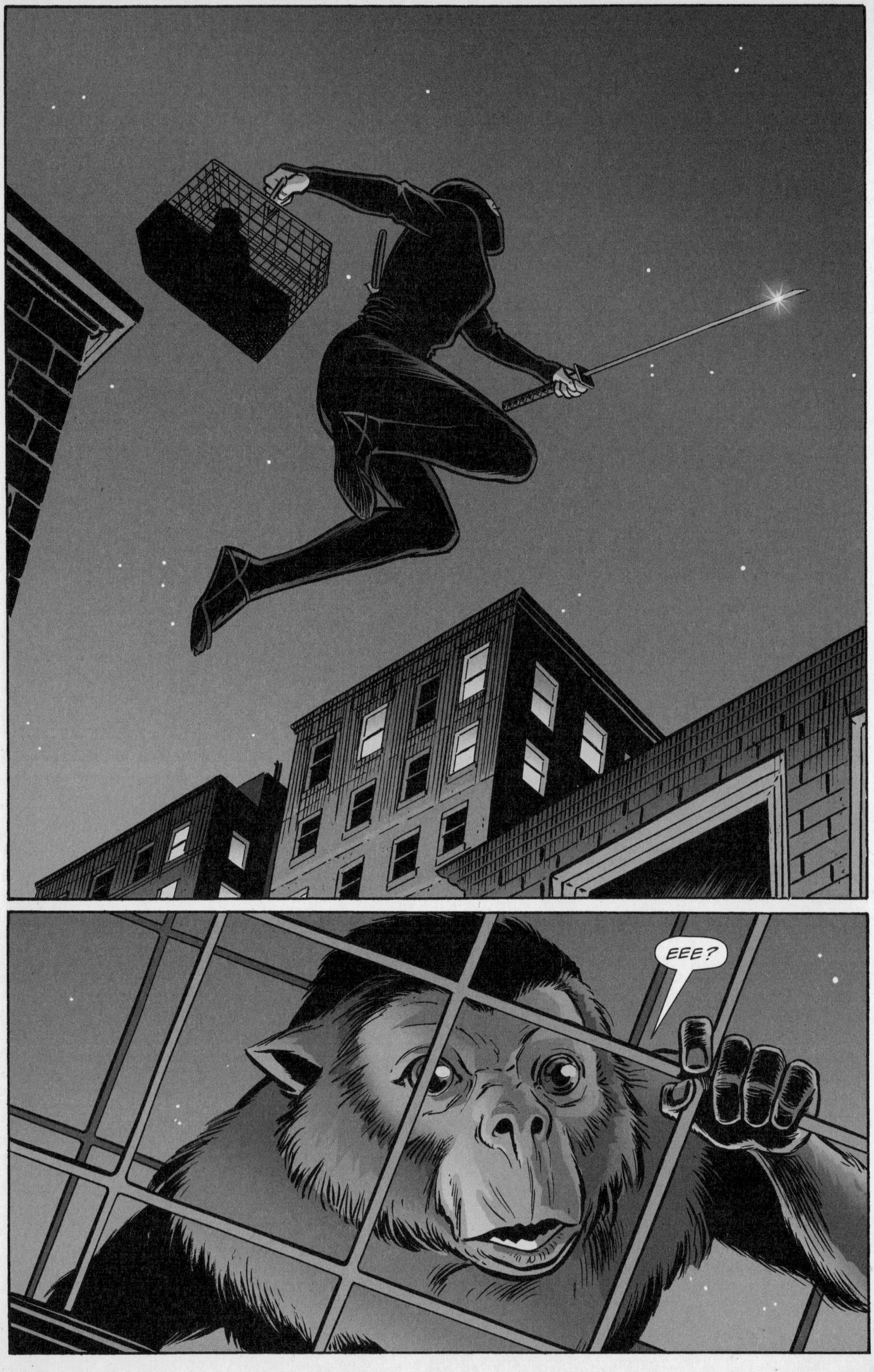
EEE?

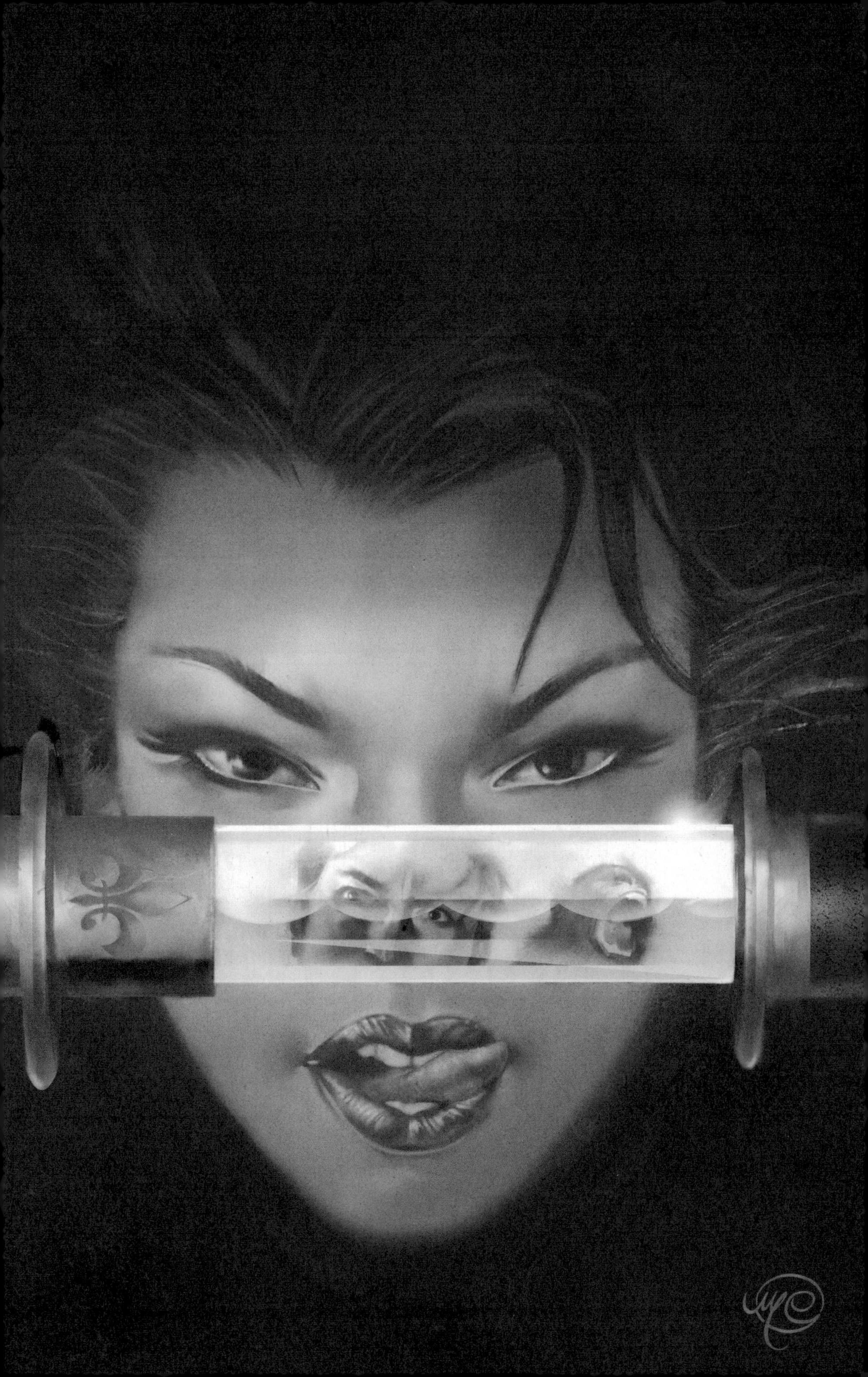

AMPERSAND!

San Francisco, California
Now

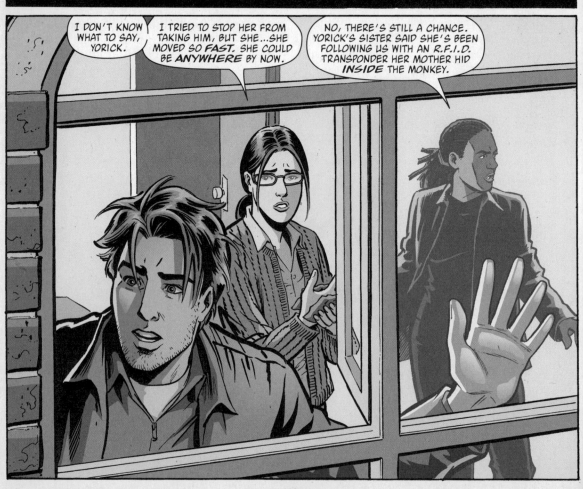

I DON'T KNOW WHAT TO SAY, YORICK.

I TRIED TO STOP HER FROM TAKING HIM, BUT SHE...SHE MOVED SO *FAST*. SHE COULD BE *ANYWHERE* BY NOW.

NO, THERE'S STILL A CHANCE. YORICK'S SISTER SAID SHE'S BEEN FOLLOWING US WITH AN *R.F.I.D.* TRANSPONDER HER MOTHER HID *INSIDE* THE MONKEY.

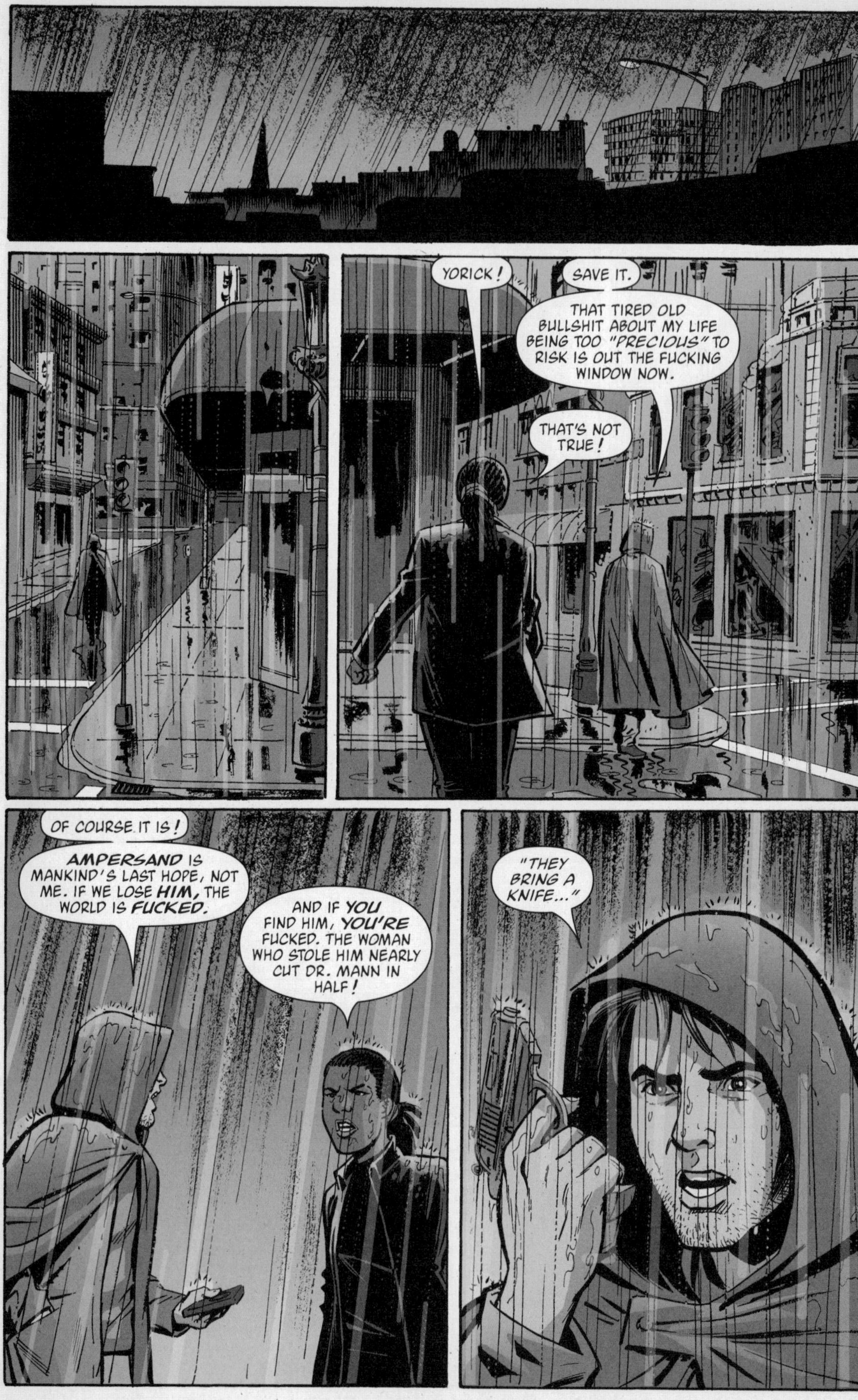
YORICK!
SAVE IT.
THAT TIRED OLD BULLSHIT ABOUT MY LIFE BEING TOO "PRECIOUS" TO RISK IS OUT THE FUCKING WINDOW NOW.
THAT'S NOT TRUE!
OF COURSE IT IS!
AMPERSAND IS MANKIND'S LAST HOPE, NOT ME. IF WE LOSE HIM, THE WORLD IS FUCKED.
AND IF YOU FIND HIM, YOU'RE FUCKED. THE WOMAN WHO STOLE HIM NEARLY CUT DR. MANN IN HALF!
"THEY BRING A KNIFE..."

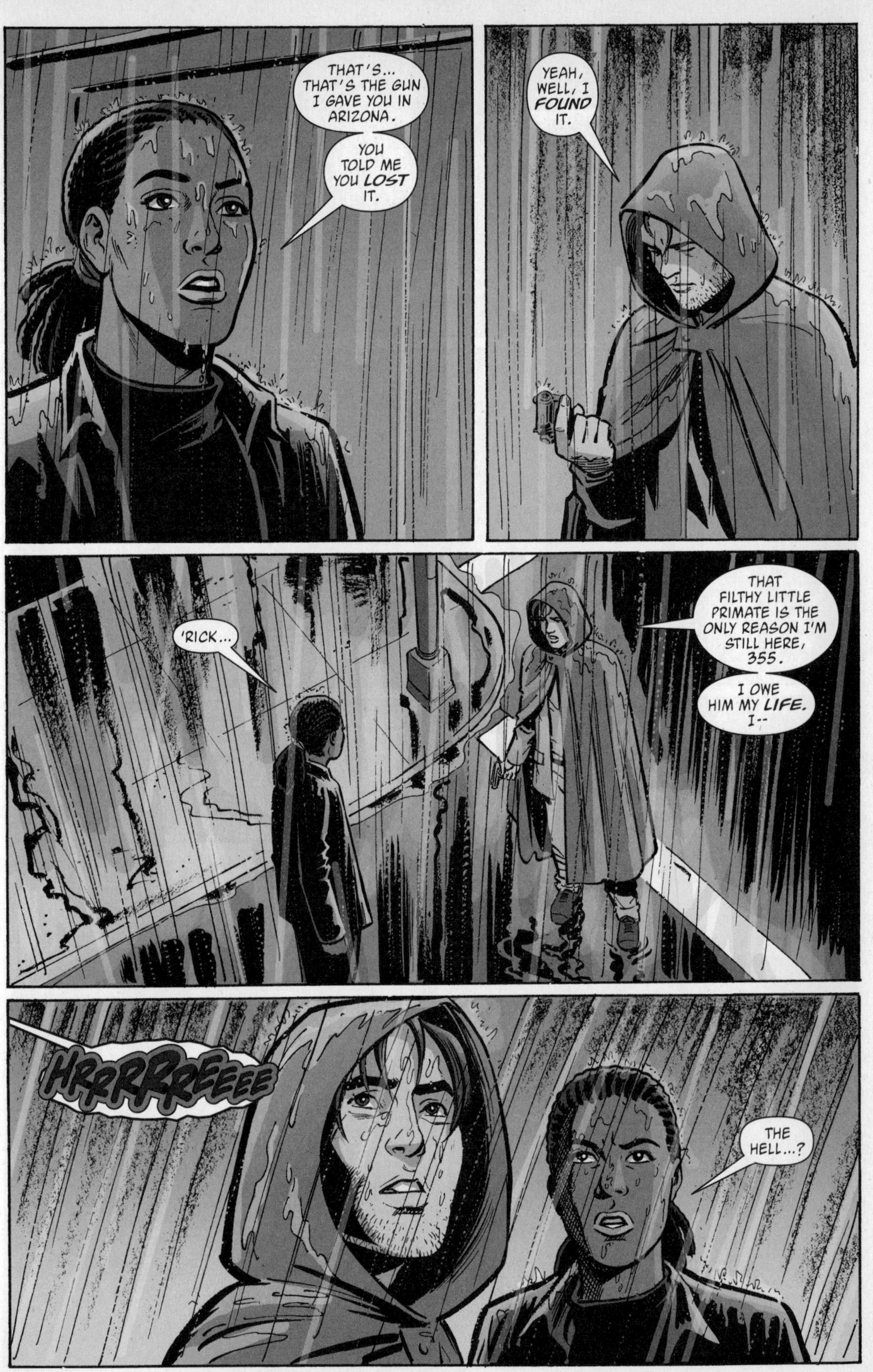
THAT'S... THAT'S THE GUN I GAVE YOU IN ARIZONA.
YOU TOLD ME YOU LOST IT.
YEAH, WELL, I FOUND IT.
'RICK...
THAT FILTHY LITTLE PRIMATE IS THE ONLY REASON I'M STILL HERE, 355.
I OWE HIM MY LIFE. I--
HRRRRREEEEE
THE HELL...?

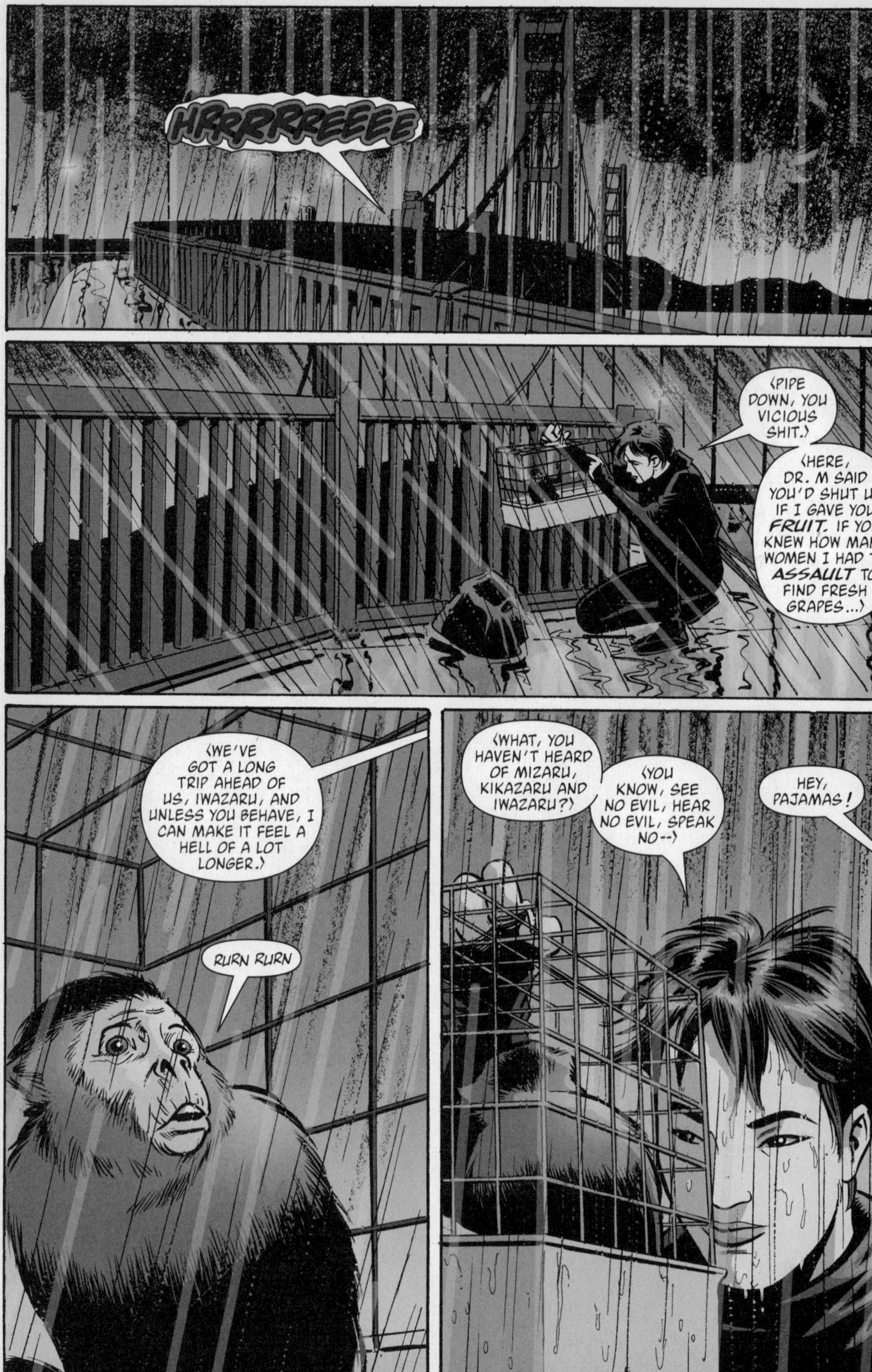
HRRRRREEEE
‹PIPE DOWN, YOU VICIOUS SHIT.›
‹HERE, DR. M SAID YOU'D SHUT UP IF I GAVE YOU FRUIT. IF YOU KNEW HOW MANY WOMEN I HAD TO ASSAULT TO FIND FRESH GRAPES...›
‹WE'VE GOT A LONG TRIP AHEAD OF US, IWAZARU, AND UNLESS YOU BEHAVE, I CAN MAKE IT FEEL A HELL OF A LOT LONGER.›
RURN RURN
‹WHAT, YOU HAVEN'T HEARD OF MIZARU, KIKAZARU AND IWAZARU?›
‹YOU KNOW, SEE NO EVIL, HEAR NO EVIL, SPEAK NO--›
HEY, PAJAMAS!

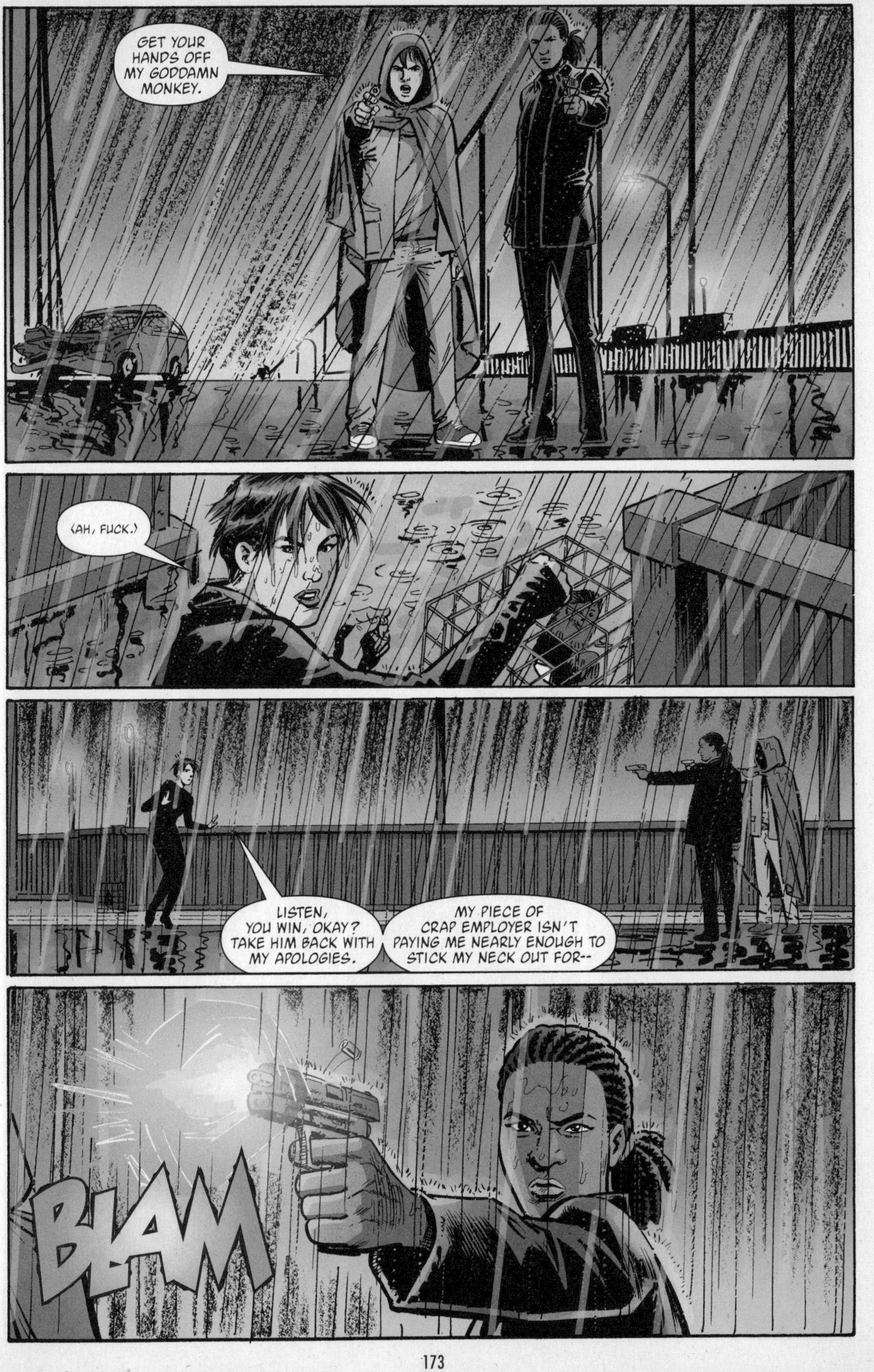

GET YOUR HANDS OFF MY GODDAMN MONKEY.
‹AH, FUCK.›
LISTEN, YOU WIN, OKAY? TAKE HIM BACK WITH MY APOLOGIES.
MY PIECE OF CRAP EMPLOYER ISN'T PAYING ME NEARLY ENOUGH TO STICK MY NECK OUT FOR--
BLAM

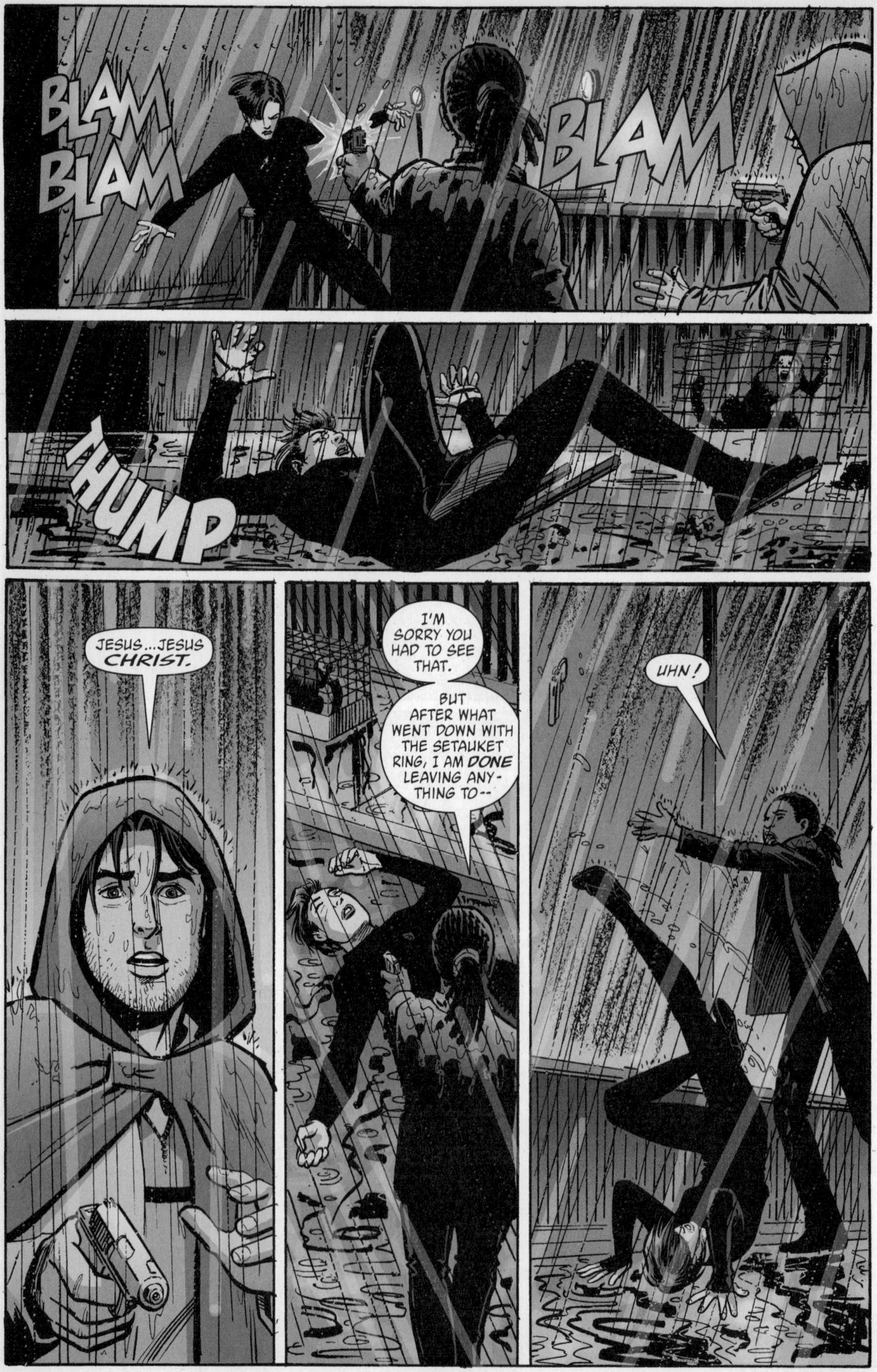

BLAM BLAM
BLAM
THUMP
JESUS...JESUS CHRIST.
I'M SORRY YOU HAD TO SEE THAT.
BUT AFTER WHAT WENT DOWN WITH THE SETAUKET RING, I AM DONE LEAVING ANY-THING TO--
UHN!

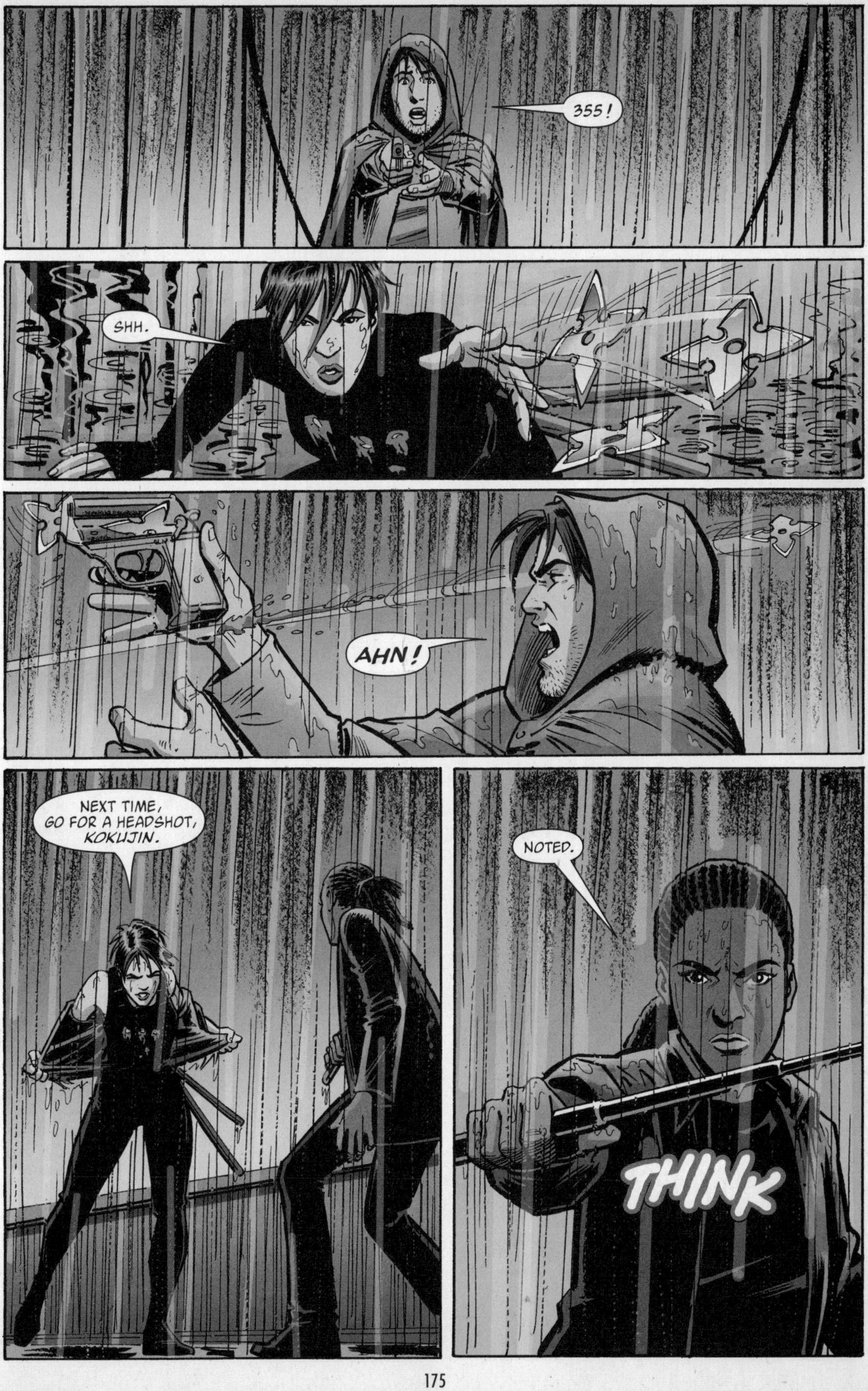
355!
SHH.
AHN!
NEXT TIME, GO FOR A HEADSHOT, KOKUJIN.
NOTED.
THINK

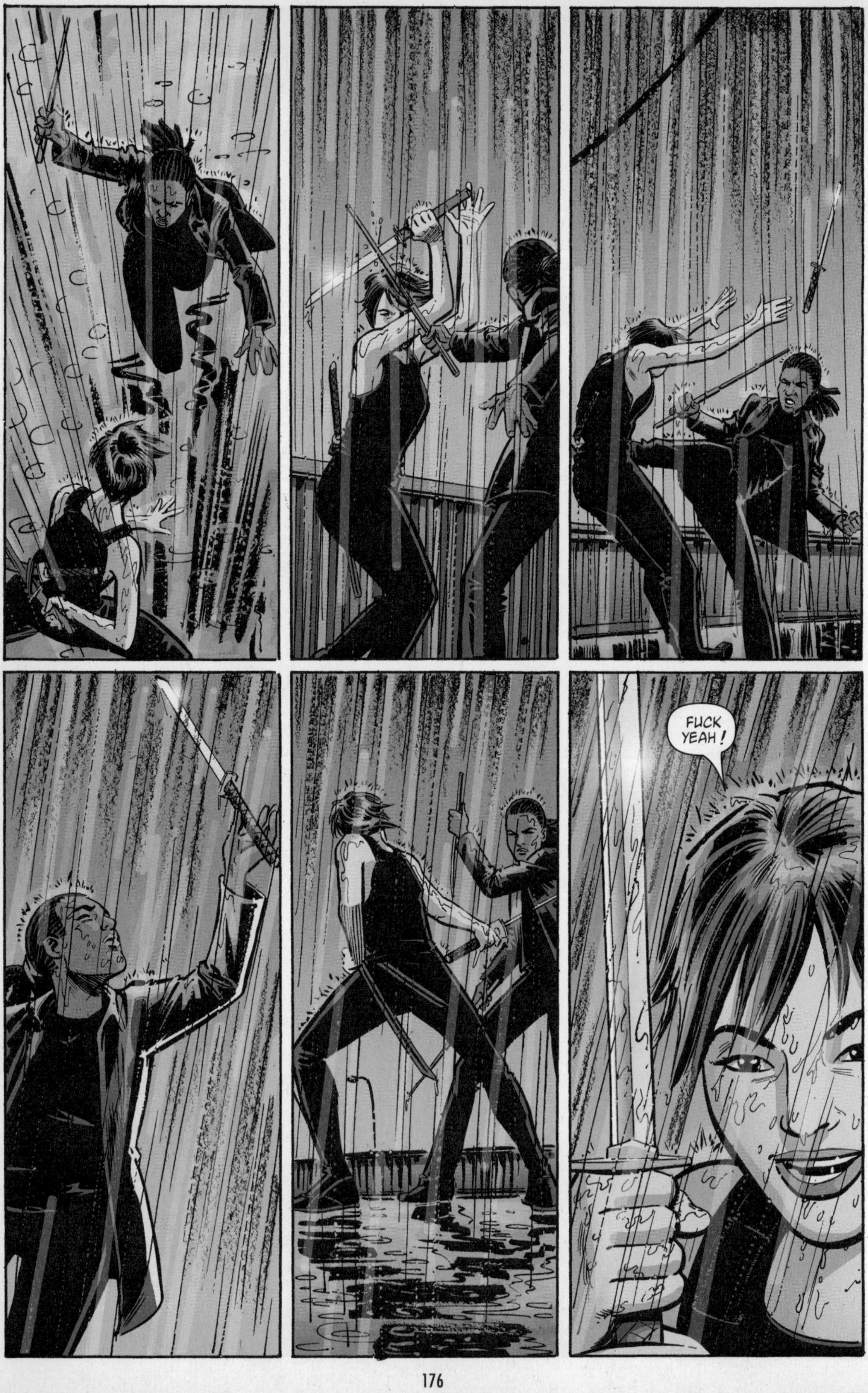
FUCK YEAH!

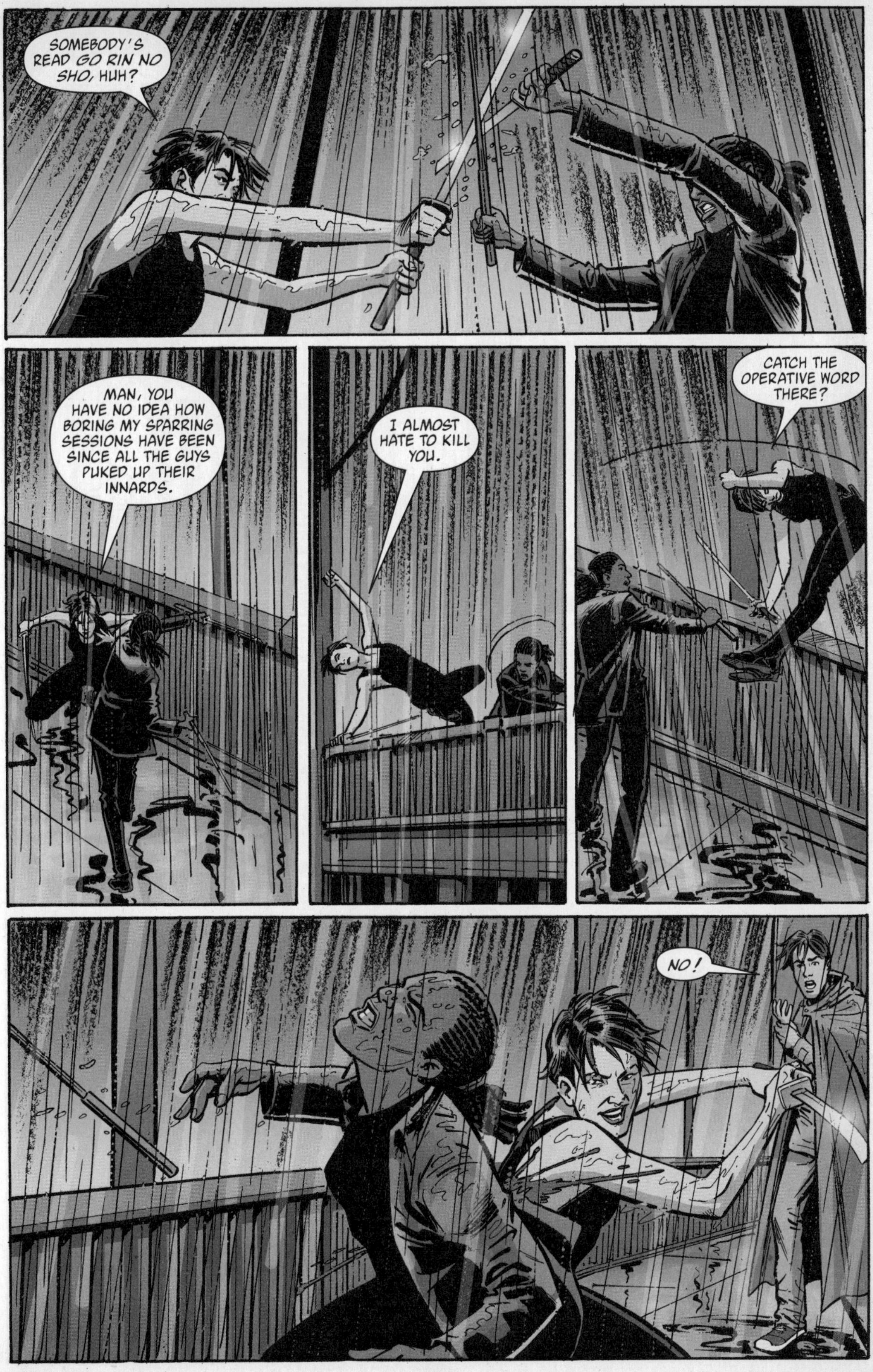
SOMEBODY'S READ GO RIN NO SHO, HUH?
MAN, YOU HAVE NO IDEA HOW BORING MY SPARRING SESSIONS HAVE BEEN SINCE ALL THE GUYS PUKED UP THEIR INNARDS.
I ALMOST HATE TO KILL YOU.
CATCH THE OPERATIVE WORD THERE?
NO!

178

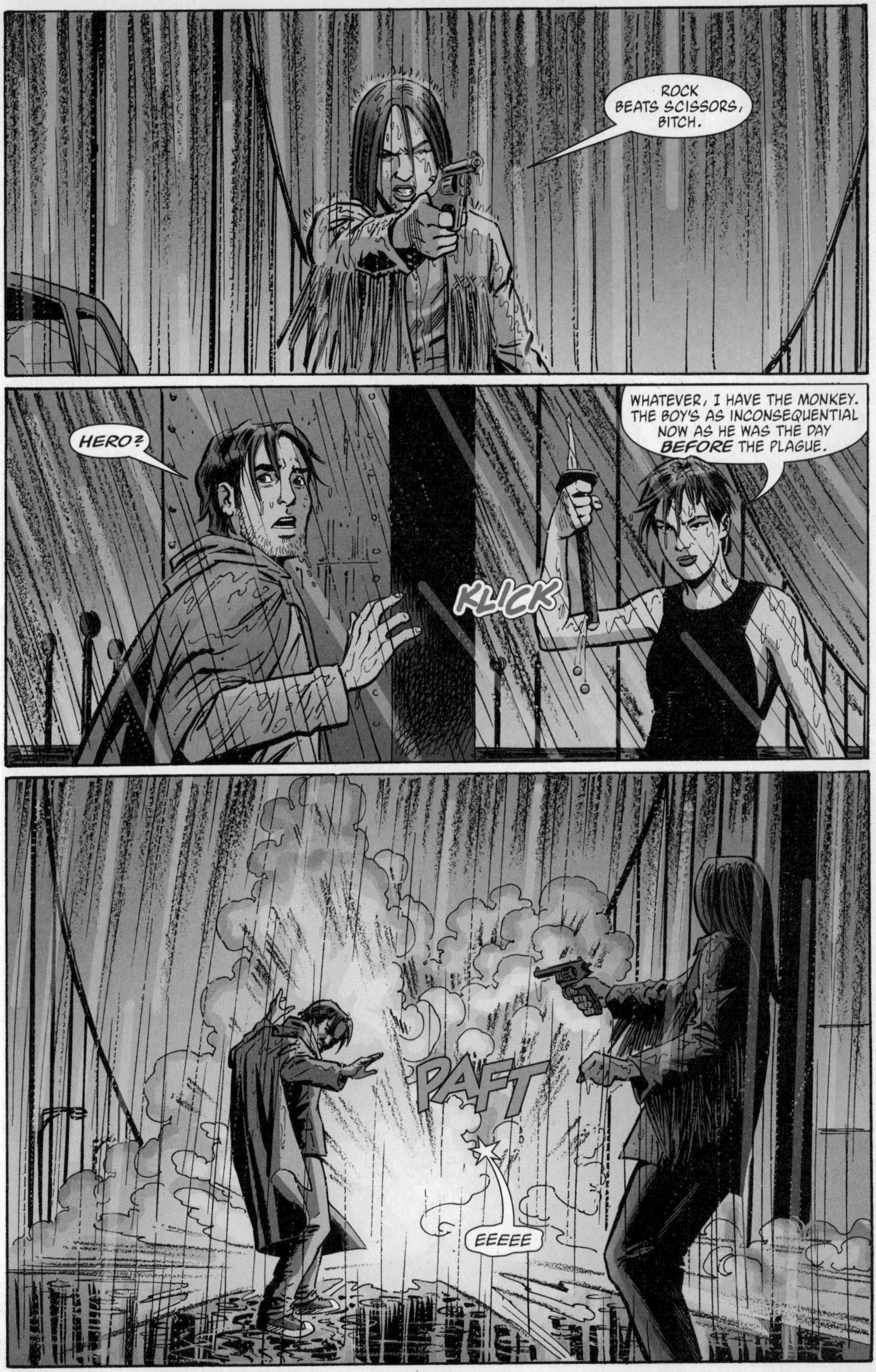
ROCK BEATS SCISSORS, BITCH.
HERO?
WHATEVER, I HAVE THE MONKEY. THE BOY'S AS INCONSEQUENTIAL NOW AS HE WAS THE DAY BEFORE THE PLAGUE.
KLICK
PAFT
EEEEE

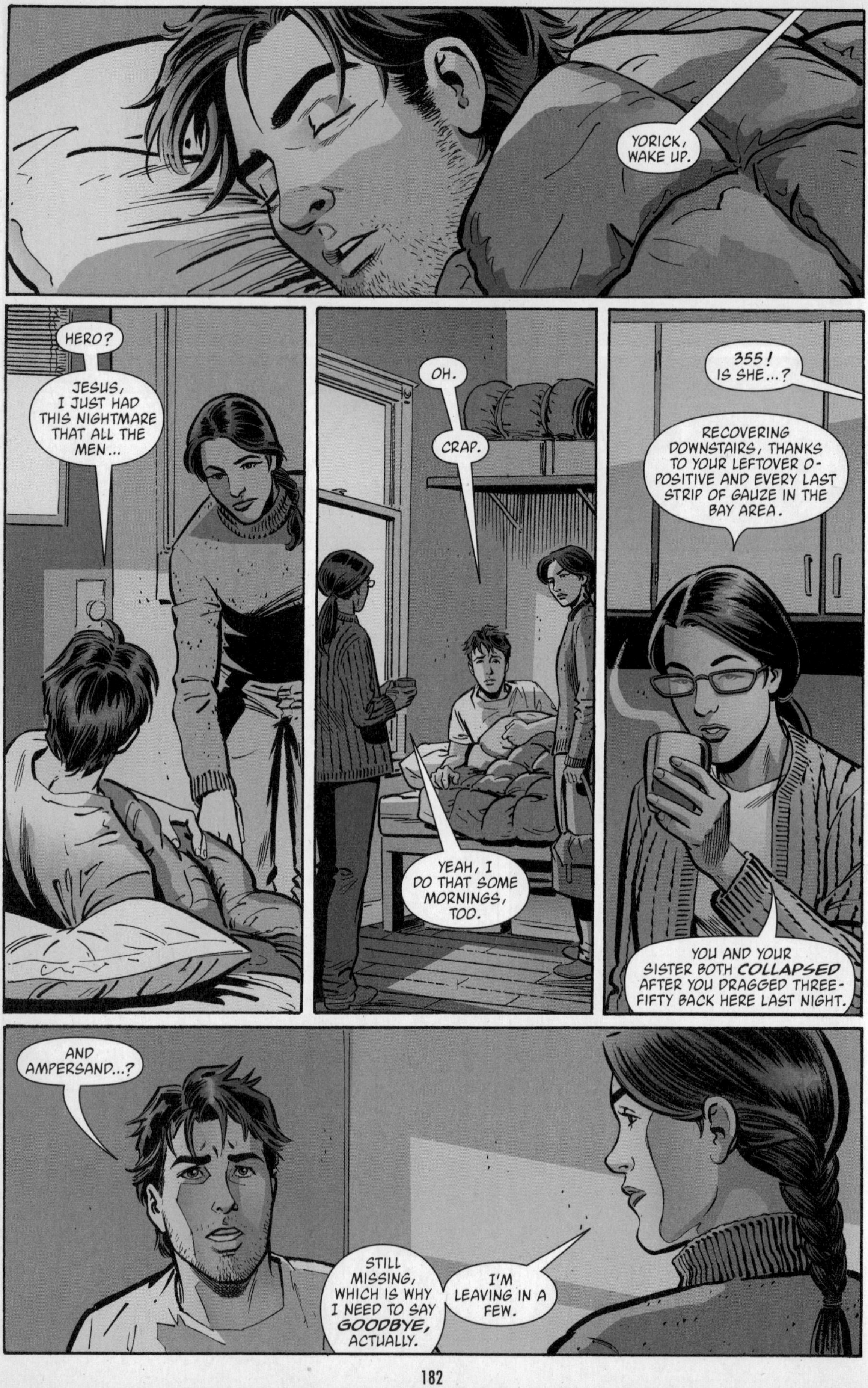
YORICK, WAKE UP.
HERO?
JESUS, I JUST HAD THIS NIGHTMARE THAT ALL THE MEN...
OH.
CRAP.
YEAH, I DO THAT SOME MORNINGS, TOO.
355! IS SHE...?
RECOVERING DOWNSTAIRS, THANKS TO YOUR LEFTOVER O-POSITIVE AND EVERY LAST STRIP OF GAUZE IN THE BAY AREA.
YOU AND YOUR SISTER BOTH COLLAPSED AFTER YOU DRAGGED THREE-FIFTY BACK HERE LAST NIGHT.
AND AMPERSAND...?
STILL MISSING, WHICH IS WHY I NEED TO SAY GOODBYE, ACTUALLY.
I'M LEAVING IN A FEW.

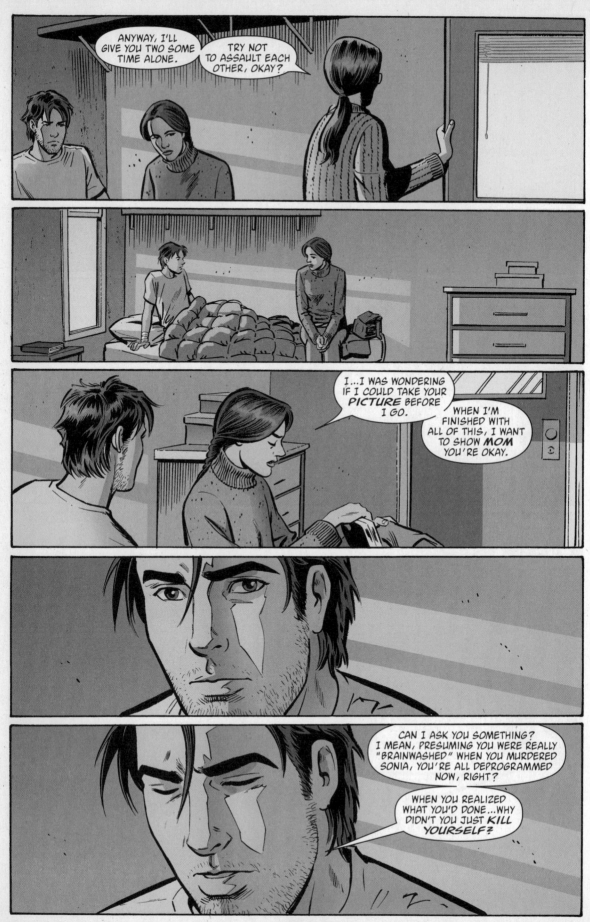

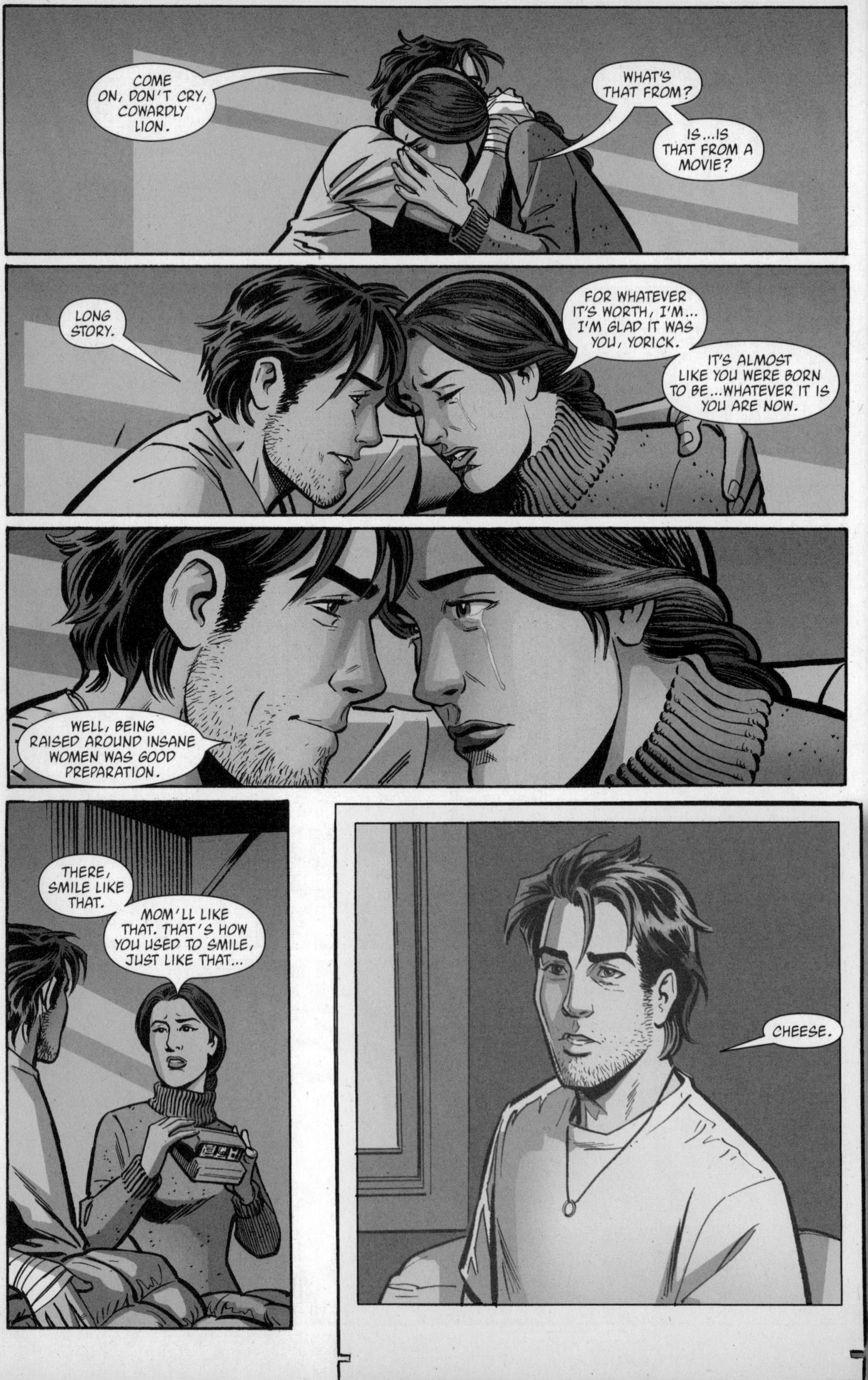
COME ON, DON'T CRY, COWARDLY LION.
WHAT'S THAT FROM?
IS...IS THAT FROM A MOVIE?
LONG STORY.
FOR WHATEVER IT'S WORTH, I'M... I'M GLAD IT WAS YOU, YORICK.
IT'S ALMOST LIKE YOU WERE BORN TO BE...WHATEVER IT IS YOU ARE NOW.
WELL, BEING RAISED AROUND INSANE WOMEN WAS GOOD PREPARATION.
THERE, SMILE LIKE THAT.
MOM'LL LIKE THAT. THAT'S HOW YOU USED TO SMILE, JUST LIKE THAT...
CHEESE.

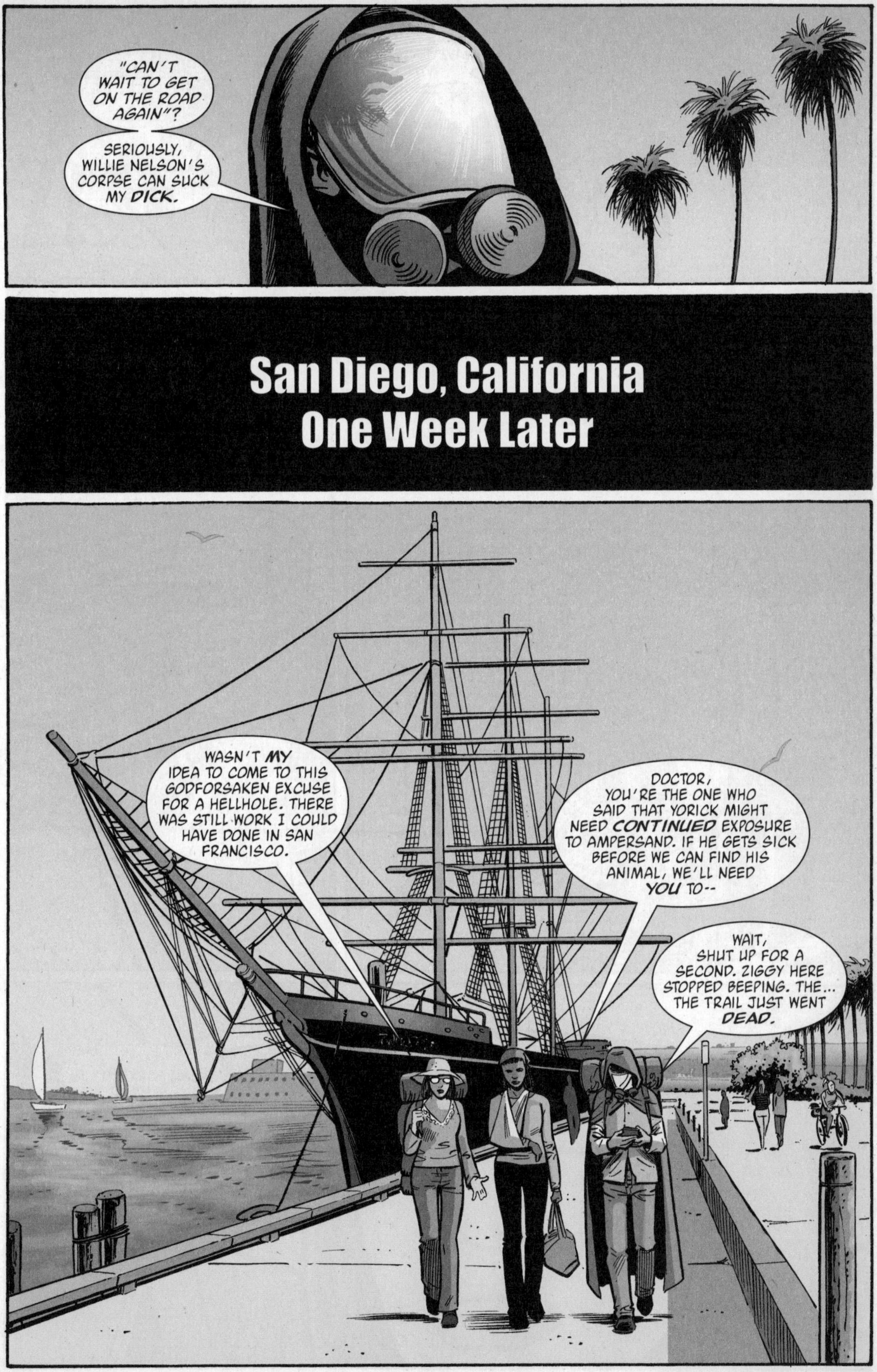
"CAN'T WAIT TO GET ON THE ROAD AGAIN"?
SERIOUSLY, WILLIE NELSON'S CORPSE CAN SUCK MY **DICK.**
San Diego, California
One Week Later
WASN'T **MY** IDEA TO COME TO THIS GODFORSAKEN EXCUSE FOR A HELLHOLE. THERE WAS STILL WORK I COULD HAVE DONE IN SAN FRANCISCO.
DOCTOR, YOU'RE THE ONE WHO SAID THAT YORICK MIGHT NEED **CONTINUED** EXPOSURE TO AMPERSAND. IF HE GETS SICK BEFORE WE CAN FIND HIS ANIMAL, WE'LL NEED **YOU** TO--
WAIT, SHUT UP FOR A SECOND. ZIGGY HERE STOPPED BEEPING. THE... THE TRAIL JUST WENT **DEAD.**

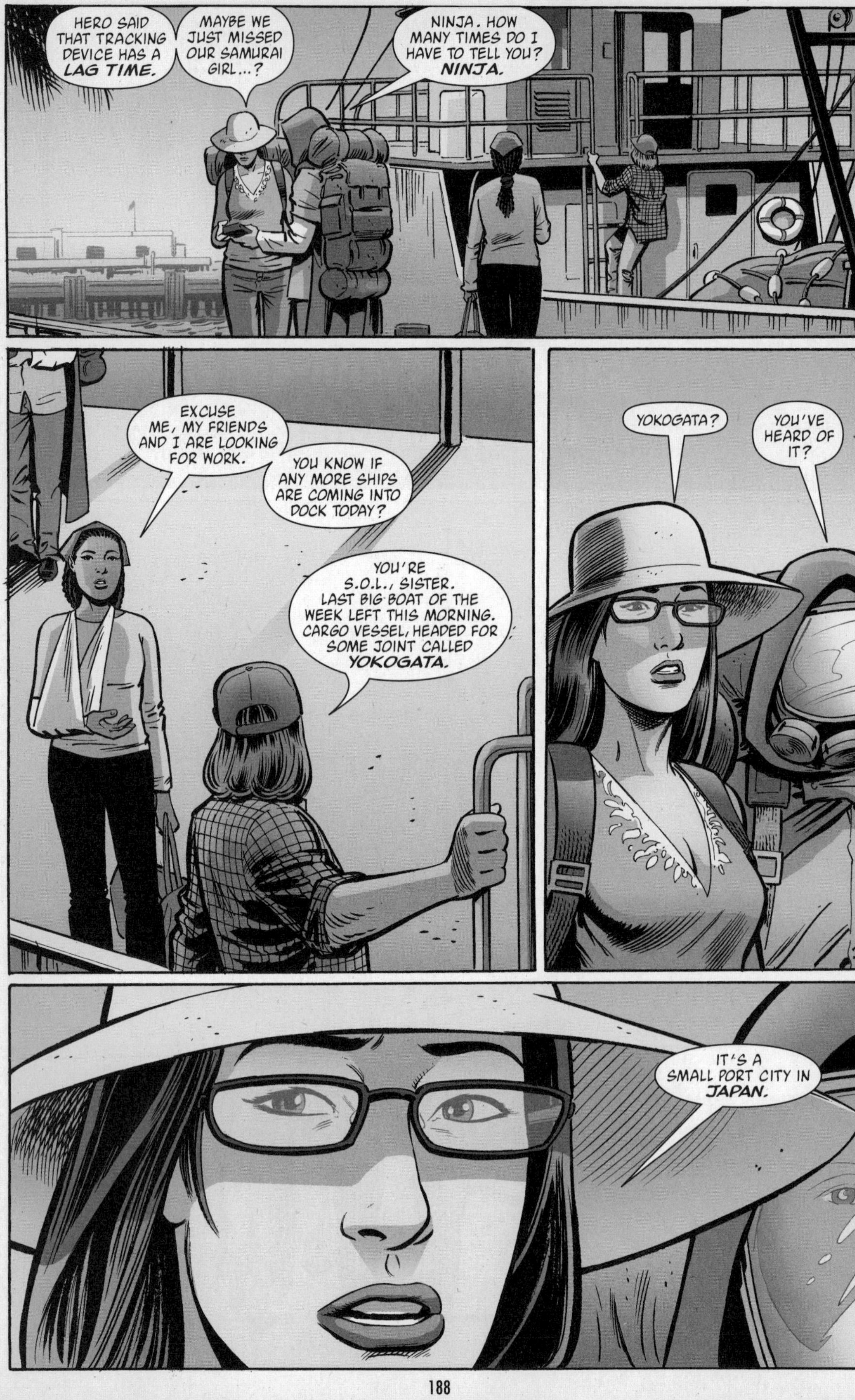
HERO SAID THAT TRACKING DEVICE HAS A LAG TIME.
MAYBE WE JUST MISSED OUR SAMURAI GIRL...?
NINJA. HOW MANY TIMES DO I HAVE TO TELL YOU? NINJA.
EXCUSE ME, MY FRIENDS AND I ARE LOOKING FOR WORK.
YOU KNOW IF ANY MORE SHIPS ARE COMING INTO DOCK TODAY?
YOU'RE S.O.L., SISTER. LAST BIG BOAT OF THE WEEK LEFT THIS MORNING. CARGO VESSEL, HEADED FOR SOME JOINT CALLED YOKOGATA.
YOKOGATA?
YOU'VE HEARD OF IT?
IT'S A SMALL PORT CITY IN JAPAN.

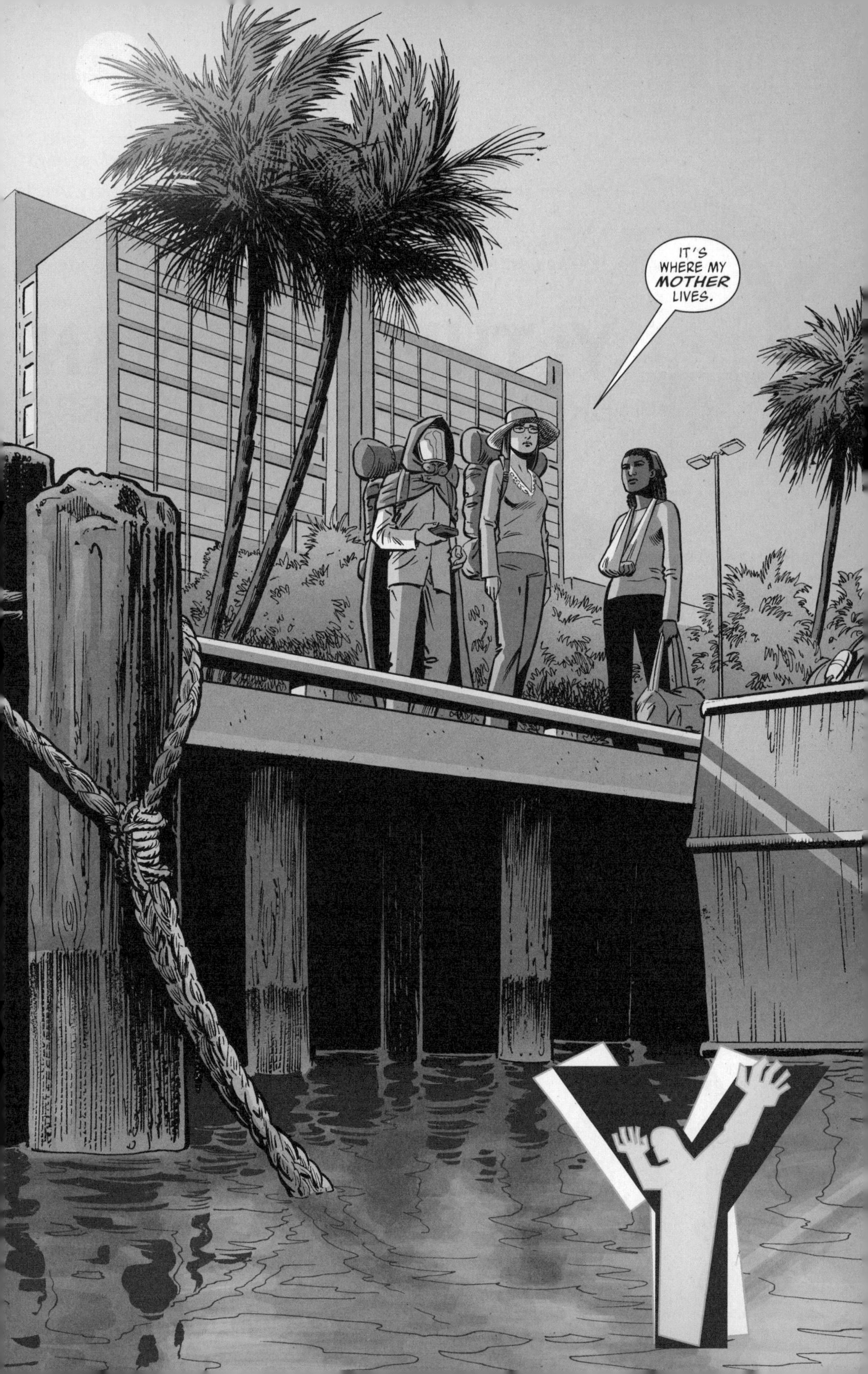
IT'S WHERE MY MOTHER LIVES.